AOL
KEYWORDS

AOL
KEYWORDS

Jennifer Watson

MIS:Press, Inc.
A Subsidiary of Henry Holt and Company, Inc.
115 West 18th Street
New York, New York 10011

copyright ©1996 by MIS:Press

Printed in the United States of America

All rights reserved. No part of this book may be reproduced or transmitted in any form or by any means, electronic or mechanical, including photocopying, recording, or by any information storage and retrieval system, without prior written permission from the Publisher. Contact the Publisher for information on foreign rights.

MIS:Press books are available at special discounts for bulk purchases for sales promotions, premiums, and fund-raising. Special editions or book excerpts can also be created to specification.

For details contact: Special Sales Director
MIS:Press
a subsidiary of
Henry Holt and Company, Inc.
115 West 18th Street
New York, New York 10011

Limits of Liability and Disclaimer of Warranty

The Author and Publisher of this book have used their best efforts in preparing the book and the programs contained in it. These efforts include the development, research, and testing of the theories and programs to determine their effectiveness.

The Author and Publisher make no warranty of any kind, expressed or implied, with regard to these programs or the documentation contained in this book. The Author and Publisher shall not be liable in any event for incidental or consequential damages in connection with, or arising out of, the furnishing, performance, or use of these programs.

All products, names and services are trademarks or registered trademarks of their respective companies.

ISBN: 1-55828-505-9

10 9 8 7 6 5 4

Associate Publisher: Paul Farrell
Executive Editor: Cary Sullivan
Editor: Laura Lewin
Copy Edit Manager: Shari Chapell
Copy Editor: Gwynne Jackson
Production Editor: Joe McPartland

Dedication

This book is dedicated to:

> Gordon, for supporting me
> Glenn, for inspiring me
> George, for encouraging me

Acknowledgments

This book is special for one important reason if no other: It is the embodiment of the support, knowledge, and community I am fortunate to have in my life. This takes the form of hundreds of friends, colleagues, and family members, most of whom I am pleased to say are on America Online. They have helped me in countless ways, and I am forever in their debt. So forgive me if I gush a bit.

Although I cannot thank everyone who had a hand in bringing this book to you, I do want to express my appreciation to those who were most instrumental:

> America Online, Inc., not for simply building an online service, but for providing an environment in which a community could be built.
>
> The thousands of community leaders and partners who originally requested a keyword list years ago. Not only did you continue to appreciate my work (and keep me going!), but you gave me the feedback I needed to update the list frequently.
>
> My two keyword assistants, Bob Strange and Valerie L. Downey, who have helped countless members with questions about keywords and helped maintain the integrity of the keyword list.
>
> Ben Foxworth, for his unwavering support in my quest for keywords and everything else that lies before me online.
>
> George Louie, not only for his patience and encouragement during the long hours of keyword gathering and writing, but for his dedicated help with the keyword database.

Dave Marx, for his time reviewing my work, his honest opinions, and his countenance.

Tom Lichty, for being my role model and mentor.

My families, offline and online. Gordon Watson, Carolyn Tody, Tom Anderson, Kim Larner, and Jeanne Beroza helped me offline, encouraging my work and doing their best to understand just what it was I did online. Online, the VLA and GMI teams not only helped test keywords, they also built amazing communities I was proud to call home. They each gave me hope, inspiration, and, best of all, a reason to persevere in the face of uncertainty.

Lyn Cameron, for giving me my own keyword, and Bill Lenoir, David Ehrlich, Jane Bradshaw, and Kathy Ryan for believing in me.

Paul Farrell, Laura Lewin, Joseph McPartland, and the crew at MIS:Press, for both the opportunity to bring this book to light and their professionalism.

The many community leaders who wrote the keyword reviews in Chapters 3, 4, and 5. Your words enrich this work beyond anything I could have done alone.

My merry band of keyword watchers who helped me find new keywords, update existing ones, and make the list as complete as possible.

Last but not least, the millions of members who make America Online the place to be in cyberspace.

Contents

Welcome 1

Chapter 1: Going Places with America Online 3

America Online 4
Behind Lock and Keyword 6
Using Keywords... 7
    Mousetraps: Using the Keyboard 9
Where Are All the Keywords?......................... 9
    Keyword Surfing................................... 13
A List of Your Own 14
    Getting to the Heart of the
    Matter: Favorite Places 15
Desperately Seeking Keywords 16
    Keyword: DEAD END 16
Using This Book.. 17
We Welcome Feedback! 19

Chapter 2: Key Chains 21

AOLholics.. 21
Explorers of Sea and Sky 22
Kidwords.. 23
LOL! (Laughers On Line) 24
Men 24

ix

Contents

Can I Have My Own Keyword? 25
Nature Lovers 25
Parents 26
Professionals 27
    Keyword Trivia 28
Readers and Writers 28
Romantics 29
    The Keyword Bizarre 30
Women 30
List Lovers 31

Chapter 3: Important Keywords 33

Chapter 4: New Keywords 47

Chapter 5: Hot Keywords 61

Chapter 6: Keywords from A to Z 81

Chapter 7: Keywords by Channel and Topic 221

General Keywords 221
C! Computers & Software 222
    General Interest Areas in
    Computers & Software 223
    Macintosh Forums in
    Computers & Software 224
    PC Forums in Computers &
    Software 226
    Special Interest Groups in
    Computers & Software 227
    Computing Company Connection 229
Digital Cities 239

Entertainment	244
Games	253
Health & Fitness	255
The Hub	256
International	257
Internet Connection	259
Kids Only	261
Learning & Culture	261
Life, Styles & Interests	266
Marketplace	278
MusicSpace	281
Newsstand	282
People Connection	288
Personal Finance	289
Reference Desk	294
Sports	295
Style	301
Today's News	302
Travel	303
Member Services	304
Special	305

Appendix A: Keyboard Shortcuts 307

Appendix B: VirtuaLingo Glossary of America Online Terms...................309

Index 317

WELCOME

Hello! If you are anything like me you are probably still standing in the bookstore, trying to decide which book you need. Even if you aren't and are now the proud owner of this book (thank you!), don't expect me to tell you how this will answer all your questions about America Online. No book can do that and, trust me, you wouldn't want one to—some of the best parts of America Online are experienced up close and personal.

What I *will* tell you is that this book can help you decide if America Online is right for you, and if so, how to find what you need without a lot of fuss. In essence, this is a directory of what's on America Online. There are many books that explain *how* to use America Online, but none that tells you *what* is available and *where* to find it as simply as the one you hold in your hands.

America Online is not only the largest and most extensive online service, it is also the fastest growing one as well. Wandering about in search of what you want is no longer practical. Many folks have come away frustrated that they could not find something online only to later realize that what they sought was there all along—they simply didn't know where to look.

You, however, are one step ahead—you've picked up this book. With it, you can bypass the extra time spent not knowing what to do with America Online and go directly to where you want to be. This book is your key to unlocking the doors to the many services, resources, and hidden treasures on America Online.

WELCOME

Even so, this isn't the kind of book you'd want to read in one sitting (unless, maybe, you're in the bathroom). Rather, treat this book as a reference. I *do* suggest you read the first chapter as that will give you a solid ground work for the information that follows. After that, feel free to bounce around, look up your topic, and cruise the table of contents to find just what you need.

Good luck in your journeys!

Jennifer Watson O;>
Screen name: *Jennifer*

Chapter 1
Going Places with America Online

I'll never forget my first visit to America Online. Back then personal computers were usually one of two things—expensive toys or expensive office equipment. We had one at work and it was both. During the day it led a life of accounts receivable and desktop publishing. At night, it came alive with dragons and rogues.

One day we received a free sign-on kit for something called America Online which, among other things, promised up-to-the-hour stock reports. This got my boss's attention and we installed it. He found his stock reports, but unfortunately, little else.

Knowing there must be more to this America Online, I returned in the evening to look around. With a few hours of aimless wandering, I found much more than dreary stock reports. I found more information to sponge, more files to download, and more things to do than I'd ever imagined.

The next day I excitedly told my boss about the wonders I'd discovered during the night. I was met with a blank stare. I realized that what intrigued me was not necessarily what he was into. He liked money matters, which I've never had much of an eye for, and thus I was unable to show him all the financial services which I now know were there.

Looking back, I can see that my inexperience with America Online cost him several opportunities and much invaluable information. Neither of us realized the extent of America Online's scope, which was significant even back then. We had the tools and the software, but no guides or references to help us find what we needed. In other words, we weren't going anywhere.

Seven years and four computers later, I practically live online. I've been to every area at least once and usually several times, if not hundreds. If there were a support group for America Online, I'd probably lead it. Thankfully, I've been able to make a living out of showing people how to do and find things online. America Online has really taken me places. And it can do the same for you.

America Online

America Online is no longer the small, intimate service it was when I first discovered it years ago. It is growing up and into its own. At the time of this writing, there are more than six million members and enough services and content to keep them all busy.

If you are not yet a member of America Online, details on how you can sign up are available in the back of the book. If you are a member, you may already have an idea of the sheer size which awaits you. To help both new and experienced members understand the scope and organization of America Online, let's take a quick tour of the features and content it offers.

"The More Windows You Open The Cooler It Gets," America Online's most well-known slogan, only describes half the picture. Among other things, the e-mail gateways, chat rooms, and Internet doors are the framework upon which the service is built. Other features include instant messages, file libraries, progressive artwork downloading, and more. All in all, America Online offers some of the best cutting-edge technology available over your modem.

America Online organizes their offerings into *channels*—think of it as your cable company on steroids. You can begin at the top with a menu of all channels by clicking the **Channels** button on your Welcome screen or selecting **Channels** from the Go To menu. Each channel contains hundreds of individual forums and areas with more information than you would ever find on a television.

CHAPTER 1 GOING PLACES WITH AMERICA ONLINE

CHANNEL SURFING

- C! Computers and Software—C! is a mecca to all things computer-related, from forums to special interest groups to company representatives. (Keyword: C!)

- Digital Cities—A new channel, Digital Cities offers links to major metropolitan communities around the country and abroad. (Keyword: DIGC)

- Entertainment—The stars really do come out on this channel, with movies, TV and more! (Keyword: E)

- Games—The ultimate toy chest with classics, trivia, contests, and the latest interactive games. (Keyword: GAMES)

- Health & Fitness—A virtual health club with innovative ways to get in shape and stay healthy. (Keyword: HEALTH)

- The Hub—A new channel, the Hub is a motley assortment of virtual "shows," ranging from the high-minded to the frivolous. More than entertainment—it is an outlook. (Keyword: HUB)

- International—The home of AOL International and information on countries around the world. (Keyword: INTL)

- Internet Connection—America Online's gateway to the Net as well as numerous resources and services to help you make the most of it. (Keyword: NET)

- Kids Only—Kids have a place of their own online, with everything from fun and games to homework help. (Keyword: KIDS)

- Learning & Culture—The educational channel with just about anything you would need to grow and enrich your life. (Keyword: LEARN)

- Life, Styles & Interests—Stop and smell the flowers along the information highway here with clubs, forums, and special communities. (Keyword: LIFESTYLES)

- Marketplace—A shopper's delight filled with brand name and specialty goods, all available to order right online. (Keyword: MALL)

Chapter 1 Going Places with America Online

- MusicSpace—Music lovers of all kinds will find their home here along with musicians and industry experts. (Keyword: MUSIC)
- Newsstand—A virtual magazine rack with not just articles and photos, but special features you'll find only online. (Keyword: NEWSSTAND)
- People Connection—The ultimate gathering place where you can chat with other members on just about every topic under the sun. (Keyword: PC)
- Personal Finance—Money matters for everyone, from advice to investment services and resources. (Keyword: MONEY)
- Reference Desk—Find what you seek here with hundreds of searchable databases. (Keyword: REFERENCE)
- Sports—Sports of every kind, plus some you've yet to discover, along with stats, games, and special events. (Keyword: SPORTS)
- Style—America Online's own fashion district showcases the latest styles from clothing and hair to trends and attitudes. (Keywords: STYLE)
- Today's News—More than just news, this channel offers photos, discussion areas, and opinion polls. (Keyword: NEWS)
- Travel—Before you go, check here for information you won't find in any guide book. (Keyword: TRAVEL)
- Member Services—Help on making the most out of America Online—free! (Keyword: HELP)

Behind Lock and Keyword

You may have noticed that after each channel, we gave a keyword in parentheses. Keywords are one of the best-kept secrets to success with America Online. They are powerful and extraordinarily simple. In essence, they are shortcuts to all the places you want to go online. They allow you to bypass extra windows and avoid artwork you don't need. And keywords don't just get you places, they help you find them as well. If you have a topic in mind, chances are it is a keyword and leads somewhere. Once you know keywords and how to use them, you can save considerable time and money.

Many keywords are obvious, such as FINANCE for the Personal Finance channel or SAILING for the Sailing Forum. There are also a great number which are not as intuitive such as EGG, which leads to the Electronic Gourmet Guide, a haven for chefs and food lovers alike. Because of the vast number of services and resources available online, many excellent areas have keywords you'd never think to try. And of course, there are keywords which are not published anywhere but are useful just the same.

With over 5000 keywords to date, memorization is not an option even if you could find them all. Luckily, you don't have to. This book is a keyword directory to America Online's many services and resources. We will show you not only how to use keywords quickly, but also how to find them through tips, techniques, and lists of keywords themselves.

Using Keywords

To use a keyword, begin by signing on to America Online. Once online, you can bring up the keyword window one of three ways:

- Select **Keyword** from the Go To menu.
- Select the **keyword** button on the FlashBar (the row of buttons at the top of your screen).
- Press the keys **Ctrl + K** (on the PC) or **Command + K** (on the Mac).

The last method is the fastest and the one I recommend. With a little practice, you can get the Keyword window up before America Online even has time to finish welcoming you.

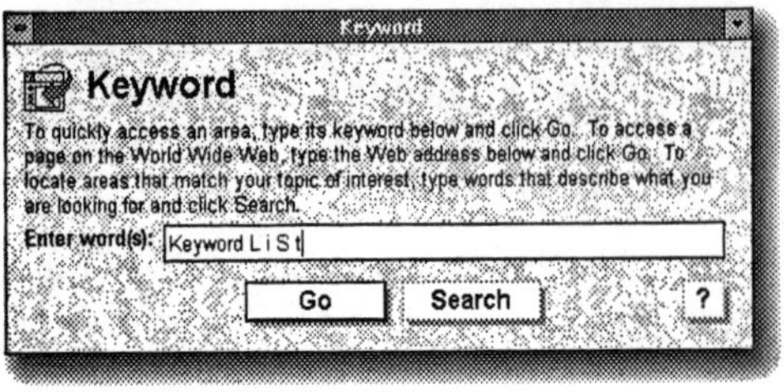

Chapter 1 Going Places with America Online

Figure 1.1 The Keyword window allows you to enter keywords and go directly to their areas.

All three ways lead to the Keyword window, your launching pad to America Online (see Figure 1.1). Once here, simply type your keyword in the box and press the **Enter** key on your keyboard or click the **Go** button in the window. America Online will instantly transport you to the keyword's area, closing the keyword window behind you to keep things neat. If the word you typed in was not actually a keyword, you will be told so immediately and the keyword you tried to use will be displayed. Should this happen, double-check that you spelled the keyword correctly.

Keywords are not case- or space-sensitive, so you can type them in any way that is convenient as was done in Figure 1.1. In addition, you can use URL addresses from the World Wide Web (WWW) as keywords—they will take you directly to the referenced WWW page using America Online's browser. URL addresses tend to be long and complicated, for example: *http://members.aol.com/jennifer/* (this leads to my home page on the WWW). We will not cover URL addresses in this book (there are many books out there that do this), but do keep in mind that you can use the Keyword window in America Online to access them.

If you look at Figure 1.1 again, you will notice two other buttons on the Keyword window: a **Search** button and a **?** button. The first button is a way to search America Online's Directory of Services. Simply type in a search word and press the **Search** button rather than the **Go** button. If there are matches, they will be displayed for you. The **?** simply explains how to use a keyword.

Mousetraps: Using the Keyboard

The mouse (or trackball) is a wonderful invention, but let's face it—it isn't always Mickey Mouse. Getting that tiny arrow in just the right spot with a mouse is not only downright challenging at times, it can be time-consuming and stressful on your wrist as well. Rather than put undue strain on your body or sanity, try using keyboard shortcuts for repetitive tasks. **Ctrl + K** (or **Command + K** on the Mac) is a keyboard shortcut and one you will soon learn to do with your eyes closed. A complete list of keyboard shortcuts is available in Appendix A at the back of the book.

If you are using Windows, you can also use the keyboard to navigate the menus and menu items which may not have keyboard shortcuts assigned to them. To do this, hold down the **Alt** key and the letter of the menu title which is underlined. The list will drop down for you, allowing you to navigate the menu items with your arrow keys. To select an item, simply press the **Enter** key.

Where Are All the Keywords?

Now that you know how to use keywords, your next step is learning how to find them. As mentioned earlier, a number of obvious destinations are already keywords. If you have an idea of the kind of area you'd like to visit, try typing in a word that describes it. For example, keyword: AUTO takes you to a window with six different auto-related areas to choose from. In addition, if you know the name of the area you are seeking, often the name itself is a keyword. For example, keyword: OMNI takes you directly to OMNI Magazine Online. Beyond this, keywords tend to become collector's items—finding them is so challenging at times that it seems natural to treasure those you have found. Up to now, that is.

CHAPTER 1 GOING PLACES WITH AMERICA ONLINE

Of all the techniques for finding keywords, the best is to simply use this book. In it are lists upon lists of not just the most useful or interesting keywords (although we have those too), but *all* the keywords on America Online known at the time of writing. The keywords in this book represent over two years of research and work; they are all yours for the taking. America Online is growing so quickly, however, by the time this book comes out there will be a slew of new keywords. To help you find the latest and greatest keywords, use the techniques and ideas that follow.

The Ultimate Keyword List Online

To keep up to date on keywords, visit the online area at keyword: KEYWORD (see Figure 1.2). In here, we keep updated versions of many of the keyword lists available in this book, plus a list of the newest keywords, changes and deletions, letters from members, and more. Our lists are updated at least twice a month and you can always learn about recent changes. The keyword lists are also available in several file formats—simple text files, database import files, Windows Help files, Mac HyperCard files, and more. And, of course, help on using and finding keywords is right here at your fingertips.

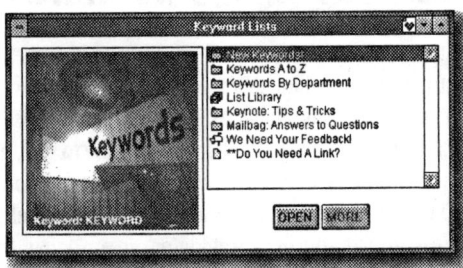

Figure 1.2 The Keyword Lists area keeps you up to date on the latest keywords.

CHAPTER 1 GOING PLACES WITH AMERICA ONLINE

 NEW—New Features & Services

America Online offers a list of new areas at keyword: NEW (see Figure 1.3). The most convenient aspect of this list is that it links to the areas themselves, allowing you to jump directly to an area with just a click of the mouse. If you take advantage of these links, make a note of the keyword given with the link so you can return later. Unfortunately, not all new areas make it into this list. Many smaller or less flashy areas don't show up here at all. But this is a good place to get a general overview of the new areas online.

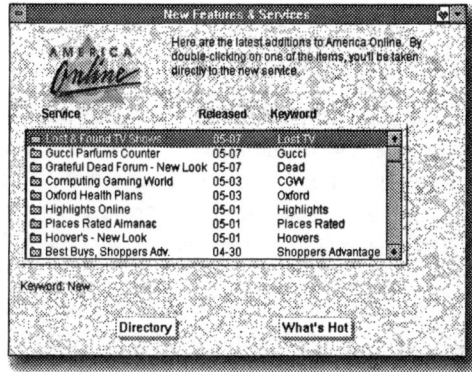

Figure 1.3 The New Features & Services area announces the most recent additions regularly.

 **SERVICES—Directory of Services**

Searching the Directory of Services is a good way to find areas you may not have yet discovered. You can search it at keyword: SERVICES or in the Keyword window (see Figure 1.4). Each area in the Directory includes a description, a keyword or two, and a way to access the area directly. As with keyword: NEW, be sure to make a note of the keyword if you choose to go directly to the

Chapter 1 Going Places with America Online

area via the description. At the time of this writing, the Directory did not include descriptions of all areas online and the newest areas were noticeably absent.

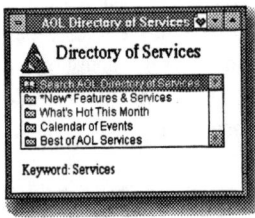

Figure 1.4 The Directory of Services allows you to search descriptions of areas online.

HOT—What's Hot on America Online

You can often glean information about interesting and unique areas at What's Hot on America Online at keyword: HOT (see Figure 1-5). This is where many of the upcoming events, new features, and special interest areas are highlighted each month. Each listing includes a short description, the keyword and a direct link. Many of the smaller or specialized areas are announced here, but again, not all will make it as space is limited. Also note that each description includes a graphic which can take some time to download if you access America Online at a slow speed.

Figure 1.5 Be sure to check What's Hot on America Online each month.

CHAPTER 1 GOING PLACES WITH AMERICA ONLINE

Other Ways to Find New Keywords

True keyword connoisseurs know that some of the best ways to find new areas online are more subtle. Here are some tips:

- Read the Welcome Screen every time you sign on. The Welcome Screen is the window that appears on your screen after you sign on with "Welcome" and your screen name at the top. New areas will sometimes show up here before they are officially announced. Special events and information frequently get spotlighted here as well.

- Check the corners of a window for keywords—they are usually placed in the lower left- or right-hand corners. If you notice one and it seems as though it could be difficult to recall later, be sure to jot it down. This is particularly important if you found the area through the Welcome Screen, as the buttons here change every 15 minutes.

- Pay attention when reading articles, watching or listening to commercials, visiting tradeshows, or talking to salespeople. Companies or associations with areas on America Online will often give their keyword and/or their World Wide Web address. Once you realize this, you'll be surprised at how often this happens.

- Read the Goodbye Screen when signing off. Future events will often be announced here along with their keywords. Again, be sure to note the keyword so you can visit when you sign on again.

 **Keyword Surfing**

For those with wanderlust, keyword surfing is a very satisfying (not to mention comfortable) adventure into the great unknown. Keyword surfing can be as simple as visiting keywords which catch your eye from one of our lists, or as challenging as trying to guess new or undiscovered keywords. And for the free-spirited surfer, there is a special keyword just

Chapter 1 Going Places with America Online

> for you—keyword: RANDOM. This keyword will take you to a random keyword somewhere online—where you will go, no one knows!
>
> One caveat: some of the areas keyword: RANDOM will take you may seem strange (they may be uncompleted areas or "skeleton keywords") or, worse yet, take you to a window without a keyword displayed. If this happens and you wish to return to it later, try guessing the keyword now rather than waiting for another day. Often the name at the top of the window is a clue to the keyword that reaches it. Keyword surfers should also be advised of high artwork levels which can cause slowdowns. But if you keep your wits about you and ride the modem carrier's wave in to shore, you may find more than you imagined. Surf's up!

A List of Your Own

Your discoveries on America Online will undoubtedly reward you with a collection of keywords that you hold near and dear to your heart. You can and probably will memorize these keywords, but there is a better way to keep a list of your frequently used keywords. The Go To menu in your America Online software can be customized with up to ten of your favorite keywords for quick access. Once a keyword is in your Go To menu, you can go right to it by pressing the **Control** key (or the **Command** key on the Mac) and a number between 0 and 9. Not only can you get to your favorite areas faster this way, but you don't need to worry about forgetting their keywords.

To customize your Go To menu, first select **Edit Go To Menu** from the menu (if you are on the Mac, it may read **Edit Favorite Places**). A window with two columns of boxes will appear—the name of the area goes in the left column and the keyword goes in the right column (see Figure 1.6). When you are finished, just click the **Save Changes** button. Your areas will appear at the bottom of the Go To menu along with the keyboard shortcut used to access them. You can update this menu at any time, including while you are offline so you can save money.

CHAPTER 1 GOING PLACES WITH AMERICA ONLINE

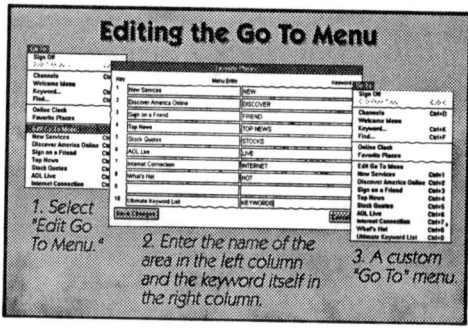

Figure 1.6 The Go To menu customized with your very own list of keywords.

Getting to the Heart of the Matter: Favorite Places

Sometimes where you want to be isn't directly accessible through a keyword. Winding your way down a twisting path of windows and prompts can be fun the first time, but a real drag after that. But never fear, help is here! A new feature called Favorite Places can get you there quicker. Favorite places (currently available in Windows, coming soon on the Mac) allow you to bookmark a window so you can return to it later on.

To mark a window, look for a small heart in the upper right-hand corner of the window. If you see a heart, click on it with your mouse and drag it to the Favorite Places icon (the folder with a heart on it) in your FlashBar (see Figure 1.7). The window will be added to your list of Favorite Places, which you can view by clicking on the same heart folder in your FlashBar. To return to a place you've marked, just double-click the name (or select the name and click the **Connect** button) in your Favorite Places folder. Alas, not all windows have this little heart on them. If your window is unadorned, back up one level and look for a heart there.

CHAPTER 1 GOING PLACES WITH AMERICA ONLINE

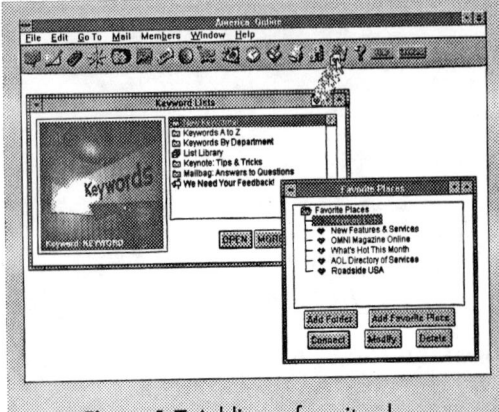

Figure 1.7 Adding a favorite place.

Desperately Seeking Keywords

If you just can't find what you are looking for and think you've exhausted all your resources, don't give up yet. Your next step is to ask someone who may know. First, try a friend or colleague who uses America Online, especially if their interests are similar to your own. Next, ask one of the many community leaders across the service, such as a Guide, a Tech Live Advisor, a forum leader or assistant, a chat host, a message board manager, or a file library manager. You can spot community leaders by their helpful natures and their screen names, which will often have a prefix of some sort such as *Guide ASC* or *Host CWC*.

If neither of these routes lead you to your destination, you can always ask us. Just send e-mail to the screen name *KEY List* with your question—please be as specific as possible. I, or one of my invaluable assistants, will endeavor to reply within 24 hours.

 **Keyword: DEAD END**

So you've typed in a keyword and the word **Invalid** screams back at you in the harsh, unearthly glow of the computer monitor. It may have even been a keyword that worked last week, or worse yet, one that appears in this book. Before you hit that brick wall, consider this: America Online is growing so fast that sometimes they need to put up a wall in order to build a bigger building.

Don't be overly discouraged by invalid keywords. First of all, check to make sure you spelled the keyword correctly. If all checks out, scan the keyword lists to see if an alternate keyword exists. This is often the case, especially if the original keyword was general. Also check for other areas that may be similar and could even contain a link to the area you are seeking.

Sometimes keywords aren't invalid but rather lead to areas which are off limits. These areas are usually construction areas for America Online staff and wouldn't be of much interest anyway. America Online *does* have an open door policy for their content online, but keep in mind that someone has to make those doors in the first place.

Using This Book

The keyword lists in this book are organized in several different ways to help you find what you need quickly. In most cases, we try to give you all synonyms of a keyword so you can choose the keyword that is easiest to type or remember. Alternate yet similar keyword spellings are indicated by parentheses—for example, BEGINNER(S) means that both keyword: BEGINNER and keyword: BEGINNERS will work. Also, note that we always give keywords in all capital letters so you can recognize them as such. You do not need to input a keyword in all caps, however; keywords are not case-sensitive.

America Online is a living, growing being in many respects, particularly when it comes to keywords. It is important to understand that keywords are added and deleted daily. You should expect to encounter keywords in this book that no longer work as well as find new keywords missing. This is where the online keyword list at keyword: KEYWORD comes in. Even so, the vast majority of keywords in this book will be valid for a long while to come.

Chapter 1 Going Places with America Online

With that said, feel free to explore each and every keyword listed in this book. Your journey is just beginning. Below is an overview of what this book offers. Any chapter will serve as an excellent starting point for your explorations.

- In Chapter 2, "Key Chains," you will find a collection of keyword lists based on specific topics, from the essential to the offbeat. There is something here for everyone!
- In Chapter 3, "Important Keywords," concise and informative descriptions of the most basic keywords online are listed in alphabetical order. Above each description is a quick-reference Ratings Bar which tells you what to expect (see Figure 1.8). The symbols on the Ratings Bar are explained at the beginning of the chapter.

| SAMPLE | 🗖 🕅 🗃 ☲ W ✧ 🕮 🕮 0:10 |

Figure 1.8 The ratings bar gives you a quick overview of important information.

- In Chapter 4, "New Keywords," the most recently introduced areas and their keywords are described and rated. Like Chapter 3, we include our ratings bar with each description.
- In Chapter 5, "Hot Keywords," we describe and classify what we feel are the most exceptional and interesting areas online. Again, the ratings bar prefaces each description.
- In Chapter 6, "Keywords A-Z," all 5000+ keywords are listed in alphabetical order, along with the area they lead to and any special notes. Begin here if you would like to browse or find out where a keyword leads before actually using it.
- In Chapter 7, "Keywords by Channel," every keyword is organized by the channel it is located in on America Online. If you have a general idea of what you are looking for but no specifics, try this keyword list first. This list is great for channel surfing, too!
- At the end of this book are two appendices. A list of keyboard shortcuts helps you navigate the online terrain

quickly and easily. And the *VirtuaLingo Glossary* deciphers AOL-speak and explains important key terms.

We Welcome Feedback!

Like America Online itself, keywords are in a state of constant flux. If you come across keywords that no longer work or lead to different areas, we want to know! We also encourage your suggestions on ways to improve our online area and future editions of this book. Please send your e-mail about this book to screen name *KEY List*. We may not be able to reply to every piece of e-mail, but you can bet it will be read! And if you report a new or recently changed keyword, we will include your screen name at the bottom of our next list.

CHAPTER 2
KEY CHAINS

America Online's greatest strength lies in its communities. They come in all shapes and sizes and may be as binding as blood or as fleeting as the seasons. To help you find your own community, we have compiled lists of keywords tailored for special kinds of people. From kids to parents, booklovers to romantics, we have something for everyone. Think of these lists as sets of keys on a ring, much like key chains—but instead of a lucky rabbit's foot, we're attaching those free AOL floppy disks everyone gets to the key rings. Hey, we wouldn't want you to misplace your keys!

Each key chain lists the keywords in alphabetical order. The actual keyword is given first, followed by the name of the area. Things we'd like to call your attention to are noted in parentheses. Keywords in bold letters are rated and described in detail within Chapters 3, 4, and 5.

AOLholics

ACCESS—Local Access Numbers
AOL BEGINNERS—The Help Desk
AOL DIAG—AOL Diagnostic Tool [Windows AOL only]
AOL ENTERPRISE—AOL Enterprise
AOL IR—AOL Investor Relations [currently on Windows AOL only]
AOL GIFT—AOL Gift Certificates
AOL GLOBALNET—AOL Globalnet (International Access Numbers)
AOLHA—Apple Aloha (for eWorld alumni)
AOL HIGHLIGHTS—America Online Highlights
AOL MAX—Family Computing: Maximum AOL
AOLSEWHERE—AOLsewhere (Connecting Abroad)
AOL SOUNDS—AOL Sound [currently on Windows AOL only]
AOL STORE—The America Online Store
AOL TIPS—Family Computing: Tip Of The Day
AOL WORLD—AOL International
ASK AOL—AOL Member Services
BEST OF AOL—The Best of America Online

Chapter 2 Key Chains

BILLING—Billing Information
CREDIT—Request Credit for Access Problems
DISCOVER—Discover America Online!
GLOSSARY—The America Online Glossary
GUIDEPAGER—Page an AOL Guide
HOT—What's Hot This Month
KEYWORD—The Ultimate Keyword Lists Online
LETTER—Community Updates from Steve Case
MEMBERS—AOL Member Directory
MHM—Members Helping Members
NEW—New Features & Services
PRESS—AOL Press Releases
SERVICES—Directory of Services
TECH LIVE—Tech Help Live
TOP TIPS—America Online's Top Tips
TOS—AOL Community Action Team
UPGRADE—Upgrade to Latest Version of AOL Software

Explorers of Sea and Sky

AMERICAS CUP—America's Cup
ASTRONAUTS—Challenger Remembered
ASTRONET—ASTRONET
ASTRONOMY—Astronomy Club
BIRDING—Birding Selections
DF SPACE—Destination Florida: Kennedy Space Center
EXCHANGE—The Exchange (Water Sports & Outdoor Activities)
FISHING—Fishing Selections
FLORIDA KEYS—The Florida Keys
FLY—Aviation Forum
FLYING—Flying Magazine
INSIDE FLYER—Inside Flyer
NSS—National Space Society
OAO—Outdoor Adventures Online
OMNI—OMNI Magazine Online
OUTDOORS—The Exchange
SAIL—Sailing Forum
SCUBA—Scuba Club
SN SPACE—Space & Astronomy
SPACE A&B—Space: Above & Beyond
STAR TREK—Star Trek Club
STARS—GALILEO Mission to Jupiter
SURF—SurfLink
TORNADO—Tornado! (various selections)
TORNADO ALLEY—Tornado Alley

UFO—Institute for the Study of Contact with Non-Human Intelligence
VAA—Virtual Airlines
VGA PLANETS—VGA Planets
WATER—Boating Online
WEATHER—Weather

(List compiled by Valerie L. Downey.)

Kidwords

ATTIC—Grandma's Attic
BLACKBERRY—Blackberry Creek
BOOKS ON BREAK—Just Books!
BRODERBUND—Brøderbund Software (KidPix and game demos)
CARTOON NETWORK—Cartoon Network
CARTOONS—The Cartoons Forum
CHILDREN'S SOFTWARE—HomePC's Children's Software
CO KIDS—Christianity Online: Kids
COMPUKIDS—CompuKids
DAVIDSON—Davidson & Associates (information on MathBlaster)
DC COMICS FOR KIDS—DC Comics for Kids
DISNEY ADVENTURES—Disney Adventures Magazine
DISNEYSOFT—Disney Interactive (demos, hints, and more)
ENCYCLOPEDIA—Encyclopedias
FAMILY PC—Family PC Online
FAO—FAO Schwarz
GAMETEK—Gametek (game demos and information)
HH KIDS—Homework Help for Kids
HIGHLIGHTS—Highlights Online for Children
KIDS—Kids Only Channel
KIDS BIZ—KidsBiz/Invention Connection
KIDS DICTIONARY—Kids Dictionary from Merriam-Webster
KIDS CHOICE—Nickelodeon's Kids' Choice Awards
KIDS QUEST—The Quest CD-ROM companion to AOL's Kids Only
KIDSOFT—Club Kidsoft
KIDS OUT—Kids Out!
KID SPORTS—New England Cable Network's Sports for Kids
KID TRAVEL—FamilyTravel Network
KIDS' WB—Kids WB (Warner Brothers) Online
KIDS WEB—Top Internet Sites for Kids
KIDZINE—ABC Kidzine
KO HELP—Kids GuidePager
MAC KIDS—Mac Kids
MCFAMILY—McFamily
MFTY—Mysteries from the Yard
NICKELODEON—Nickelodeon Online

Chapter 2 Key Chains

NINTENDO—Nintendo Power Source
ODYSSEY—Odyssey Project
PETS—Pet Care Forum
PHOTORAMA—Kids Photorama
POGS—KidBiz POGS Area
RINGLING—Ringling Brothers and Barnum & Bailey Circus Online
SCHOLASTIC—Scholastic Network Preview Area
SCOUTING—Scouting Online
STUDY Break—Compton Encyclopedia's Study Break
TOY—Pangea's ToyNet
TOYS—Collector's Corner

LOL! (Laughers On Line)

60—60-Second Novelist
AOOL—America Out of Line
BURP—AOL Plays With Sounds [currently on Windows AOL only]
CARTOON NETWORK—Cartoon Network
CARTOONS—The Cartoon Forum
COMEDY—Comedy Pub
COMEDY CENTRAL—Comedy Central
COMICS—Comics Areas
DILBERT—Dilbert
FUNNIES—The Funny Pages
HECKLERS—Hecklers Online
IMPROV—The IMPROVisation Online
INTOON—InToon with the News
JOKES—JOKES! etc.
MAD MAGAZINE—Mad Magazine
NEWS GRIEF—News Grief
SF—Science Fiction & Fantasy Forum (see Comic Book Forum)
SOUNDBITES—Soundbites Online
THE HUB—The Hub
TV SPOOFS—TV Spoofs!
WWN—Weekly World News

(List compiled by George Louie.)

Men

CO MEN—Christianity Online: Men's Fellowship
MARS—Men Are From Mars, Women Are From Venus
MEN—The Exchange: Communities (Men's Board)
MEN'S HEALTH—Men's Health Forum
MEN'S HEALTH WEB—Men's Health Internet Sites
PEN—Personal Empowerment Network (Men's Health)

🗝 Can I Have My Own Keyword?

While this is one of the most frequently-made requests concerning keywords, the answer is no. It is not possible to request your own keyword unless you are a contracted partner with America Online and charged with building an online area. Not only would it be impractical to allow individuals to have their own keywords (what would the keyword lead to?), it would be confusing as well—keywords would probably lead to unexpected places not designed for general consumption. And as America Online grows larger, keywords will become a commodity and something to be managed carefully lest we fall into chaos.

Even so, there is one way to have your own keyword of sorts. As mentioned in Chapter 1, World Wide Web addresses (URLs) can be input as keywords. As every member has the option of creating a World Wide Web page (which have URLs), you could have your own keyword to your page. It would probably look something like this: *http://members.aol.com/jennifer/*, which is the URL keyword to my own page. For more information on creating your own World Wide Web page, see keyword: MY HOME PAGE or keyword: MY PLACE.

Nature Lovers

ASTRONOMY—Astronomy Club
BACKPACKER—Backpacker Online
BIRDING—Birding Selections
CAMP—Explorers' Camp
EFORUM—Environmental Forum
EXCHANGE—The Exchange: Interests/Hobbies (Special Interests)
GARDEN—The Garden Spot
HOBBY—Hobby Central (Outdoors)
LONGEVITY—Longevity Online (Food, Fitness, Travel)
MOUNTAIN—iSKI
NAS—National Academy of Sciences

Chapter 2 Key Chains

NATURE—The Nature Conservancy
NATURE CO—The Nature Company
ODYSSEY—The Odyssey Project
OUTDOOR—Outdoor Adventure Online
OUTDOOR FUN—The Exchange: Outdoor Fun
PICTURES—Pictures of the World
SCI AM—Scientific American
SCIENCE—Science & Nature
SPACE—Space Exploration Online
SUNSET—Sunset Magazine
WEATHER—Weather News

Parents

ADOPTION—Adoption Forum
AOL FAMILIES—AOL Families area
BLACK VOICES—Orlando Sentinel Online: (Black Family Today)
CHILD SAFETY—Child Safety Brochure
CHILDREN'S HEALTH—Children's Health Forum
CO FAMILY—Christianity Online: Family
COL EDUCATION—Chicago Online Education Guide
COMPUKIDS—CompuKids
DIS—DisABILITIES Forum (especially message boards)
EDUCATION—Education department
EXCHANGE—The Exchange (Home/Health/Family in Home & Careers; Support Groups Board; African-Americans, Hispanic, Men, Women, Generation X & The Thirties in Communities; Exchange Overflow Board)
FAM HOT—What's Hot!
FAMILY COMPUTING—Family Computing Resource Center
FAMILY FINANCES—Real Life
FAMILY GAMES—Family Computing Forum: The Rec Room
FAMILY LIFE—Family Life Magazine Online
FAMILY NEWS—Family Computing Forum: News & Reviews
FAMILY PC—FamilyPC Online
FAMILY ROOM—Family Computing Forum: Family Room
FAMILY SHOWCASE—Family Product Showcase
FAMILY TRAVEL—Family Travel Network
FLORIDA—Destination Florida
FOTF—Focus on the Family
GIFTED—Gifted Online
HEALTH—Health Channel
HEM—Home Education Magazine
HOMESCHOOL—Homeschooling Forum
HOME VIDEO—Home Video

CHAPTER 2 KEY CHAINS

HOMEWORK—Homework Help Choices
IMH—Issues in Mental Health (Parenting & ADD Boards)
JCPENNEY—JCPenney
JEWISH NEWS—Jewish News (Jewish Family & Life! Magazine)
LONGEVITY—Longevity Magazine Online
MARRIAGE—Marriage Partnership Magazine
MCFAMILY—McFamily Community
MED—Mac Education & Technology Forum
MOMS ONLINE—Moms Online
MONTESSORI—Montessori Schools
NETNOIR—NetNoir (In General Messages Board)
NPC—The National Parenting Center
ONLINE PSYCH—Psych Online
OPRAH—Oprah Online (In Helpline)
PARENT ADVICE—Princeton Review Informed Parent
PARENT SOUP—Parent Soup
PARENTAL CONTROL—Parental Controls
PARENTING MAGAZINE—Parenting Magazine Online
PHS—Practical Homeschooling
PRESCHOOL—Preschool/Early Childhood SIG
SCRAPBOOK—Member Scrapbook (show off your family!)
SCREEN NAME—Add, change, or delete screen names
SMART WATCHING—The ABC Classroom
STUDY—Study Skills Service
TOY—Pangea ToyNet
TPN—The Prayer Network
WOMANS DAY—Woman's Day Online
WOMEN—Women's Interests

(List compiled by Valerie L. Downey.)

Professionals

ATT—AT&T Products & Services
AZ BIZ—Arizona Central: Work Pl.
BUSINESS—Business News
BUSINESS FORUM—Business Forum
BUSINESS RANKINGS—Business Rankings
BUSINESS SCHOOL—Business School Test Prep Areas
BUSINESS SENSE—Business Sense Inc.
BW—Business Week Online
CLASSIFIEDS—AOL Classifieds
CRAIN'S SMALL BIZ- Crain's Small Business
FEDEX—Federal Express Online
GOVERNMENT RESOURCES—Your Government Resources
HOC—Home Office Computing Online

Chapter 2 Key Chains

INC—Inc. Online
INDUSTRIES—Your Industry
LEGAL PAD—The Legal Pad
LIN—Legal Information Network
LUNCH—Your Business Lunch
NBR—Nightly Business Report
NOLO—Nolo Press Self-Help Law Center
OFFICE—Office Max Online
REAL LIFE—Real Life
RESOURCES—Your Resources
SBA—U.S. Small Business Administration
STRATEGIES—The Business Strategies Forum
TAX—Tax Forum
VOICE—Your Voice
WHITE PAGES—Pro CD's Phone Book
YB—Your Business
YELLOW PAGES—American Business Information Yellow Pages

Keyword Trivia

Think you know your keywords? Or just want to exercise your imagination? This trivia quiz tests your knowledge of America Online and, of course, keywords. You'll find the answers online at keyword: KEYWORD (check in the Keynote area) or within the keyword lists themselves. A score of 3 or above qualifies you as a Keyword Maven.

1. Where does keyword: SATAN lead?
2. What single area has the most keywords (not counting sub-areas)?
3. What is the shortest keyword?
4. What is the longest keyword?
5. Where does keyword: FREE lead?

Readers and Writers

AFTERWARDS—Afterwards Cafe
BOOK—The Book Nook
BOOKNOTES—Barron's Booknotes

Chapter 2 Key Chains

BOOKS—Books & Writing
BOOKS & CULTURE—Christian Books & Culture
BOOKS ON BREAK—Just Books!
BOOKSHOP—Mysteries from the Yard
BOOKSTORE—Online Bookstore
CRITICS—Critics' Choice (check under the Books icon)
DR WHO—Doctor Who Online
ETEXT—PDA Forum's Palmtop Paperbacks
EW—Entertainment Weekly (see Books under The Guide)
GAY BOOKS—Lambda Rising Bookstore Online
HATRACK—Hatrack River Town Meeting (Orson Scott Card)
HOBBY—Hobby Central (Writing)
L&C STORE—Learning & Culture Store
LITERACY—Adult Literacy & Education Forum
NOVEL—60-Second Novelist
OMNI—OMNI Magazine Online (Science fiction, fantasy and horror)
READING—Saturday Review Online
READING ROOM—The Reading Room
ROGUE—Rogue Print
ROMANCE GROUP—Writers Club: Romance Writers & Readers
SF—Science Fiction & Fantasy Forum
SN LIT GAME—Bookwoman's Literature Game
STAR WARS—Star Wars Fan Forum
TIMES BOOKS—The New York Times: Books of The Times
WRITE—Writers Chat
WRITER—The Writers Club

Romantics

ASTROMATES—ASTRONET: ASTROMates
CARDS—Hallmark Connections
DATING—Romance Connection
DC PERSONALS—Digital City Personals
FLOWERS—1-800-Flowers
GALLERY—AOL Portrait Gallery
HEART TO HEART—Gay & Lesbian Community Forum: Heart to Heart
IMH—Issues in Mental Health (Relationships message board)
JEWISH SINGLES—Jewish Community Forum: Jewish Singles
LOVE—Love@AOL
LOVE ONLINE—ABC's Love Online
LOVE SHACK—The Love Shack [currently on Windows AOL only]
LOVE ZONE—HealthZone: The Love Zone
MARRIAGE—Marriage Partnership Magazine
MARS—Men Are From Mars, Women Are From Venus
NETGIRL PERSONALS—NetGirl: Personals

Chapter 2 Key Chains

PEOPLE—People Connection
RELATIONSHIPS—Relationships area
ROMANCE—Romance Channel
ROMANCE STORE—Romance Store
STD—Sexually Transmitted Diseases
WASH PERSONALS—Washington Digital City: Personals
WEDDING—Wedding Workshop

The Keyword Bizarre

With the sheer number of keywords out there, you would expect there to be some oddball keywords. And sure enough, there are. For some comic relief, check out the keywords below. Can you guess where they go? You may be surprised. (No peeking in the back!)

<><
:)
AOL DEAD
BURP [currently on Windows AOL only]
CHOCOLATE
CRISPY
ELVIS
FORSOOTH
GET A LIFE
HACK
HOT CHAT
JENNY FLAME
JIM'S BRAIN
JUST DO IT
LUST
MOO
PEANUTS
PLAYMATES
RAW
SCOUNDREL
SEX
STUMP
THE COSMIC MUFFIN
UNDIES
UNIVERSE
WEIRD
WORRY
WRONG!
YOUR MOMMA
ZEN

Women

ABC WOMEN—ABC Woman's Sports
BETTER LIVING—Woman's Day Ideas for Better Living
CO WOMEN—Christianity Online: Women's Fellowship
COMMUNITIES—The Exchange: Communities (Women's Board)
ELLE—Elle Magazine Online
JEWISH NEWS—Jewish News (LILITH: Jewish Women's Magazine)
MARS—Men Are From Mars, Women Are From Venus

CHAPTER 2 KEY CHAINS

MOMS ONLINE—Moms Online
TCW—Today's Christian Woman Magazine
WOMAN—Woman's Day Magazine Online
WOMAN BOARDS—Women's Interests' Message Boards
WOMAN COLLECTIONS—Women's Interests' Arts and Letters
WOMAN NEWS—Women's Interests' News
WOMAN VOICES—Women's Interests' Organizations
WOMEN—Women's Interests
WOMEN'S HEALTH WEB—Women's Internet Sites
WOMEN CLASS—Women's Interests' Courses
WOMEN ROUND—Women's Interests' Community
WOMENS HEALTH—Women's Health Forum
WOMENS SPACE—Women's Space (Lesbian Issues)
WOMEN WEB—Women on the Web
WSF—Women's Sports World

List Lovers

Have you compiled your own list of keywords for a certain topic? Let us know and we may put it online to share with others. Just e-mail your list to screen name *KEY List* along with a description and why you think others would find it useful.

CHAPTER 3
IMPORTANT
KEYWORDS

Like phone numbers, there are important keywords everyone should know. And like a phone book, we've put them near the front for quick reference. This chapter describes and rates each of these essential keywords on America Online. Each keyword's description is introduced by a *ratings bar* which gives a general overview of the area and important information to help you decide whether it has what you seek (see Figure 3.1).

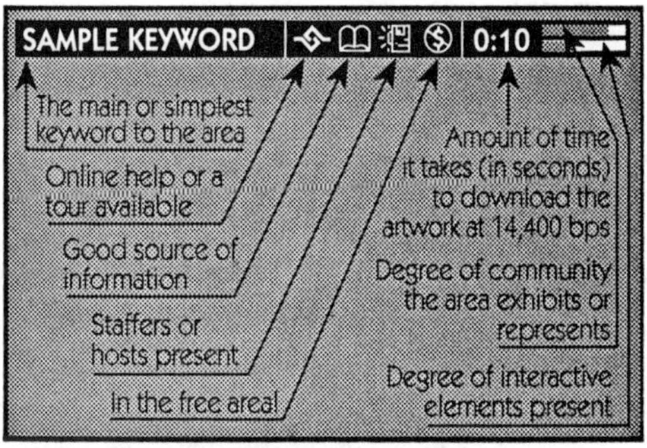

Figure 3.1 The ratings bar.

The keywords were chosen and reviewed by a group of experienced and respected community leaders. Each of them reviewed an area with which they were familiar, but never an area to which they had an official connection. Their chorus of voices is much more harmonious than anything I could have done on my own. My sincere thanks to Valerie L. Downey, Mary Gay, Elizabeth Homza, Ken Kippenbrock, Laura Kramarsky, Dave Marx, William Mason, Miriam Nathan, Amanda Randall, Eva Shaderowfsky, Gwen Smith, Bob Strange, and Bradley Zimmer.

CHAPTER 3 IMPORTANT KEYWORDS

ACCESS | 2:00

If you can't connect to America Online, you can't use keywords at all. But if you *can* connect, keyword: ACCESS is the place for the lowdown on upgraded connections. Find and/or request new access numbers. Report trouble with your current number. Learn to connect via TCP/IP. Traveling or moving? You'll find domestic and international access numbers. The single biggest weakness? Its excellent technical help has been buried in How to Connect. keyword: HIGH SPEED is another area that provides help in the same vein. ACCESS is biased in favor of your *phone* connection, while HIGH SPEED is biased in favor of *modem* problems. What if you choose the wrong one? Don't worry; they're connected to each other!

Alternate keywords: ACCESS NUMBERS, AOLNET, CALL, CONNECTING, NUMBERS, PETITIONS, PHONE HELP, PHONE NUMBER(S), PHONES, TELEPHONE, TELEPHONE NUMBERS.

Reviewed by Dave Marx.

BILLING | 0:05

Designed for easy use, keyword: BILLING allows you to change your password or address, check your billing information, and view the billing terms of your account. You will also be able to keep track of time spent online by using the detailed billing and current billing options; these are especially helpful if you have a multiple-user account. For answers to everything from how to keep track of your bill to how to get 15 free hours, check out the Commonly Asked Questions section. If you can't find the answers you're looking for there, write to the staff and they will gladly answer all your questions.

Alternate keywords: None.

Reviewed by Mary D. Gay.

BUDDY | 1:00

America Online members tend to find as many friends online as they do good resources and information. Keeping track of your friends is now easier than ever with "Buddy Lists" at keyword: BUDDY. Buddy List will tell you

CHAPTER 3 IMPORTANT KEYWORDS

exactly when your friends (or family members, colleagues, clients—anyone you designate) sign on and off. Just go to keyword: BUDDY, create your list, and view it. As soon as one of your buddies signs on or off, Buddy List will let you know by showing (or removing) their name in your list. It has options such as **Show me my buddy list as soon as I sign on**, and you can block other members from putting you on their list. If you used **Locate Member Online** every five minutes in the past, you won't know how you did without Buddy Lists. And if you are new, consider yourself fortunate.

> **NOTE:** At the time of this writing, Buddy Lists were only available for Windows. This feature will be added to the Macintosh software later in 1996.

Alternate keywords: BL, BUDDIES, BUDDY LIST(S), BUDDY MAIN (BUDDY VIEW, BV).

Reviewed by Bob Strange.

CLOCK | 0:00

Hey, what time is it? It's the day we change our clocks. Is it an hour forward or an hour back? Spring forward, fall back—or the other way around? You were to meet someone online at 7 P.M. sharp. Is your clock or watch accurate? The last time you signed up for a class online you were 15 minutes late, but your clock said it was the right time. Aargghhhhh! Never fear. The online clock is always here! Just use keyword: CLOCK

Alternate keyword: ONLINE CLOCK.

Reviewed by Eva Shaderowfsky.

CREDIT | $ | 0:03

Yes, it happens every so often: You download that interactive multimedia presentation of Proust's masterworks but discover it won't run because the file is somehow corrupted. Or your bill says you were online for 72 hours last night. What can you do? Try keyword: CREDIT! This handy credit request form lets you inform America Online of problems due to system slowness, "Host failed to respond" notices, interrupted/corrupted downloads, and billing

CHAPTER 3 IMPORTANT KEYWORDS

errors. Be prepared to type in the date and time the problem occurred and the number of minutes lost. As an additional bonus, keyword: CREDIT is in a free area, so you aren't charged for time asking for charges to be dropped!

Alternate keywords: CREDIT REQUEST, DOWNLOAD CREDIT.

Reviewed by Gwen Smith.

DICTIONARY — 0:20

How *do* you spell that? It happens to all of us. We just don't know or can't recall how to spell a word. You are online, talking to that special someone or a business contact, and you don't want to seem ignorant. What can you do? Try keyword: DICTIONARY. There are several dictionaries, including a collegiate version for adults. If you don't know how to spell the word, type in what you think may be the first three letters and an asterisk (*), then press the **Enter** key. It also includes complete definitions! There are also kid's and medical dictionaries! Need help with all those complex Wall Street or fancy Internet terms? There are dictionaries for those as well!

Alternate keywords: (COLLEGIATE, COLLEGIATE DICTIONARY, KIDS DICTIONARY, MEDICAL DICTIONARY, MW DICTIONARY, WSW).

Reviewed by Ken Kippenbrock.

DISCOVER — 0:15

Before you can go far, you need to explore the terrain and discover what awaits you on your journey. You can do this and more at keyword: DISCOVER. Discover America Online is an area all about America Online. Dubbed "Member Orientation," this area designed especially for new members and was formerly known as the Orientation Express. In here you will find a well-written tutorial which introduces you to the many features and resources available. In addition, there is a chat room where you can talk to other explorers. Discover America Online even brings some of the more unique areas online to you. Other links include the America Online Store (keyword: AOL STORE), the Find feature (keyword: FIND), and more!

CHAPTER 3 IMPORTANT KEYWORDS

Alternate keywords: DISCOVER AOL, NEW MEMBER, NEWBIE, ORIENTATION EXPRESS

Reviewed by Jennifer Watson.

DOWNLOAD 101 | 0:10

What could be better than five excellent free lessons? That's exactly what you'll find at keyword: DOWNLOAD 101. If you haven't downloaded yet, go there! If you're a veteran downloader, you still won't believe how much well-written, well-organized information is there for the taking. You'll find a superb step-by-step demonstration of file searching in Lesson 2 and a free download library for your practicing pleasure. Download 101 covers the bases, from "What is Downloading?" to finding, downloading, and using downloaded files, to "Troubleshooting, Tips and Tricks." keyword: DOWNLOAD 101 is the place to go to get started downloading and the place to return again and again for a wide range of knowledge on the topic.

Alternate keyword: DOWNLOAD HELP.

Reviewed by Dave Marx.

FILE SEARCH | 0:00

America Online is one of the best places to get shareware, and keyword: FILE SEARCH will help you find just what you're looking for! Want a game to help you procrastinate? A word processing program to help you write that paper? A benchmark program to see the speed of your new hardware purchase? Just head over to keyword: FILE SEARCH and enter the description of what you need. The search engine will present a list of choices. Although the database does not include the company-run libraries—you have to go directly to those yourself—it does list the software that has been uploaded to America Online computing forums by members.

> **NOTE** This keyword will present you with only the software for the computer system you are using to access it; if you are using a Mac you will only see Mac software, and vice versa with the PC.

Alternate keywords: QUICKFIND, QUICKFINDER.

Reviewed by Laura Kramarsky.

CHAPTER 3 IMPORTANT KEYWORDS

GUIDE PAGER | 0:05

Guide Pager is an area where members can request the assistance of a Guide. An *America Online Guide* is a Community Leader who roams the People Connection and outlying areas, helping members find their way around and making sure that everything is going smoothly. In the Guide Pager area, members can also report Terms of Service (commonly abbreviated "TOS") violations, set parental controls, change passwords, and ask questions of the Community Action Team, which is responsible for maintaining the Terms of Service. There is also a link to Member Services. Plenty of information is available in all these categories at the click of a button.

Alternate keyword: GUIDE PAGE.

Reviewed by Amanda Randall.

HELP | 0:05

HELP!!! This is *the* keyword for America Online Customer Service and Technical Support. With more than eighteen different help areas, including an online reference manual (keyword: QUESTIONS), live technical support (keyword: TECH LIVE), the MEMBERS HELPING MEMBERS message board (keyword: MHM), free lessons at DOWNLOAD 101 (keyword: DOWNLOAD 101), or a new ACCESS number (keywords: ACCESS, AOLNET), this is the place to go for help. To top it all off, it's free! Visit keyword: HELP, stay all day, and learn how to get the most from your membership. The Help Area is very well organized, providing multiple routes to every area. There's even a Search tool to find whatever you need. This area will not answer your general computing questions, and there are many excellent help resources elsewhere on America Online that should also be here. But for comprehensive, authoritative assistance with your America Online experience, you won't find anyplace else like it.

Alternate keywords: ASK AOL, ASK AMERICA ONLINE, CUSTOMER SERVICE(S), FEEDBACK, FREE, HOTLINE, INFO SHOP, INFORMATION, ONE STOP SHOP INFO, MEMBER, MEMBER SERVICES, SERVICE, SUPPORT, SYSOP.

Reviewed by Dave Marx.

CHAPTER 3 IMPORTANT KEYWORDS

HELP DESK 0:10

Libraries, uploads, downloads, compression, installation, upgrades. What does it all mean? Your computer is confusing enough, but now you're on America Online and feeling completely lost? Don't panic! Take a deep breath and try keyword: HELP DESK, where you'll visit the Computing and Software Beginner's area Help Desk. No matter what your computer or software, the Help Desk is full of simple straightforward instructions that will help you with America Online and your computer system, including downloading and uploading help, hints and tips, and answers to just about every question you'll bump into along the way. Every night, live help with knowledgeable forum staff is available with a click of a single icon to a conference room. You'll feel welcome because you are, and so are your questions. Here's where you'll find answers!

Alternate keywords: AOL BEGINNERS, BEGINNER(S), FORUM HELP, GETTING STARTED, MAC HELP, PC HELP, STARTER.

Reviewed by Miriam Nathan.

HIGH SPEED 0:00

The High Speed Access area is a very close cousin to keyword: ACCESS. keyword: HIGH SPEED's specialty is connecting to America Online at the highest possible speed—and especially modem and connection problems. The help here is oriented toward the technical do-it-yourselfer. You'll find instructions, modem profiles, FAQs galore, access numbers, and links to the America Online Store's Modem shop and to modem manufacturers on America Online and the Internet. The organization of the technical information is somewhat better than ACCESS, but the organization of the access number information is inferior. In the end, either keyword will do the job.

Alternate keywords: GRANDE VITESSE, MODEM HELP.

Reviewed by Dave Marx.

HOLIDAY n/a

America Online loves to celebrate holidays! If it is near a major (or even minor) holiday, try keyword: HOLIDAY or

Chapter 3 Important Keywords

the name of the holiday itself. While the areas change with each holiday, you will usually discover great hard-to-find information about the holiday itself, interactive events and contents, message boards, libraries, chat rooms, and more! Some of the big holidays can become quite elaborate, with other areas contributing to the festivities in unique and creative ways. On the downside, artwork can also be very elaborate at keyword: HOLIDAY so be prepared to wait. Happy holidays!

Alternate keyword: HOLIDAYS (others vary with the holiday).

Reviewed by Jennifer Watson.

HOT

You may be surprised at how much is happening on America Online. Take a gander at keyword: HOT for a glimpse. At What's Hot on America Online, you'll find both descriptions and links to special events, promotions, new areas, and more. Each description includes a graphic in addition to text, so be forewarned you will need to wait for it to download. If you find an area that looks interesting, be sure to note the keyword given at the bottom so you can return again later. Not all "hot" areas are listed here—space is limited—but you'll find a great cross section that can keep you busy for hours.

Alternate keyword: WHATS HOT.

Reviewed by Jennifer Watson.

MEMBERS

You know your friend has an America Online account but you don't know his or her screen name. What can you do? You might want to begin your quest at keyword: MEMBERS, by searching through the Member Directory. All members are given the option of creating a member profile for each screen name. You can create, edit, delete, or view your own profile at keyword: MEMBERS, and you can try a Member Directory search, which might lead you to your long-lost friend! The search engine supports Boolean and wildcard searches and will return as many as 250 matches. Some searches are less successful than

CHAPTER 3 IMPORTANT KEYWORDS

you'd like, because members aren't required to have a profile, nor are they obliged to use their full names. But it's a great place to start. Good luck!

Alternate keywords: DIRECTORY, MEMBER DIRECTORY.

Reviewed by Elizabeth Homza.

MHM

Confused? Lost? A bit overwhelmed by this big community? Why not pay a visit to the Members Helping Members (MHM) message boards? MHM is a place to ask questions and learn nearly anything you might need to know about America Online. Many people find themselves sometimes needing a little help with something, whether they are new or experienced users. Post a question! The questions are answered by other members like yourself who are happy to provide friendly assistance. Everyone here remembers what it was like to be new or to need a hand! Separate MHM areas are maintained for Macintosh and Windows users, and you will be automatically taken to the MHM area appropriate for the America Online platform you are using. This also ensures the answers are specific to your America Online software and computer. MHM is a happy, friendly place, full of knowledge and helping hands. And remember: the only stupid question is the one that's never asked!

Alternate keywords: None.

Reviewed by Elizabeth Homza.

NEW

Do you like to stay on top of things? At keyword: NEW you can see the latest services and areas offered on America Online. Each listing gives the keyword used to get to the area and the date the area opened. Double-clicking on a listing takes you directly to that area. NEW also offers links to America Online's Directory of Services and the current month's What's Hot listing. Don't be the last to know! Visit keyword: NEW regularly and be among the first to discover America Online's newest features!

Alternate keywords: None.

Reviewed by Valerie L. Downey.

Chapter 3 Important Keywords

PARENTAL CONTROLS | 0:30

Are your children safe? With millions of people online, who knows what type of people they will come across. In order to help you protect your children, a set of tools called *Parental Controls* has been developed by America Online. Available in the Parental Controls area are links to popular areas concerning online security, including Steve Case's monthly letter and the Terms of Service area. In addition, there are staffed message boards for posting your own questions about security or the tools and an Online Safety Tips area. There are also special tools! The first tool is for younger children; it allows you to restrict their access to the Kids Only Channel. It is highly recommended that you do this for children under twelve. The remaining tools let you selectively block or unblock areas of the service, such as chat rooms, Instant Messages, or Internet newsgroups.

Alternate keyword: PARENTAL CONTROL.

Reviewed by Bradley Zimmer.

PASSWORD | 0:00

Your password is literally your key to signing onto America Online, and it's important to change your password often to help keep that key as secure as possible from unauthorized persons. keyword: PASSWORD is the place to make that happen! Here, you'll find brief rules, tips, and cautions to read before selecting a password. When you're ready, you simply click on **Change Password**, make your choice, and then confirm it! This section of America Online is in the free area, so you won't be charged while you take your time and decide what your password will be. Choose wisely at keyword: PASSWORD!

> **NOTE** Your password is a secret, and you should never give it out to anyone, even if someone posing as America Online staff asks for it. If you are asked for your password, report it immediately at keyword: GUIDE PAGER.

Alternate keyword: CHANGE PASSWORD.

Reviewed by William Mason.

42

Chapter 3 Important Keywords

PRESS 0:05

If you'd like to read what's happening "behind the scenes" at America Online, try keyword: PRESS. Collected here in the America Online Press Release Library are press releases on new features and partners, financial statements, announcements of new membership plateaus, and more! You might find out what new alliances America Online has struck in the online industry or read about an upcoming forum before its debut. You can search the library of releases for a topic of your choice. keyword: PRESS will tell you what's coming before it happens. The presses are never on hold at America Online's Press Releases!

Alternate keyword: PRESS RELEASE.

Reviewed by William Mason.

QUESTIONS 0:00

The centerpiece of America Online's Member Services is the One-Stop Infoshop at keyword: QUESTIONS. You'll find the answers to all your Customer Support and Technical Support questions behind fourteen handy on-screen buttons organized by topic. Each topic area includes a Suggestion box and a Write to Our Staff feature. To top it all off, the time you spend here is not charged to your account. You can spend days reading the answers available at keyword: QUESTIONS and you'll be none the poorer for the experience! I can't find enough good things to say about QUESTIONS. If I had to recommend one Help resource on America Online, this would be it. Be sure to check it out!

Alternate keywords: ASK STAFF, QUESTION, WRITE TO (OUR) STAFF.

Reviewed by Dave Marx.

SERVICES 0:00

It's huge! America Online is a very big city with many places to go, people to see, and things to do. Where can you look for areas that match your interests? America Online maintains a searchable directory of much of its content at key-

CHAPTER 3 IMPORTANT KEYWORDS

word: SERVICES. A search on any topic(s) will return a list of areas that might be of interest, and a short description of each area is available. Not all areas make it into the Directory of Services, and some don't get updated as frequently as they should. Along with the directory, the Directory of Services offers useful summary information grouping popular areas into lists such as What's Hot This Month, New Features & Services, Calendar of Events, and Best of America Online Services. There's something for everyone!

Alternate keywords: DIR OF SERVICES, DIR OF SVCS, DIRECTORY OF SERVICES, DONT MISS, FIND, NOW PLAYING, SERVICES DIRECTORY.

Reviewed by Elizabeth Homza.

TECH LIVE

For human assistance, come to TECH LIVE. Staffed 20 hours a day, the friendly "TLAs" field questions about America Online's software and services while the "AOLTechs" *also* help with your America Online–related modem and computer hardware problems. TECH LIVE can get very busy and chaotic, and waiting times may stretch to 20 minutes or more. Watch the Techs helping others while you wait—it's an education in itself. Meantime, you can browse keyword: QUESTIONS without losing your place in line; time spent in TECH LIVE is not charged to your account. The real trick is getting there—they try very hard to divert you to written Help before you can enter.

> **NOTE** At the time of this writing, these keywords did not take your directly to the front door of Tech Live—you had to navigate through a few windows first.

Alternate keywords: CS LIVE, TECH HELP LIVE.

Reviewed by Dave Marx.

TOP TIPS

Wish you knew more about America Online? Want to share your knowledge with others? Now you can, at keyword: TOP TIPS. In this area you will find useful tips

CHAPTER 3 IMPORTANT KEYWORDS

about America Online offered by other members. Each tip is accompanied by a graphic example and, when appropriate, a link to the area featured. You can submit your own favorite tips and win free online time. Unfortunately, the area isn't kept as current as it should be; for example, the keyword list in this area is almost a year old at the time of this writing. Most of the tips are timeless, however. Definitely worth a visit or three.

Alternate keywords: BEST TIPS, HOW TO, NAVIGATE.

Reviewed by Valerie L. Downey.

TOS

If you love "fine print," this is the place! America Online's Terms of Service (TOS) are the rules of the road and service agreement for America Online's members. If you can't abide by these rules you can be "TOSsed" offline, so it pays to review. On the flip side, when others misbehave, come here to check the rules and report to America Online's Community Action Team—the folks who enforce TOS. Three big buttons lead to the **Terms of Service**, **Rules of the Road**, and **Online Conduct**. The fourth button is for reporting TOS violations and asking TOS, Billing, and General questions (all via e-mail). The biggest problem is that you can't get immediate help with troublemakers. For that, you need to know about keyword: GUIDEPAGER.

Alternate keywords: TERMS, TERMS OF SERVICE, TOS ADVISOR.

Reviewed by Dave Marx.

TOUR

Looking for America Online in all the wrong places? Try the America Online Highlights tour. It wends its way through twelve different features of the service, allowing you to break off at any time and explore on your own. The places you stop at on the tour are considered only samples of what you'll find here and are not intended to give you a broad overview. While this tour can be a fun introduction for newcomers, it will most likely leave you with a limited view of America Online. Note also that each tour

Chapter 3 Important Keywords

stop requires an art download, making for a choppy tour indeed. If you are looking for a real tour of America Online, I recommend Tom Lichty's *Official America Online Tour Guide*, Published by Ventana Press

Alternate keyword: AOL HIGHLIGHTS.

Reviewed by Jennifer Watson.

| UPGRADE | -◇- | $ | 1:00 |

Are you driving yesterday's America Online software? America Online upgrades its programs at least once a year, adding nifty new features and improving technical performance. This is the place to come to get a free download of the latest America Online software and an overview of its new features. You may also find a software "patch" for fixing problems with the current software. keyword: UPGRADE won't win any awards for scintillating content, but it often has links to demos of the latest features. Its biggest failing? Inadequate help texts for installation and solving installation problems. A lot of folks end up getting their installation help at keyword: TECH LIVE.

Alternate keyword: NEW AOL.

Reviewed by Dave Marx.

CHAPTER 4
NEW KEYWORDS

New keywords are special. They may be announced with great fanfare or steal quietly onto scene. More often than not they are exchanged by members with pride and excitement, heralding in a new place with wonders yet unknown. While we cannot include *all* new keywords here, we are honored to present a broad cross-section of both the not-to-be-missed and the missed-the-mark. Remember, you can learn about most new keywords at keyword: NEW (although not all make it there). Also keep in mind that new areas don't always make it and may disappear shortly after debut.

Each keyword's description is introduced by a Ratings Bar which gives you a general overview of the area and its offerings (see Figure 4.1). The ratings bar is helpful in deciding whether or not an area is of interest to you *before* spending the time to visit it.

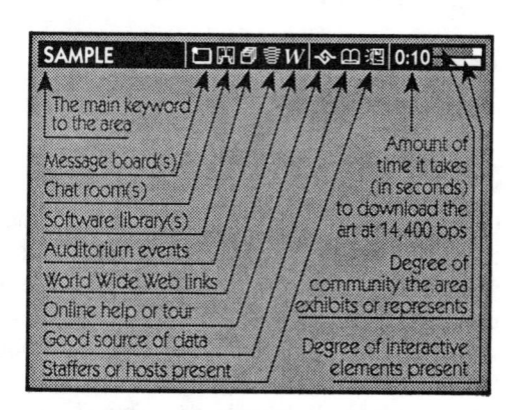

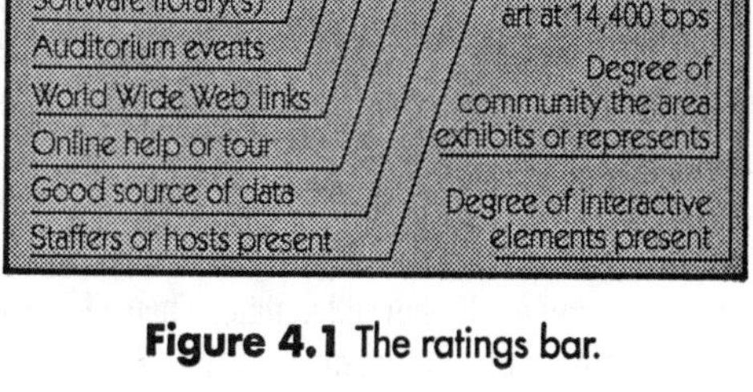

Figure 4.1 The ratings bar.

The new keywords were chosen and reviewed by a group of colleagues and friends, all respected leaders in the America Online community. Each of these folks reviewed

Chapter 4 New Keywords

an area with which they were familiar, but never an area to which they had an official connection. My sincere thanks to Stacy Brice, Valerie L. Downey, Dave Marx, Lauren Sebel, Gwen Smith, Kate Tipul, Stephen Urban, and Bradley Zimmer.

AAA — 5:30

Going on a trip? Need help planning your trip? AAA may be able to help you out at keyword: AAA. Here you will find information on everything from where to stay when you get to your destination, to where to dine, to what to see. You will also find information on construction hotspots so that you can avoid those long waits on the interstate sitting in your car. AAA also keeps you aware of *Traffic Traps*, which are "locations where natural or artificial conditions are used to entrap unsuspecting motorists, particularly strangers, and/or strict enforcement practices are followed primarily to generate revenue rather than improve traffic safety." AAA also offers Car Care Tips and Bridge & Ferry information. Do keep in mind that many of the special services require that you be a AAA member.

> **NOTE:** At the time of writing, AAA is only available on America Online for Windows.

Alternate keywords: 3A, A3, TRIPLE A.

Reviewed by Bob Strange.

AIR WARRIOR — W — 3:00

Close your eyes for just a moment. Now picture in your mind a clear blue sky. Big white clouds for miles. You are sitting in the cockpit of your authentic WWII fighter plane, cruising along at 5000 feet. Not a care in the world. Then, you hear a low hum in the distance. You look around but can't see anything anywhere. The hum gets louder and louder but still nothing. Then all of a sudden, out of nowhere, a Korean War fighter plane swoops down from above you and fires its guns. You push your flight stick down and nosedive just in time to avoid the ammunition from the other plane. Pretty exciting, huh?

CHAPTER 4 NEW KEYWORDS

Well that is the feeling you get when you play Air Warrior. The new multiplayer online game on America Online, Air Warrior is a game unlike those you may have seen on other online services. This game features real-time multiplayer online play, adjustable levels of play to be enjoyable to both beginners and veterans, the most comprehensive viewing system of any air combat simulator, and more. You also have your choice of 27 different WWI, WWII and Korean War fighters and bombers to take into action. The thing that makes this game exciting to play is that you are flying against other members online, which makes the play unpredictable and exciting. If you love the thrill of combat and the feeling you get when you accomplish what seems to be an impossible mission, then you have to check out keyword: AIR WARRIOR.

> **NOTE** At the time of writing, AAA is only available on America Online for Windows.

Alternate keyword: KESMAI.

Reviewed by Bob Strange.

AOL WORLD   W   4:00

Ever want to travel across the oceans but couldn't afford it? Now you can at keyword: AOL WORLD! This is your one stop flight to the U.K., France, Japan, Germany, Canada, and the USA. You'll find International News, Chat, Sports, Message Boards, and more! Join in on conversations in a particular country or check out the global chat room and make America Online friends from all over the world. More than 60 different countries are represented here. Where will this passport to the world take you today?

Alternate keywords: AOL INTERNATIONAL, FRANCE, GERMANY, INTL, INTERNATIONAL (US), JAPAN, GERMANY.

Reviewed by Lauren Sebel.

ARFA   W   0:10

If you've been sitting in front of the computer too much lately, get out your running shoes and use keyword: ARFA, the American Running & Fitness Association. AR&FA's

Chapter 4 New Keywords

goal is to improve the health of Americans by promoting safe exercise, which they do admirably in their online area. Their collections of information are organized into eight main topics: Running, Cycling, Swimming, Training, Sports Injuries, Diet & Nutrition, General Fitness, and Motivations & Mental Strategy. Their articles will not only help you stay safe, but offer advice on existing conditions as well as help you improve your performance and enjoyment. Where else could you find tips on staying in shape while you stay online?

Alternate keywords: None.

Reviewed by Jennifer Watson.

ASTRONET — W — 3:00

ASTRONET is a star-studded production—stars in the zodiac, that is. America Online's mecca to all things astrological. Beyond what you'd expect to find here—horoscopes and astrology readings—there are several surprises as well. Several independent magazines on astrology make their home here and there are a number of special-interest areas on everything from medical astrology to ancient Chinese astrology. And don't miss "The Cosmic Muffin," a nationwide radio show now online. ASTRONET is an expansive area, with regularly hosted chats, active message boards, an even a matchmaking area (ASTROMates). Remember, "it is a wise person who rules the stars and a fool who is ruled by them."

Alternate keywords: ASTROLOGY, WELCOME TO PLANET EARTH, ZODIAC.

Reviewed by Jennifer Watson.

ATTIC — n/a

Grandma's Attic is a magical place just for kids. Like a real attic, this area houses special things to be treasured and preserved. Of particular interest are the chests of information scattered about on a variety of subjects such as animals, clouds, sports, dreams, crafts, magic tricks, music, science, and more. There is even a castle, designed and illustrated by kids themselves—plus games, contests, and activities. One of the best things

CHAPTER 4 NEW KEYWORDS

about the Attic is that there is a real Grandma here, and Grandma's kids help keep the Attic alive and well. This is not just *for* kids, it is also *by* kids.

Alternate keyword: None.

Reviewed by Jennifer Watson.

CGW | 2:00

If you like to play computer games, visit the Computer Gaming World at keyword: CGW. In Game Tracks you can see the latest about games in development. Find out what's hot in the Game Review area. Read the diary of a game designer and discuss the games you like to play on the message boards. You can also find tips to help improve your play and, in the Game Poll area, you can even rate the games you play. At present CGW is just getting off the ground and is working out some bugs. Some areas seem a little slow but the potential is there!

> **NOTE:** At the time of this writing, AAA is only available on America Online for Windows.

Alternate keywords: CG, COMPUTER GAMING (WORLD).

Reviewed by Valerie L. Downey.

FLASH | 0:00

How can I explain this place? Let's quote the proprietors: "This area is designed to provide a forum for music industry professionals to talk about music in cyberspace, as well as discussion of the interactive cyber novel 'Shooting to The Top: A Music Industry Crime Story.' In its first month only fifty messages were posted regarding the novel, although the music industry chit-chat was a bit livelier. Lacking everything but a message board and the aforementioned novel, with a keyword that has no relation to its content and a mediocre cyber novel thinly connected to the topic of its message boards, this is a forum going nowhere fast.

Alternate keyword: MAM.

Reviewed by Dave Marx.

Chapter 4 New Keywords

FULL D 2:00

Have you ever considered buying America Online? No…not the company, but stock in it? In order to better serve its stockholders or those who wish to research the company's performance first, America Online has created Investor Relations. This forum has specific information on every detail of America Online, Inc.—both current and archived. Also included are reports and analyses from independent firms. Before you pick up the phone to call your broker, be sure to stop by here first to consider adding AMER to your portfolio!

> **NOTE:** At the time of this writing, AAA is only available on America Online for Windows.

Alternate keywords: AOL INVESTOR RELATIONS, AOLIR, FD, FULL DISCLOSURE, INVESTOR RELATIONS, IR.

Reviewed by Bradley Zimmer.

GOOD LIFE 1:30

Are you living the good life? The folks at Your Good Life belief that a good life centers around balancing your physical, personal and professional sides. With that in mind, their online area's mission is to provide daily support and motivational articles, networking opportunities, exposure to new ideas, mentorship, career opportunities, and strategies to reach your personal and physical goals. One of my favorite parts of this area is the weekly spotlight on members—their success stories are inspiring and uplifting. The area is a bit weak on content yet, but the promise is there.

Alternate keywords: None.

Reviewed by Jennifer Watson.

HIGHLIGHTS 5:00

Remember when you were a kid and the best part about going to the doctor was knowing you would get to read the *Highlights* Magazine while you waited? Well, now you can read it right here online! Once at the main screen, it is a

CHAPTER 4 NEW KEYWORDS

feast for the eyes! Click on **Our Own Place** and you'll discover art, poetry and stories by kids. Move to **Boredom Busters** and you'll find a crafts area, mindteasing activities, picture puzzles and more! There's a library here too, full of articles and pictures. Click on the blinking **Special Features** star and you'll find non-fiction and short stories and science questions answered. Who can forget Goofus and Gallant? Click on the **Timbertoes & More** icon and you'll find all the great Highlights cartoons and hidden pictures. Make sure you sign your kids up for the Highlights Newsletter and leave a message for other kids at the Post It section! One of the best features is the Ask Highlights section where you can get safety tips from Goofus and Gallant, find technical help, meet the editors, or get advice. Highlights remains fun with a purpose.

Alternate keywords: HFC, HIGHLITES, HIGHTS ONLINE.

Reviewed by Lauren Sebel.

INTOON

If you like a good laugh at the expense of today's popular and political leaders and events, then keyword: INTOON is for you! INTOON is an area featuring the political cartoons and satire of Mike Keefe, whose work is seen in newspapers across the nation. Not content to focus solely on Mike Keefe, it also provides biographies, photos, and the all important sample cartoons from other leading editorial cartoonists, as well as links to other cartoon-themed websites. Also provided are weekly cartoon contests, message boards for political debate, and discussion of cartooning. Also, a caveat: as this area is by and about political cartoonists, you can expect to see a lot of online-viewable art scattered throughout the area.

Alternate keywords: DEPIXION, EDITORIAL CARTOONS, MIKE KEEFE, TOON, TOONZ.

Reviewed by Gwen Smith.

JEWISH

Whether you're Jewish or not, you're bound to feel welcome here. If you're looking for answers about Judaism, a chat (including scheduled youth chats and singles activ-

CHAPTER 4 NEW KEYWORDS

ities for all ages), information on Israel, travel, education, family, food, or holidays and spirituality, you'll find it. There's a variety of resources, message boards, chat activities and even a mailing list to keep members in touch. The area is attractively presented with original artwork—Mac members will encounter almost no artwork download wait times, but PC members should expect to wait a bit. Visit soon, and check out **This day**, where you can find a short quote, a Torah reading, a historical event, a trivia question, and a new joke every day.

Alternate keywords: JCOL, JEWISH COMMUNITY.

Reviewed by Sue Boettcher.

KIDCARE

If you care about kids, then KidCare is the place for you. It is devoted to children's health and well-being. In KidCare you have an opportunity to exchange experiences, ideas, and information about raising healthy kids. Find out how to deal with finicky eaters and how to make doctor visits go smoothly. Learn about physical and cognitive development. Find out how to deal with sexuality and dating issues. KidCare focuses on five main areas: Growth & Development, Staying Safe & Well, Sickness & Symptoms, Fitness, and Nutrition. You can find out what toys are safe for children and learn how to talk with your child about sex, drugs, and violence. You can find current news items in HealthBytes and take the Rate Your Plate quiz to find out how nutritious your meals are. Read special stories provided by others and write of your own experiences. So, whether you're a parent, grandparent or just interested in kids, visit KidCare to show how much you really care.

Alternate keywords: None.

Reviewed by: Valerie L. Downey.

LATINO

Los Latinos de America Online: here's your chance to be a star. Every week you can find new biographies or profiles at HISPANIC Online—will you be featured there? Use keyword: LATINO to travel to HISPANIC Online, the gathering place for Latinos on America Online. HISPANIC Online is the electronic branch of the national HISPANIC Magazine. You will find information and links to all Latino interests plus a guide to Latino-related areas on the World Wide Web. Find out which issues in news, politics, education, and entertainment relate to the Latino community. Be sure to check regularly to see who is being given the big Basta and who gets the cheering Bravo!

Alternate keywords: HISPANIC MAGAZINE, LATINA.

Reviewed by Valerie L. Downey.

LOVE@AOL

On a journey searching for the right significant other or true love? Lost but destined to find that single soulmate? Look no further and find your Love@AOL! Love@AOL is filled with many ways to find that person especially for you. Included are steamy messages boards packed with persons with interests of all kinds, likes, and dislikes. Learn the definitions of love, get love tips, shop for the perfect love gift, maybe win a romantic vacation, and much more. Browse around and get love down to a science. Go ahead and send one or many of the Show'n'Tell pictured members a fill-in-the-blank precreated message or an in-your-own-words love letter to strike up a fire. Hey, if all else fails on the journey for love, call a LoveDr and try the hosted nightly The Hot Bed conference room chat for a live interactive way to find your Love@AOL! You may just get yourself a date, get hitched—who knows what else!

Alternate keywords: AMOR(E), DATE, DATING SERVICE(S), LOVE(R), LOVE AT AOL, LUST, LUV, MATCHMAKER, MATCHMAKING, PASSION.

Reviewed by Stephen Urban.

PARASCOPE

Do you believe everything the government told us about the Roswell Incident? Do you have a paranormal experience to share? Have you ever had a close encounter of any kind? If you'd like to learn more about these and countless other mysterious happenings, then ParaScope is the

Chapter 4 New Keywords

place for you. With great graphics, and wonderfully interactive with weekly polls, contests and games, this area is sure to delight those who feel something is very definitely going on "out there." But this place isn't all fun and games—there is hard-core, documented information in the Dossier section that is sure to chill even Oliver Stone. If the thought of conspiracies, cover ups and unexplained phenomena keep you up nights, then set your sights on ParaScope. But be careful—you never know who might be watching over your shoulder.

Alternate keywords: ALIENS, CONSPIRACY, PARANORMAL, PERISCOPE, PS, PSCP, SCOPE, STRANGE, WEIRD.

Reviewed by Kate Tipul.

PARENT SOUP

So, parents, what's your favorite soup? You name it, keyword: PARENT SOUP has it! The Soup community is a diverse and well-seasoned one with new flavors being thrown in all the time. All parents are welcome. Single parents mingle at the Meet Market while others chat in the Rumpus Room. Find out how to relax with monkey exercises. Test your knowledge in PARENT SOUP—THE GAME! And, after a particularly difficult and trying day, a Primal Scream in the Chill Out room may be in order. Add an ingredient, take an ingredient, stir and taste.

Alternate keywords: PARENTS SOUP, PARENT'S SOUP.

Reviewed by Valerie L. Downey.

PLACES RATED

So you decided to take a vacation! Or maybe move to another city! Either way, Places Rated Almanac is the resource to turn to for help with the big decision of "Where to?" Besides being able to search by specific details such as crime rate, availability of the arts, or climate, you may also search by city or state to view all of the statistics about an area. For instance, a search on a random city had well over 125 statistics. However, the one thing you won't find here is an opinion. All ratings are made using facts and statistics, including the Overall Rating list.

Chapter 4 New Keywords

> **NOTE:** At the time of publication, only the United States and Canada are included in the Almanac.

Alternate keyword: PLACES RATED ALMANAC.

Reviewed by Bradley Zimmer.

PRESCHOOL | 0:00

If you've ever had to work with preschoolers then you know it's both challenging and rewarding. You also know that it helps to have as much assistance as possible. Never fear—help is here at keyword: PRESCHOOL, the Preschool/Early Childhood Special Interest Group (a branch of the Mac Education & Technology Forum). Share ideas and information with others on message boards focusing on preschool learning, Montessori methods, and Waldorf Education. One of the best things you'll find here is a wealth of Mac software to use with preschoolers. Come check it out, but be prepared to do some file downloading—some of the programs are hard for even adults to resist.

Alternate keyword: EARLY ED(UCATION).

Reviewed by Valerie L. Downey.

STRAIGHT DOPE | 1:00

Do you know Cecil Adams? Remember, he sat behind you in English class. The guy with the funny looking…okay, just kidding, really he's the world's smartest human! Use keyword: STRAIGHT DOPE and get the opportunity to search Cecil's brain. Hear his answers to questions such as where does belly button lint come from, how do you hypnotize a chicken, and have chastity belts ever been used on men? Find out if anything is worn under a kilt and if a 90-lb chimp can clobber a full-grown man. Of course if you already know the answers and think you are smarter than Cecil, see if you can stump him—go ahead, try it! I dare you!

Alternate keywords: DOPE, CECIL, CECIL ADAMS.

Reviewed by Valerie L. Downey.

Chapter 4 New Keywords

TPI 3:00

What's the latest trivia game to hit America Online? Trivial Pursuit Interactive. NTN, that trivia purveyor extraordinaire, has dished-up another hot title. Show up on time (times for scheduled games are posted) and you'll find NTN's not-so-trivial, mainstay Countdown transformed into Trivial Pursuit with those six famous categories, colored wedges, the works! A glance at the rules tells another story. Each round of the game is played differently, mostly in ways only remotely related to the original board game. This one is for heavy-duty players only. At this writing the game is brand new, but it looks like NTN will run this as a special, big-prize, evening-prime-time-only attraction. At noontime Countdown will be the only game in town.

> **NOTE:** At the time of this writing, AAA is only available on America Online for Windows.

Alternate keyword: TRIVIAL PURSUIT.

Reviewed by Dave Marx.

WWN 0:15

Online imitates offline as the blazing headlines of the Weekly World News greet you at keyword: WWN. No longer do you need to surreptitiously read this paragon of American culture while standing in the check-out lane. Just like the pulp version, every off-the-wall column and audacious article of the tabloid are right here for the reading. The area is refreshingly low on artwork, too, so you won't be caught in a download when your mother-in-law walks into the room. And as always with online magazines, there are several features you won't find anywhere else, including regularly-hosted chats and the Alien Diary (you'll find out). So dig in and enjoy. The Weekly World News may be tacky, but it is 100 percent American.

Alternate keywords: ASK SERENA, BATBOY, BIGFOOT, DEAR DOTTI, ED ANGER, ELVIS, NESSIE, SATAN, SIDESHOW, VAMPIRE, WEEKLY WORLD NEWS.

Reviewed by Jennifer Watson.

CHAPTER 4 NEW KEYWORDS

YOUR BIZ   0:30

If you've ever wished for just *one* place to turn to where you could find all the help you needed to start a small business or make one more successful, Your Business—America Online's small business resource, is the place for you! Under one roof, you'll find the tools you need to reach the people and businesses that can help you succeed. Including access to business strategies for *your* industry, Your Business includes information and resources in all sorts of areas, designed to help you think about, establish and maintain your own business—and flourish in it. Be sure to join in the many and varied topical discussions hosted here, and subscribe to *Your Newsletter*, the weekly news digest. As an entrepreneur or small business owner, there's no need to go it alone any more!

Alternate keywords: BUSINESS CENTER, E-ZONE, ENTREPRENEUR ZONE, EZ(ONE), MSBIZ, MSBC, SBC, SMALL BUSINESS, THE ENTREPRENEUR ZONE, THE ZONE, YB, YOUR BUSINESS.

Reviewed by Stacy Brice.

ZD NET   6:00

Do you crave additional computer equipment? If so, check out ZDNet, which is a production of Ziff-Davis. Especially designed for the home computer user to help them get the most out of their computing experience, ZDNet has much to offer. Be the first to find out what is happening in the computing industry. Let Dr. Download answer your software questions. Learn how to customize Windows 95 or make your PC printer talk like a Mac in ZDNet's Tweak area. Post your technical questions on the message boards and you'll likely get an answer in short order. Visit the Crave area for useful product reviews and advice. Spend some time at ZDNet and soon you'll be amazing your friends with your wealth of knowledge!

Alternate keywords: ZD, ZIFF.

Reviewed by Valerie L. Downey.

Chapter 5
Hot Keywords

Remember Saturday morning cartoons? We all had our favorite cartoons and we'd regale anyone who would listen to their plots and hijinks. Like those old favorites, these keywords are tried and true. We don't think you can miss with any of them. Each of the hot keyword's descriptions are introduced by a ratings bar, which gives a general overview of the area as well as other important information (see Figure 5.1).

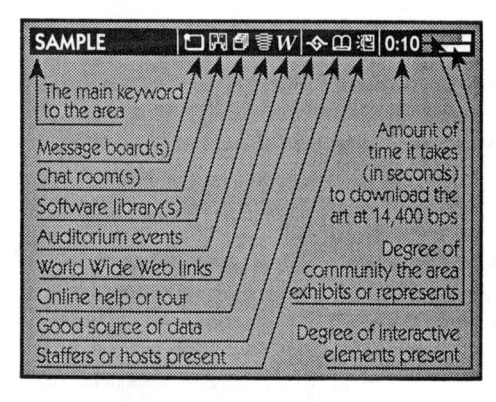

```
SAMPLE                                          0:10
 ↑
 The main keyword
 to the area
                                        Amount of
 Message board(s)                       time it takes
 Chat room(s)                           (in seconds)
                                        to download the
 Software library(s)                    art at 14,400 bps
 Auditorium events
                                        Degree of
 World Wide Web links                   community the area
                                        exhibits or represents
 Online help or tour
 Good source of data                    Degree of interactive
                                        elements present
 Staffers or hosts present
```

Figure 5.1 The ratings bar.

Each of the hot keywords described here was chosen and reviewed by an experienced community leader on America Online, all of whom volunteer their time online to help others and improve the service. Each of them reviewed a favorite area of theirs, but never an area to which they had an official connection. My sincere thanks to Sue Boettcher, Stacy Bribe, Kate Chase, James Corning, Valerie L. Downey, Tim Hayes, Warren Holzem, Elizabeth Homza, Genevieve Kazdin, Laura Kramarsky, Carol Kummer, George Louie, Dave Marx, Miriam Nathan, Hal Rosengarten, Terry Stader, Bob Strange, Kate Tipul, and Kimberly Trautman.

Chapter 5 Hot Keywords

AAC

Ever been stumped by a homework assignment? Help is only a mouse click away at the Academic Assistance Center (AAC). Specialists in many subject areas volunteer their time to provide assistance, live and via e-mail, to students of all ages. The online teacher will not do the work for you, but will instead guide and assist you in finding the answer. The AAC Academy Tutoring Rooms provide live help through out the day and night. Private tutoring is also available. Academic contests offer you the chance to put your skills to work and win free time on America Online. The AAC is also home to the Teacher Pager, where you can send e-mail to a teacher online and get help fast. It's a very popular feature which receives over 3,000 questions per day. The next time you run into a problem, remember, help is readily available at the AAC!

Alternate keywords: RESEARCH, TUTORING.

Reviewed by Valerie L. Downey.

ADOPTION

Adoption affects many families in one way or another. Information related to all aspects of adoption can be found here—and the staff is well-experienced. The Search activity has a remarkable capability to help those looking for their birth family (and an incredible success rate!). With numerous weekly chats (although the schedule is presently outdated), everything from the political ramifications of adoption to the raising of adopted children is discussed. If you are considering adoption, have been adopted, are looking for your birth family, or have given a child up for adoption, you will want to visit this area. There is heart here.

Alternate keywords: None.

Reviewed by Genevieve Kazdin.

AOL LIVE

Michael Jackson. Sandra Bullock. President Clinton. Aerosmith. These are just a few of the guests who have appeared in AOL Live, your one-stop link to America

CHAPTER 5 HOT KEYWORDS

Online's live events. This area is America Online's largest gathering place, and is surely the best place to go to find real-time interaction with some of the world's most interesting and intriguing personalities. Along with live events, AOL Live offers calendars of current and coming attractions, chat schedules, an Intermission section full of interesting information about the area, games, contests, and message boards. The Events Transcripts area is well-designed, and the archives are searchable, in case you missed a favorite event! So, comb your hair, splash on some cologne, and head out for a night on the town in AOL Live. You won't be disappointed!

Alternate keywords: AOL LIVE!, AUDITORIUM, BOWL, CENTER STAGE, CHAT SCHEDULE, COLISEUM, CS, LIVE(!), GLOBE, LIVE TONIGHT, ODEON, SHOWS.

Reviewed by Elizabeth Homza.

APPLE COMPUTER

Looking for a system update or other software direct from Apple? Need a quick question answered? Apple Computer is the place to go! Here you will find press releases and product information, Tech Support FAQs (Frequently Asked Questions), and a link to Apple's Tech Info Library on the Web with developer information and all software updates Apple releases for both Macs and PCs. There are also links to Apple-run websites and information for Apple/Mac professionals. It's one-stop shopping for your Mac!

Alternate keywords: None.

Reviewed by Laura Kramarsky.

CAMPUS

Adult Education classes, a chat about the latest Broadway play, and an evening conversing in German or Latin. All this and much more are available at the Online Campus. More than 100 self-enrichment courses are offered, all with a private teacher at a moderate fee. The Campus is also the gateway to the Afterwards Cafe, the Bull Moose Tavern, and the International House, three of the most intriguing intercultural forums online. In Scholars' Hall

Chapter 5 Hot Keywords

there is access to weekly Home Schooling classes and topical lectures. Learn how to navigate the Internet or talk to a member of AOL Germany. The Online Campus offers an innovative online experience for all.

Alternate keywords: CLASSES, IES.

Reviewed by Hal Rosengarten.

CE

In the world of gadgets and things for your home, your car, your office and the beach, there is only one place to check them out—Consumer Electronics at keyword: CE. You don't have to be a technogeek to enjoy this area. It has information on the practical electronic items as well as the bizarre. But the technogeek will be happy to wander these corridors, too! Make sure you check out the Gadget of the Month area. Here is where you find the Forum Leaders selection of the month, and Ed has some great gadgets. From the smallest cellular telephone to baby monitors, you'll find reviews on the hottest electronics here.

Alternate keywords: ALARM, AUTO SOUND, BEEPER, CELLULAR (PHONE), CONSUMER ELECTRONICS, HOME AUDIO, PAGER, SECURITY.

Reviewed by Terry Stader.

CLASSIFIEDS

Need a place to dispose of your childhood toys, or do you need to buy new toys like a Pentium-based computer or Power Macintosh? The America Online Classifieds forum is the place to go. Here you'll find eight sections: Business, Collectibles, Computers, Employment, General, Habitats, People, and Vehicles, which organize message boards containing thousands of ads. Because the ads are message board posts, anyone with something to sell can put an ad online, but once online you can't remove the ad. Instead, you'll have to wait until it's displaced by newer ads (a process that takes only two to four days in the more popular sections, but which might take a month or more in a slower section). Like a newspaper, America Online's classifieds are text-only, so you can't post the picture of that hula girl lamp you're selling. Unlike a newspaper, there are no extra charges for an ad on America Online. Like many, you're probably worried about dealing with people you can't see; however, I've found that with a few precautions the classifieds are safe. In fact, I've bought and sold three computer systems and numerous peripherals. So if you've got something to sell, need to find a particular item, or just like looking over other people's offerings, visit the Classifieds.

Alternate keywords: AOL CLASSIFIED(S), CLASSIFIED, CLASSIFIEDS ONLINE.

Reviewed by George Louie.

CNN

Cable News Network (CNN) is undoubtedly the world's leading news gathering organization. If you are an educator, you can bring the power of CNN right into your classroom with the CNN Newsroom Program, courtesy of Turner Educational Services, Inc. Each day, CNN broadcasts a 30 minute news program at 4:30–5:00 A.M. Eastern Time. Educators can tape the show on VCR, and incorporate it into their classroom curriculum any time of the day. What a great way to present current events—gone are the days of newspaper clippings! In addition, a daily Classroom Guide is available for downloading and distributing to the students. There are message boards for both teachers and students to discuss the daily events, as well as a place to sign up for virtual field trips (the only way to go!). Get your class involved and check out the CNN Newsroom. Who knows, you just might learn something along the way.

Alternate keywords: CNN GUIDES, CNN NEWSROOM, DEMOCRACY, NGUIDES

Reviewed by Kate Tipul.

COMPUTING

Ever needed help? Want to know more about how to use your computer to the fullest extent? This is the place for you! The Computing Channel features tons of forums and subforums in which you can learn about, discuss and get help with topics ranging from Software and Internet Sites, to Graphics Art and Development, to Business and Communication & Networking! Among the greatest

CHAPTER 5 HOT KEYWORDS

benefits of the channel is the presence of the Family Computing Forum, *the* place for families online. The channel's layout is intuitive and easy to navigate, even for the most novice user. The channel even has its own spotlight, updated periodically to show you cool new areas in the Computing Forums. If you ever wanted to know anything about computers, or if you ever wanted to find a place online to share your vast knowledge of them, this is definitely the place to be!

Alternate keywords: C!, COMPUTER(S), COMPUTER FORUM, COMPUTER(S) & SOFTWARE, COMPUTING & SOFTWARE, SIFS, SIGS, TECHNOLOGY.

Reviewed by James Corning.

CONTESTS

Congratulations! You just won $25,000 and a year's worth of FREE time on America Online. Sounds good, doesn't it? Well, all this and more can be yours if you enter some of the great contests you can find at keyword: CONTESTS. Whether you enjoy trivia contests, photo contests, or a great scavenger hunt, you will love America Online's Contest Area. You could win everything from cold hard cash to free online hours to the getaway vacation of your dreams. And with so many different categories out there, you are bound to win something. There is even a feature that lets you quickly and easily find the type of contest you are looking for. Could you be our next big winner? Come to keyword: CONTESTS and find out.

Alternate keywords: CONTEST, CONTEST AREA, WINNER.

Reviewed by Bob Strange.

CRUISE

Ready for a vacation? What about a cruise? Let the Cruise Critic help pick the right cruise for you. Use the interactive ship finder to narrow your selections. All cruises and cruise ships are not the same, so if you want to make the most of your vacation—to have the vacation of a lifetime—you need to find the one that is best for you. Do you want to vacation on a cruise ship or a river boat, a freighter or an expedition vessel? Do you want a singles cruise or

Chapter 5 Hot Keywords

will the family be along? Let the Cruise Critic reviews help you decide which cruise to take. Read reviews by people who have been there, and offer reviews of cruises you've taken. Visit the Cruise Critic now and start making those vacation plans. After all, you don't want to miss the boat!

Alternate keywords: CRUISES, CRUISE CRITIC(S), SHIP CRITIC(S).

Reviewed by Valerie L. Downey.

DEAD

Jerry Garcia may be gone and the group might never be the same, but The Grateful Dead keep on truckin' at keyword: DEAD. Shop for hot T-shirts and other memorabilia, including some with the original artwork of R. Crumb. Find tour dates for former Dead performers' new bands and special tribute events. Exchange messages with other Deadheads and post your thoughts in the Garcia Tribute Area. Download original artwork celebrating three decades of The Dead's music. You might even discover why The Grateful Dead are as well-known—in some circles—for their charitable acts as they are for their signature musical and psychedelic landscape.

Alternate keywords: :), GRATEFUL DEAD, THE DEAD.

Reviewed by Kate Chase.

DIGITAL CITIES

Where you live, online! Covering the country, community by community, is the goal of Digital City. Concentrating on individual cities, the Digital Cities bring specific local information: news, weather, classifieds, personal ads, entertainment, culture, appropriate web sites, and live chat. This keyword brings you to the staging area from which you can find individual cities. Presently still under development, we can expect more communities soon. If you are traveling, learn about your destination. If you are a resident, see what you have been missing!

Alternate keywords: DCN, DIGC, DIGCITY, DIGITAL CITY (US), DIGITAL USA.

Reviewed by Genevieve Kazdin.

Chapter 5 Hot Keywords

DISABLITIES 0:30

The disABILITIES forum, as its name implies, concentrates both on empowering the disabled and on changing society's view of disabilities in general. Every possible resource is available in the disABILITIES forum, including medical databases, support groups, software, organizations that serve the disabled community offline as well as online, and web links for further exploration. The term *disability* covers a great deal of ground in this forum: physical, developmental, and general disabilities all have their own boards, and the forum hosts deal with a variety of health issues and concerns such as attention deficit disorder, epilepsy, chemical sensitivities, blindness, chronic pain, spinal cord injuries, amputations, muscular dystrophy—just about any kind of physical, emotional, or combination health problem. The forum is a place where people can not only discuss their disorders, but also get information on assistive technologies and medications to help control the problems they are having and debate and discuss political, sociological and sexual implications associated with disabilities. All in all, a pitstop not to be missed on the information superhighway.

Alternate keywords: BLIND, DIS(ABILITY), PHYSICALLY DISABLED.

Reviewed by Laura Kramarsky.

FC 2:00

Looking for an area for the whole family? Where the content is geared towards everyone? Look no further—just visit the Family Computing Forum! Here you can meet other families who share your interests, talents, and online experiences. Chat rooms, family software, message boards, and numerous contests await you in this exciting forum. Best of all, this huge area is constantly monitored to ensure that everything gets a "G" rating—thanks to a batch of highly talented and friendly hosts. So come on down, and make sure you bring the whole family!

Alternate keywords: FC, FC FORUM.

Reviewed by Tim Hayes.

CHAPTER 5 HOT KEYWORDS

FOOL W 0:25

Fools, ahoy! If you're not a fool, you can become one easily at The Motley Fool, an unconventional but successful approach to investing. You can attend Fool's School and learn the thirteen steps to investing foolishly and foolish job hunting tips! Motley Fool works to help you obtain financial information and learn the techniques of investing—foolishly, of course! You also have the opportunity to win free America Online time while learning and having fun playing the daily investment game, playing the portfolios, or playing other games. Make sure to visit Fooldom, a instructive and entertaining place, where the biggest fool wins!

Alternate keywords: COOKIE, COMMONS, COSTARD, FESTE, FOOLISH, LAVATCH, LAUNCE, MFOOL, MOTLEY (FOOL), THE MOTLEY FOOL, TODAY(S) PITCH.

Reviewed by Valerie L. Downey.

FREESHOP 0:15

Everybody loves free stuff, and there is a lot of free stuff at The Free Shop Online! Free software, free information, free catalogs, and even free samples can be ordered from this special shop. You'll even find an occasional contest to enter, too. Each time I return to The Free Shop, I find myself ordering something new. My mailbox has been full ever since.

Alternate keyword: FREESHOP ONLINE.

Reviewed by Warren Holzem.

GEMSTONE 2:00

Imagine a world of fantasy and adventure, warriors and wizards. Now imagine that this intricate world exists online—and rather than computer-generated characters, there are thousands of real people online, joining forces to fight beasts and share heroic quests. This and more can be found in Gemstone III, a text-based adventure game that takes place in a medieval time period. Players can create their own characters and advance through the game by hunting creatures and performing deeds. Gemstone has a highly-developed community—assistance is available both from the GameMasters and your

CHAPTER 5 HOT KEYWORDS

fellow adventurers. Beware: this game is highly addictive. Don't say we didn't warn you.

Alternate keywords: GEMSTONE III, GS3.

Reviewed by Jennifer Watson.

GENDER

Want to visit one of the friendliest places on America Online? Keyword: GENDER takes you to the Transgender Community Forum (TCF), a branch of the Gay & Lesbian Community Forum. Whether you are transgendered or not doesn't make any difference because *all* are welcome here. The TCF offers support, education, and outreach. If you have questions about gender therapists, SRS Surgeons, hormone use, or legal issues, you can find answers here. Whether you come to TCF for a brief visit or plan on making it a regular part of your life, be sure to visit the Gazebo chat room early in your trip. While the TCF has much to offer, the *best* thing about it is its people. So, come sit a while, make friends, and share laughter and love!

Alternate keywords: CROSSDRESSER, CROSSDRESSING, F2M, GLCF TCF, M2F, TCF, TG, TRANSGENDER, TRANSSEXUAL, TRANSVESTITE.

Reviewed by Valerie L. Downey.

GLCF

Wow! That's about the best word I can come up with to describe the Gay and Lesbian Community Forum. If you're of the alternative lifestyles and looking for a home online, this is surely it. In the GLCF you'll find chats, conferences, gaymes, resources of all sorts, places to put up a personal ads, AIDS/HIV, support, gender, friend and community boards—you name it, they've got it! It's all packed into one easy-to-navigate area, run by the neatest folks you'll ever want to meet. Be sure to visit the GLCF often.

Alternate keywords: GAY, LESBIAN, BISEXUAL, QUEER, PINK TRIANGLE, PROUD, BI, LAMDA, HOMOSEXUAL, TRIANGLE, PRIDE.

Reviewed by Stacy Brice.

CHAPTER 5 HOT KEYWORDS

GRANDSTAND

Are you a sports fanatic? Do you spend your life playing and/or watching sports? If so, then The Grandstand's the place for you! Keep up with and discuss your favorite sports here. It doesn't matter whether your favorite takes place on a field, court, rink, or track; you can find it in The Grandstand—from baseball, basketball, and golf to martial arts, motor sports, and figure skating! You're not limited to reading or talking about sports, you can play them here as well! Become a star in one of the fantasy or simulation games found at The Grandstand. You'll find both competition and the opportunity for prizes in the Cyber Sports Tournaments at The Grandstand. So, come on, put on any necessary equipment, take your place, and let the game begin!

Alternate keyword: THE GRANDSTAND.

Reviewed by Valerie L. Downey.

HATRACK

If you enjoy writing and community, this is the place for you. Hatrack, built around the "Alvin Maker" books of Orson Scott Card, is a township in an alternate America of the 1830's. Card takes an active interest in this, his own community, and uploads his own works in progress to one library in Hatrack, while the Hatrack citizens themselves have places to upload their works. Hatrack is fairly evenly divided between historical and modern areas. On one hand are the 1830s "in character" boards and conferences, where people post back and forth, creating a story and a world by writing chapters with their characters; on the other are contemporary boards and conferences where people discuss what is on their minds today. The only things that are required for citizenship in Hatrack are an active imagination and a respect for your fellow town denizens, so move in today!

Alternate keywords: ALVIN, ENDER, HATRACK RIVER TOWN, ORSON SCOTT CARD.

Reviewed by Laura Kramarsky.

CHAPTER 5 HOT KEYWORDS

HH KIDS

"Dad? What's a flywheel?" "I don't know—can't you look it up?" For an elementary or middle school student, keyword: HH KIDS (Homework Help for Kids) will have the answer! A division of the AAC (Academic Assistance Center), Homework Help for Kids is tailor-made for the Kids Only crowd. It's a clean, simplified route to online Reference works, Teacher Pager, grade-appropriate tutoring live and via message board, plus age-appropriate Academic Games. What's missing? A clear explanation of the difference between the Academic Assistance Center and Homework Help for Kids. A younger child will be way over his/her head at Academic Assistance Center, and vice-versa, but nobody bothers to explain that, *or* provide a path from one area to the other.

Alternate keywords: None.

Reviewed by Dave Marx.

HOMESCHOOL

Whether you're thinking about homeschooling, already homeschooling, or simply curious about the concept, the homeschooling forum is the place for you! Here you can search for an e-mail pal for your child, find a local support group, get the latest state law information, and download resource catalog and mailing lists, lesson ideas, and tips for new homeschoolers. Staff members are friendly, knowledgeable, and helpful, so be sure to ask them for a free copy of the forum's fantastic newsletter, *Homeschool Cyber-News*. The homeschooling community is as incredibly diverse online as it is offline so the chat conversation is always informative and lively. Where else could you find the best comebacks to the S-word question?

Alternate keyword: HOMESCHOOLING.

Reviewed by Kimberly Trautman.

INTERNET

So you say you want to surf the Net but you're scared to get your feet wet? Keyword: INTERNET has it all laid out and within reach. In just a single click you can suddenly find yourself browsing the World Wide Web, rummaging through Gopher/WAIS databases, reading the latest messages in the Humor Newsgroups, or downloading photos from NASA's FTP sites. And what's more, it's easy! With a click in the list box, you will find help, resources, information on conducting business on the Internet and top picks to choose from. Even searching the entire Internet is just a few clicks away. So you'll hang ten and have fun, because it's all well within reach at the Internet Connection.

Alternate keyword: INTERNET CENTER, INTERNET CONNECTION, NET.

Reviewed by Miriam Nathan.

KIDS WB

When I go to KIDS WB (WB stands for Warner Brothers), my mood becomes as bright as the visually stimulating screen. How can anyone not be excited by the bright colors, and flurry of activity on the screen? KIDS WB is fun! The Activity Center features games and contests that will keep your kids busy when the well-staffed conference room is closed. The numerous message boards are well monitored, and allow serious yet entertaining discussions to flourish. As an adult, my favorite part of KIDS WB is The Shows. Here I can download photos, sounds, and even animation clips from the Animaniacs, Earthworm Jim, and even classic Warner Brothers cartoons. There's even technical help available for the multimedia-challenged. Obviously, KIDS WB is part of Pinky and The Brain's plot to take over the world.

Alternate keywords: KIDS' WB, KIDS' WEB!

Reviewed by Warren Holzem.

LONGEVITY

Is your lifestyle healthy? You can rate your personal health now at *Longevity Online*, a magazine devoted to healthy lifestyles. Learn how to reduce your risk of cancer and heart disease. Longevity is devoted to helping you take control of your health and add healthy years to your life. Find information about fitness, family health, vitamins, sexual well-being, and alternative medicine. There are even recipes available for great tasting healthy foods.

Chapter 5 Hot Keywords

Longevity offers the opportunity to exchange ideas on topics such as herbal medicine, cosmetic surgery, spas, the mind-body connection, and even on pet health! Plus there are weekly chats on a variety of topics, all with friendly hosts. After all, don't you want to know more about smile therapy and how to get a "bare-able" belly?

Alternate keywords: ANTIAGING, ANTI-AGING, ANTI-OXIDANTS, HERBS, HOMEOPATHIC REMEDIES, MASSAGE, PLASTIC SURGERY, SPA(S), VITAMINS, WELLNESS, WORKOUTS, YOUNGNESS, YOUTHFUL.

Reviewed by Valerie L. Downey.

NYT | 5:00

"All the news that's fit to print" now playing on a computer screen near you! That's what you'll find here, when you visit THE NEW YORK TIMES online! You no longer have to be a native New Yorker to read the latest daily edition of this premiere newspaper; you'll even get late updates to the day's breaking news stories. . . something your local paper might not even do! Search the files for past articles from such popular features as The Science Times and Arts and Entertainment. Or just catch up with the news of the day, from Page One to The Week In Review. One of the world's greatest newspapers, now delivered to *your* door!

Alternate keywords: @TIMES, ATTIMES, NEW YORK CITY, NEW YORK TIME.S, NY TIMES, NYC NYT, NYNEX, TECHNOTORIUM, TIMES, TIMES NEW

Reviewed by Carol Kummer.

ODYSSEY | W | 0:30

Cuddle a baby chimp on the deck of a riverboat in Zaire. Help feed 27,000 catfish on the Mekong river. A photo is almost like being there. You've seen the great photos in magazines like National Geographic and Life...have you ever wondered what happens to the ones that *aren't* published? The Odyssey Project is an attempt by the artists to put world-class photojournalists' work out where everyone can enjoy it. Here you can find The Odysseys: quality picture stories; OdyBooks: CD-ROMs, CDs, and tapes;

OdyGallery: monthly exhibitions; and much, much more! The Odyssey is ever-changing, a visual feast!

Alternate keywords: ODY, ODYSSEY PROJECT, THE ODYSSEY PROJECT.

Reviewed by Sue Boettcher.

OMNI

OMNI Magazine has an honorable tradition of providing superior science and science fiction literature and information. Due to publication costs, though, it has stopped actual monthly circulation except online. Here you have immediate choices of Science Fiction, UFOs, OMNI Chat, OMNI Online, OMNI Shopping, and a menu of special features. OMNI Online contains the Continuum, with fascinating tidbits about the latest scientific breakthroughs in fields ranging from medicine to materials science to astronomy and antimatter, where you'll find articles, discussion, and more focusing on the unexplainable: UFOs, alien visitation, psychic powers, dreams, ghosts, and other paranormal phenomena. It only takes a few minutes to discover why OMNI is subtitled *The Tool for the Twenty-First Century*, but it will take hours to fully appreciate the valuable information and the enjoyable stories included in OMNI Online.

Alternate keywords: OMNI MAG, OMNI MAGAZINE, OMNI ONLINE.

Reviewed by Hal Rosengarten.

OSO

Not just for Floridians, keyword: OSO transports you to the electronic extension of the Orlando Sentinel newspaper. OSO is a high-energy, newspaper-style area with heaps of information about any topic under the sun. While the focus is on items of interest to Floridians, others will find plenty to sink their teeth into. Find advice about topics ranging from sex to pets. Read about art museums, galleries, shows, and festivals. As is typical of any newspaper, you'll find columnists, cartoons, news, editorials, weather, and classifieds. In addition, you'll find special things you'd never find in a newspaper, such as

CHAPTER 5 HOT KEYWORDS

file libraries and the e-mall, where you can shop online for services and products.

Alternate keywords: ORLANDO (SENTINEL).

Reviewed by Valerie L. Downey.

REAL LIFE — 0:50

In debt? Got those credit card blues? Have any questions about retirement, insurance, or mutual funds? The "Real Life...It's More than a Game" Money Forum offers help and advice on all types of money matters. Geared for the average Joe or Jane, you can find information on wedding planning, investments, real estate, bankruptcy, and credit repair. Just about any money matter you can think of is covered in one of Real Life's six basic areas—education, job, relationships, home, family, and retirement. The list of topics covered by chat hosts and guests in the daily online talk shows is endless! Real Life is also prepared to show you the humorous side of money matters—yes, there really is one! So, don't be intimidated by the financial world, let Real Life help you take control of your money!

Alternate keywords: FAMILY FINANCES, INSURANCE, JOB, RETIREMENT, RL.

Reviewed by Valerie L. Downey.

SATURDAY — 0:15

A favorite long-time periodical is at home online. Holding to founder Norman Cousin's standard that art and culture belong to all, participation is encouraged with chats and the publishing of members' writings. Although there is nothing specifically set aside for young members, comments and contributions from kids are treated with respect. The chat schedule is active and varied with a comprehensive schedule posted and knowledgeable hosts to lead conversation. Speak your mind about the arts—and be listened to!

Alternate keywords: FAMILY FINANCES, FINANCIAL PLANNING, INSURANCE, JOB, PLANNING, RETIREMENT, RL, YM, YOUR MONEY.

Reviewed by Genevieve Kazdin.

CHAPTER 5 HOT KEYWORDS

SPACE

Ever wanted to talk to an astronaut? You can do it here, at SPACE EXPLORATION ONLINE from The National Space Society, where there is an astronaut of the month to answer questions. Space Online also provides information on current and past space exploration activities including political action alerts, detailed information about each Space Shuttle and Mir mission, and twice-weekly Space chats. The libraries are stuffed with space photos, and a collection of space news from pro-space organizations rounds out the collection. Space Exploration Online is the next best thing to being there yourself!

Alternate keyword: NSS.

Reviewed by Sue Boettcher.

TREK

Space, the final frontier. These are the voyages of the Star Trek Club. Its continuing mission, to keep you entertained on America Online. Okay, so that isn't quite how the story goes. But if you are a Star Trek fan you should check out the Star Trek Club at keyword: TREK. The Star Trek Club has everything a Trekkie could ever want. It has a great message board, where you can discuss everything from the classic Star Trek episodes to the Next Generation show to the Deep Space Nine episodes. There are even message boards that discuss the Star Trek movies. Another great thing the Star Trek Club has (and this is one of my favorites) is the Record Banks. Here you will find files that you can download: everything from pictures of your favorite Star Trek characters, to stories written by other America Online members. And there is also a chat room called The Bridge where you can go to chat with others in real-time conversation. There are also trivia games that are played every Friday and Saturday evenings in The Bridge. So beam up to the Star Trek Club now, at keyword: TREK.

Alternate keywords: STAR TREK CLUB, TREK.

Reviewed by Bob Strange.

Chapter 5 Hot Keywords

UCX

Want to go to college, right here online? You can do it, with the University of California's Center for Media and Independent Learning. You start the course when you want to, and take up to a year to complete it. And you receive college credit at the end! You do your assignments at home, at your own pace, and e-mail them to your instructor. The final exam is taken under the supervision of an approved proctor. Courses fall into six categories and range from The Art of Film to Pollution Prevention to The Psychology of Communication. If you want to go to the University of California, and can't get there yourself in person, try this!

Alternate keywords: CMIL, UCAL.

Reviewed by Sue Boettcher.

WEB DINER

Grab yourself a seat at the Web Diner counter, tuck that napkin in your shirt and prepare for a veritable feast of information on creating and maintaining your very own home page. Order yourself a Blue Plate Special, which are daily links to websites offering home page tips, tricks or free software. Perhaps you'd care for something a la carte such as Web Soup for information of a more technical nature. Don't forget to top it all off with a slice of Easy As Pie graphics to give your page that finishing touch. Message boards, chat rooms, and expert help from the staff will make you want to drop by often. Whether you are a novice or a pro at HTML, a stop at the Web Diner is sure to leave you satisfied.

Alternate keywords: DINER (CREW), HTML HELP, WEB BIZ, WEBD, WEB HELP.

Reviewed by Kate Tipul.

WOMEN

Safe, comfortable, alive and ever-changing: that's the Women's Interests Forum. It's a place where you can meet other women, investigate your life interests, communicate and find support for your concerns, find people and places and things to rejuvenate your spirit, and feel free to be who you are. The forum is growing at an enormous rate, and wonderful changes are evident, almost daily. All women will find something here, but it's especially wonderful for the America Online newcomer who can join the Street Smarts program and learn to navigate the halls of America Online wisely and happily. Be sure, too, to visit Evenings With Eva—a lovely setting to explore women's issues. Whatever your interests are, there's something here for you!

Alternate keyword: WOMENS.

Reviewed by Stacy Brice.

WRITERS

Keyword: WRITERS is America Online's central resource for writers, both those who do it for a living and those who write strictly for the passion of the craft. Talk to other writers, download articles and short stories, or participate in a group discussion on playwriting or technical editing. Locate addresses of competitions and writers' groups (professional unions, too). Link up with editors looking for submissions. You can find notices of paying markets, ads for writing jobs, special writers' Web sites, and check for special events. You will find that top authors often appear online to discuss their work and offer suggestions for how you can make it, too.

Alternate keywords: WRITER(S), WRITER'S (CLUB), WRITING.

Reviewed by Kate Chase.

Chapter 6
Keywords from A to Z

Looking for the definitive source of keywords? The following list includes *every* known keyword on America Online at the time of writing, organized alphabetically with the keyword first. Entries with an asterisk (*) are in a free area and may be accessed without the standard conect charges. Comments are given in brackets.

Key to comments:

WAOL = Windows AOL

MAOL = Mac AOL

GAOL = GEOS AOL (also known as DOS AOL)

Platform-dependent = Works differently based on your computer type

@AOL DEAD—AOL Live Auditorium
@AOL LIVE—AOL Live Auditorium
@BOWL—The Bowl auditorium
@COLISEUM—The Coliseum Auditorium
@CYBER RAP—Cyber Rap Auditorium
@CYBERPLEX—Cyberplex Auditorium
@GLOBE—The Globe Auditorium
@INC LIVE—Inc Live Conference Room
@MAINSTAGE—Main Stage Auditorium
@NEWS ROOM—The News Room Auditorium
@ODEON—The Odeon auditorium
@ROTUNDA—Rotunda Auditorium
@THE.MOVIES—@the.movies
@THE MOVIES—@the.movies
@THE NEWS ROOM—The News Room Auditorium

Chapter 6 Keywords from A to Z

@TIMES—@times/The New York Times Online

@TIMES CROSSWORD—The New York Times Crosswords

@TIMES STORE—@times: Store

:)—Grateful Dead Forum

;)—Hecklers Online

;-)—Hecklers Online

;-D—Virtual Christian Humor

<><—Christianity Online

1-800-TREKER—800-TREKKER: 24 Hour Sci-Fi Collectibles Hotline

1-800-TREKKER—800-TREKKER: 24 Hour Sci-Fi Collectibles Hotline

1010—A Day in the Life of Cyberspace

17—Seventeen Magazine Online

1995—1995: The Year in Review

20—Twentieth Century Mutual Funds

20/20—ABC News-On-Demand

20TH—Twentieth Century Mutual Funds

21ST—Twentieth Century Mutual Funds

24 HOURS—24 Hours of Democracy Web site

25 REASONS—Best of America Online showcase

2MARKET—Marketplace Gift Service

3-D—3D Forum

3-D RENDERING—3D Forum

3A—AAA Online

3D—3D Forum

3D AUDIO—SRS Labs

3D REALMS—Apogee/3D Realms Support Center

3D RENDERING—3D Forum

3D SIG—3D Special Interest Group

3D SOUND—SRS Labs

3D-RENDERING—3D Forum

3DO—The 3DO Company

4DDA ENTRY—Mac Business Forum [*MAOL only*]

4RESOURCES—AT&T Home Business Resources

5TH GENERATION—Symantec

60—60-Second Novelist

60 SECOND NOVELIST—60-Second Novelist

Chapter 6 Keywords from A to Z

60 SECONDS—60-Second Novelist

7 WONDERS—Seven Wonders of the Web

777-FILM—MovieLink

777-FILM ONLINE—MovieLink

7TH—Seventh Level Software

800—AT&T 800 Directory Web Site

800 DIRECTORY—AT&T 800 Directory Web Site

800 FLOWERS—800-Flowers

800-FLOWERS—800-Flowers

800-TREKER—800-TREKKER: 24 Hour Sci-Fi Collectibles Hotline

800-TREKKER—800-TREKKER: 24 Hour Sci-Fi Collectibles Hotline

90210—90210 Wednesdays

90210 WEDNESDAYS—90210 Wednesdays

95 APPLY—AOL for Windows 95 Beta Test Application [*WAOL only*]

9600—High Speed Access*

9600 ACCESS—High Speed Access*

9600 CENTER—High Speed Access*

99.1—WHFS 99.1 FM

A&B—Simon & Schuster College Online

A'S—Major League Baseball Team: Oakland Athletics

A-LIST—Style Channel

A3—AAA Online

AAA—AAA Online

AAC—Academic Assistance Center

AAFMAA—Army and Air Force Mutual Aid Association

AAII—American Association of Individual Investors

AAPMR—American Academy of Physical Medicine and Rehabilitation

AARP—American Association of Retired People

AARP ANNUIT—AARP Annuity Program

AARP ANNUITY—AARP Annuity Program

AARP BANK 1—AARP Credit Card Services

AARP FUND—AARP Investment Program

AARP HART—AARP Auto & Homeowners Program

AARP HARTFORD—AARP Auto & Homeowners Program

AARP LIFE—AARP Life Insurance Program

Chapter 6 Keywords from A to Z

AARP NY LIFE—AARP Life Insurance Program
AARP PRU—AARP Group Health Insurance
AARP SCUDDER—AARP Investment Program
AATRIX—Aatrix Software, Inc.
ABBATE VIDEO—Abbate Video
ABC—ABC Online
ABC AUDITORIUM—ABC Online Auditorium
ABC AUTO RACING—ABC Sports REV Speedway
ABC BASEBALL—ABC Sports Major League Baseball
ABC BETA—ABC Online: Beta Area
ABC CLASS—The ABC Classroom
ABC CLASSROOM—The ABC Classroom
ABC COLLEGE FOOTBALL—ABC Sports College Football
ABC CROWN—ABC Triple Crown
ABC DAYTIME—ABC Daytime/Soapline
ABC ENTERTAINMENT—ABC Prime Time
ABC EVENTS—ABC Online Auditorium
ABC FIGURE SKATING—ABC Sports Figure Skating
ABC FOOTBALL—ABC Sports College Football
ABC GMA—ABC Good Morning America
ABC GUESTS—ABC Online Auditorium
ABC HELP—ABC Online Help
ABC HOCKEY—ABC Sports Hockey / NHL Online
ABC KIDS—ABC Kidzine
ABC KIDZINE—ABC Kidzine
ABC LOVE—ABC Love Online
ABC NEWS—ABC News-On-Demand
ABC NEWS VIEWS—ABC Online: News Views
ABC NHL—ABC Sports Hockey / NHL Online
ABC PRIME TIME—ABC Prime Time
ABC RADIO—ABC Radio
ABC SOAPS—ABC Daytime/Soapline
ABC SPORTS—ABC Sports
ABC SPORTS STORE—ABC Sport Store
ABC STARS—ABC Online: Stars and Shows [*WAOL only*]
ABC STATION—ABC Online: Stations
ABC STATIONS—ABC Online: Stations
ABC TRACK—ABC Track

Chapter 6 Keywords from A to Z

ABC TRANSCRIPTS—ABC Online Auditorium
ABC TRIPLE—ABC Triple Crown
ABC TRIPLE CROWN—ABC Triple Crown
ABC VIDEO—ABC Online: Video Store
ABC WOMEN—ABC Sports Women's Sports
ABC WOMEN'S—ABC Sports Women's Sports
ABF—Help Desk [*Platform-dependent*]
ABI—Business Yellow Pages
ABI YELLOW PAGES—Business Yellow Pages
ABM—Adventures by Mail
ABOVE THE RIM—NESN: New England Basketball
ACADEMY—Starfleet Online
ACADEMY AWARDS—Academy Awards
ACCESS—Accessing America Online*
ACCESS ERIC—AskERIC
ACCESS EXCELLENCE—Access Excellence
ACCESS NUMBERS—Accessing America Online*
ACCESS.POINT—access.point
ACCESS SOFTWARE—Access Software
ACCESSPOINT—access.point
ACCOLADE—Accolade, Inc.
ACCORDING—Company Research Message Boards
ACCORDING TO BOB—Company Research Message Boards
ACE VENTURA—EXTRA Online
ACE VENTURE STORE—EXTRA Online
ACER—Acer America Corporation
ACLU—American Civil Liberties Union
ACS—American Cancer Society
ACSNATL—American Cancer Society
ACT—Kaplan Online/SAT, ACT
ACTING—The Casting Forum
ACTIVISION—Activision
ACTORS—The Casting Forum
ACTRESSES—The Casting Forum
ACUBED—America-3: The Women's Team
AD SIG—Advertising Special Interest Group
AD&D—AD&D Neverwinter Nights
ADAMS—Cindy Adams: Queen of Gourmet Gossip

Chapter 6 Keywords from A to Z

ADD—AD&D Neverwinter Nights
ADDONS—BPS Software
ADOBE—Adobe Center Menu
ADOBE PHOTOSHOP—Adobe Center Menu
ADOPTION—Adoption Forum
ADVANCED—Advanced Software, Inc.
ADVANCED GRAVIS—Advanced Gravis
ADVANCED LOGIC—Advanced Logic Research
ADVENTURE—Outdoor Adventures Online
ADVENTURES BY MAIL—Adventures by Mail
ADVERTISING—Advertising Special Interest Group
ADVERTISING SIG—Advertising Special Interest Group
ADVICE—Advice & Tips
ADVISOR—Top Advisor's Corner
ADVISORS—Top Advisor's Corner
ADVSOFT—Advisor Software
AE—Awakened Eye Special Interest Group
AECSIG—Architects, Engineers and Construction Special Interest Group
AEN—American Entertainment Network
AF'S SECRET BARGAINS—Arthur Frommer's Secret Bargains
AFFINIFILE—Affinity Microsystems
AFFINITY—Affinity Microsystems
AFRICA—Afrocentric Culture
AFRICAN—Genealogy Forum
AFRICAN AMERICAN—The Exchange: Communities Center
AFRICAN-AMERICAN—Afrocentric Culture
AFROCENTRIC—Afrocentric Culture
AFT—American Federation of Teachers
AFTEREFFECTS—AfterEffects
AFTERWARDS—Afterwards Cafe
AGOL—Assemblies of God Online
AGRICULTURE—NAS Online
AHS—American Hiking Society
AI INC—Hecklers Online: Antagonistic Trivia
AIDS—AIDS and HIV Resource Center
AIDS DAILY—AIDS Daily Summary
AIDS QUILT—Gay & Lesbian Community Forum Aids Scrapbook

Chapter 6 Keywords from A to Z

AIQ—AIQ Systems
AIQ SYSTEMS—AIQ Systems
AIR JORDAN—Michael Jordan Area
AIR WARRIOR—Air Warrior
AIRCRAFT—Flying Magazine
AIRCRAFTS—Flying Magazine
AIRPLANE—Aviation Forum
AIRPORTS—Flying Magazine
AIRSHOWS—Aviation Forum
AKIMBO—FullWrite
ALA—America Lung Association
ALADDIN—Aladdin Systems, Inc.
ALARM—Consumer Electronics
ALASKA—Digital Cities: Alaska
ALASKA DC—Digital Cities: Alaska
ALASKA DCITY—Digital Cities: Alaska
ALASKA DIGC—Digital Cities: Alaska
ALASKA DIGITAL CITY—Digital Cities: Alaska
ALBANY—Digital Cities: Albany NY
ALBANY DC—Digital Cities: Albany NY
ALBANY DCITY—Digital Cities: Albany NY
ALBANY DIGC—Digital Cities: Albany NY
ALBANY DIGITAL CITY—Digital Cities: Albany NY
ALBANY NY—Digital Cities: Albany NY
ALBUQUERQUE—Digital Cities: Albuquerque/Santa Fe NM
ALBUQUERQUE DC—Digital Cities: Albuquerque/Santa Fe NM
ALBUQUERQUE DCITY—Digital Cities: Albuquerque/Santa Fe NM
ALBUQUERQUE DIGC—Digital Cities: Albuquerque/Santa Fe NM
ALDUS—Adobe Systems' Inc.
ALF—American Leadership Forum
ALIENS—Parascope
ALL MY CHILDREN—ABC Daytime/Soapline
ALL STAR—MLB All-Star Ballot
ALLYN & BACON—Simon & Schuster College Online
ALOHA—Apple Aloha for eWorld Alumni
ALPHA TECH—Alpha Software Corporation
ALPT—The Grandstand's Simulation Golf
ALR—Advanced Logic Research

Chapter 6 Keywords from A to Z

ALTERNATIVE MEDICINE—Alternative Medicine Forum
ALTSYS—Altsys Corporation
ALUMNI—Alumni Hall
ALUMNI HALL—Alumni Hall
ALVIN—Hatrack River Town Meeting
ALYSIS—Alysis Software
AM GLOSSARY—AnswerMan: Glossary
AMATEUR RADIO—Ham Radio Club
AMBROSIA—Ambrosia Software
AMC—ABC Daytime/Soapline
AMERICA ONLINE STORE—America Online Store
AMERICA OUT OF LINE—ABC Online: America Out Of Line
AMERICA'S CUP—America's Cup
AMERICA3—America-3: The Women's Team
AMERICAN AGENDA—ABC News-On-Demand
AMERICAN AIRLINES—EAASY SABRE Travel Service
AMERICAN ART—National Museum of American Art
AMERICAN ASTROLOGY—Astronet
AMERICAN DIABETES—American Diabetes Association
AMERICAN DIALOGUE—American Dialogue
AMERICAN EXPRESS—ExpressNet (American Express)
AMERICAN HISTORY—National Museum of American History
AMERICAN INDIAN—The Exchange: Communities Center
AMERICAN LUNG—American Lung Association
AMERICAN LUNG ASSOC—American Lung Association
AMERICAN WOODWORKER—American Woodworker
AMERICAS CUP—America's Cup 1995
AMERICON—America Online Gaming Conference
AMEX—ExpressNet (American Express)
AMEX ART—ExpressNet Art Download*
AMOR—Love@AOL
AMORE—Love@AOL
AMPLIFIERS—Stereo Review Online
ANALOG—Science Fiction & Fantasy
ANDERTON—Craig Anderton's Sound Studio & Stage
ANDY PARGH—Andy Pargh/The Gadget Guru
ANGELS—Major League Baseball Team: California Angels
ANIMAL—Pet Care Forum

Chapter 6 Keywords from A to Z

ANIMALS—Pet Care Forum
ANIMATED SOFTWARE—Animated Software
ANIMATION—Graphic Forum [*Platform-dependent*]
ANIME—Wizard World
ANOTHER CO—Another Company
ANSWERMAN—Answer Man
ANTAG—Hecklers Online: Antagonistic Trivia
ANTAGON—Hecklers Online: Antagonistic Trivia
ANTAGONIST—Hecklers Online: Antagonistic Trivia
ANTAGONIST TRIVIA—Hecklers Online: Antagonistic Trivia
ANTAGONISTIC TRIVIA—Hecklers Online: Antagonistic Trivia
ANTI-AGING—Longevity Magazine Online
ANTI-OXIDANTS—Longevity Magazine Online
ANTIAGING—Longevity Magazine Online
ANTIQUES—The Exchange: Collector's Corner
AOL BEGINNERS—Help Desk [*Platform-dependent*]
AOL BUSINESS—AOL Enterprise
AOL CANADA—AOL Canada
AOL CLASSIFIED—AOL Classifieds
AOL CLASSIFIEDS—AOL Classifieds
AOL CRUISE—AOL Member Cruise
AOL DEAD—AOL Live Auditorium
AOL DIAG—AOL Diagnostic Tool [*WAOL only*]
AOL DINER—Everything Edible!
AOL EDUCATION—America Online Education Initiative
AOL ENTERPRISE—AOL Enterprise
AOL ENTERPRISES—AOL Enterprise
AOL FAMILIES—AOL Families
AOL FULL DISCLOSURE—AOL's Full Disclosure for Investors
AOL GAME FORUMS—Games Channel
AOL GIFT—AOL Gift Certificates
AOL HIGHLIGHTS—AOL Highlights Tour
AOL INTERNATIONAL—International Channel
AOL INVESTOR RELATIONS—AOL's Full Disclosure for Investors
AOL ISRAEL—Israel
AOL ISREAL—Israel
AOL LIVE—AOL Live!
AOL MAX—Family Computing Forum: Maximum AOL

Chapter 6 Keywords from A to Z

AOL MEMBER CRUISE—AOL Member Cruise

AOL MFC—AOL Mutual Fund Center

AOL MOVIES—@the.movies

AOL PREVIEW—Upgrade to latest AOL software

AOL PRODUCTS—America Online Store

AOL ROADTRIP—AOL Roadtrips [*WAOL only*]

AOL SOFTWARE SHOP—AOL Software Shop

AOL SPORTS LIVE—AOL Sports Live

AOL STORE—America Online Store

AOL TIPS—Family Computing Forum: Tip of the Day

AOL WORLD—International Channel

AOLGLOBALNET—AOLGLOBALnet International Access*

AOLHA—Apple Aloha for eWorld Alumni

AOLIR—AOL's Full Disclosure for Investors

AOLNET—AOLNET

AOLSEWHERE—AOLsewhere

AOOL—ABC Online: America Out Of Line

AOP—Association of Online Professionals

APDA—Apple Professional Developer's Association [*MAOL only*]

APOGEE—Apogee/3D Realms Entertainment

APPLE—Apple/Macintosh Forums

APPLE COMPUTER—Apple Computer

APPLE UPDATE—Apple System 7.5 Update

APPLEBIZ—Apple Business Consortium

APPLESCRIPT—AppleScript Special Interest Group

APPLICATIONS—Business/Applications Forum [*Platform-dependent*]

APPLICATIONS FORUM—Business/Applications Forum [*Platform-dependent*]

APPMAKER—Bowers Development

APPS—Applications/Business Forum [*Platform-dependent*]

APRIL—AOL's April Fool Area [*May disappear without notice*]

APRIL FOOL—AOL's April Fool Area [*May disappear without notice*]

APRIL FOOLS—AOL's April Fool Area [*May disappear without notice*]

ARCADE—Games Forum [*Platform-dependent*]

ARCHITECTURE—Home Magazine Online

ARFA—American Running & Fitness Association

Chapter 6 Keywords from A to Z

ARGOSY—Argosy
ARIEL—Ariel Publishing
ARIZONA—Arizona Central
ARIZONA CENTRAL—Arizona Central
ARM—AOL's Real Estate Center
AROUND THE HORN—NESN: New England Baseball
ARSENAL—Arsenal Commmunications
ART—Graphic Forum [*Platform-dependent*]
ARTEMIS—Artemis Software
ARTHUR FROMMER—Arthur Frommer's Secret Bargains
ARTICULATE—Articulate Systems
ARTIFICE—Artifice, Inc.
ARTIST—Artists on America Online
ARTIST GRAPHICS—Artist Graphics
ARTIST'S SPOTLIGHT—Artist's Spotlight
ARTISTS—Artists on America Online
ARTISTS SPOTLIGHT—Artist's Spotlight
ARTS—Afterwards Cafe
ARTSPEAK—The Hub: ArtSpeak
ASC TECH—Alpha Software Corporation
ASC TS—Alpha Software Corporation
ASCD—Assoc. for Supervisor & Curriculum Development
ASFL—The Grandstand's Simulation Football
ASI—Articulate Systems
ASIAN—The Exchange: Communities Center
ASIMOV—Science Fiction & Fantasy
ASK AMERICA ONLINE—Member Services*
ASK AOL—Member Services*
ASK CS—Member Services*
ASK SERENA—Weekly World News
ASK STAFF—Questions*
ASK TODD—The Image Exchange: Ask Todd Art
ASK TODD ART—The Image Exchange: Ask Todd Art
ASKERIC—AskERIC
ASNE—Newspaper Association of America
ASSASSINS—Assassins
ASSEMBLY—Development Forum [*Platform-dependent*]
ASSN—Christianity Online: Associations & Interests

Chapter 6 Keywords from A to Z

ASSN ONLINE PROF—Association of Online Professionals
AST—AST Support Forum
ASTROGRAPH—Astrograph
ASTROLOGY—Astronet
ASTROMATES—Astronet
ASTRONAUTS—Challenger Remembered
ASTRONET—Astronet
ASTRONOMY—Astronomy Club
ASTROS—Major League Baseball Team: Houston Astros
ASYLUM—Snowboarding Online
ASYMETRIX—Asymetrix Corporation
AT—Hecklers Online: Antagonistic Trivia
AT ONCE—atOnce Software
AT TIMES—@times/The New York Times Online
AT&T—AT&T
ATAGONISTS—Hecklers Online: Antagonistic Trivia
ATG—Hecklers Online: Antagonistic Trivia
ATHEISM—Religion & Ethics Forum
ATHLETICS—Major League Baseball Team: Oakland Athletics
ATLANTA—Digital City Atlanta GA
ATLANTA BRAVES—Major League Baseball Team: Atlanta Braves
ATLANTA DIGITAL CITY—Digital City Atlanta GA
ATLANTIC—The Atlantic Monthly Online
ATLANTIC MONTHLY—The Atlantic Monthly Online
ATLANTIC ONLINE—The Atlantic Monthly Online
ATLUS—Atlus Software
ATT—AT&T
ATT WIRELESS—AT&T
ATTICUS—Atticus Software
AUDIO—Stereo Review Online
AUDITORIUM—AOL Live!
AUG—User Group Forum
AUSTIN—Digital Cities: Austin TX
AUSTIN DC—Digital Cities: Austin TX
AUSTIN DCITY—Digital Cities: Austin TX
AUSTIN DIGC—Digital Cities: Austin TX
AUSTIN DIGITAL CITY—Digital Cities: Austin TX
AUSTIN TX—Digital Cities: Austin

Chapter 6 Keywords from A to Z

AUSTRALIA—Australia
AUSTRIA—Austria
AUSTRIAN—Genealogy Forum
AUTO—AutoVantage
AUTO RACING—AOL Auto Racing
AUTO SOUND—Consumer Electronics
AUTOCAD—CAD Resource Center
AUTODESK—Autodesk Resource Center
AUTOEXEC—Tune Up Your PC
AUTOMATE—Affinity Microsystems
AUTOMATION—Affinity Microsystems
AUTOMOBILE—Car/Cycle Selections
AUTOMOTIVE—Car/Cycle Selections
AUTOS—Road & Track Magazine
AUTOVANTAGE—AutoVantage
AV—AutoVantage
AV FORUM—Aviation Forum
AVIATION—Aviation Forum
AVID—Avid Technology
AVID DTV—Avid Technology
AVOCAT—Avocat Systems
AVOCAT SYSTEMS—Avocat Systems
AVON—Avon
AWAKE EYE—Awakened Eye Special Interest Group
AWAKENED EYE—Awakened Eye Special Interest Group
AWAY—AOLsewhere
AX GARDENING—Arizona Central: House/Home
AZ ALT—Arizona Central: ALT.
AZ ALT.—Arizona Central: ALT.
AZ ASU—Arizona Central: Sports
AZ AT EASE—Arizona Central: At Ease
AZ BENSON—Arizona Central: Sound Off
AZ BEST—Arizona Central: The Best
AZ BIZ—Arizona Central: Small Business
AZ BUSINESS—Arizona Central: Your Money
AZ CACTUS—Arizona Central: Cactus League (Classifieds)
AZ CALENDARS—Arizona Central: Plan On It
AZ CARDS—Arizona Central: Sports

Chapter 6 Keywords from A to Z

AZ CAROUSING—Arizona Central: Carousing
AZ CARTOON—Arizona Central: Sound Off
AZ CENTRAL—Arizona Central
AZ COLUMNS—Arizona Central: Sound Off
AZ COMMUNITY—Arizona Central: Your Community
AZ COMPUTERS—Arizona Central: Computers
AZ CONCERTS—Arizona Central: Carousing
AZ COUCHING—Arizona Central: Couching
AZ DESTINATIONS—Arizona Central: Destinations
AZ DIAMONDBACKS—Arizona Central: Sports
AZ DINING—Arizona Central: Dining
AZ EATS—Arizona Central: Dining
AZ EDITORIALS—Arizona Central: Sound Off
AZ ENTERTAINMENT—Arizona Central: At Ease
AZ FILMS—Arizona Central: Films
AZ FUN—Arizona Central: Plan On It
AZ GOLF—Arizona Central: Golf
AZ HIGH SCHOOLS—Arizona Central: Preps
AZ HOME—Arizona Central: House/Home
AZ HOUSE—Arizona Central: House/Home
AZ KTAR—Arizona Central: KTAR Talk Radio
AZ LETTERS—Arizona Central: Sound Off
AZ LIFE—Arizona Central: Your Life
AZ MONEY—Arizona Central: Your Money
AZ MOVIES—Arizona Central: Films
AZ NEWS—Arizona Central: Newsline
AZ NEWSLINE—Arizona Central: Newsline
AZ OPINIONS—Arizona Central: Sound Off
AZ PENELOPE—Arizona Central: Dining
AZ PHOTOS—Arizona Central: Photos
AZ PREPS—Arizona Central: Preps
AZ SCHOOLS—Arizona Central: Schools
AZ SCOREBOARD—Arizona Central: Scoreboard
AZ SCORES—Arizona Central: Scoreboard
AZ SMALL BUSINESS—Arizona Central: Small Business
AZ SOUNDOFF—Arizona Central: Sound Off
AZ SPORTS—Arizona Central: Sports
AZ SPORTS CALENDARS—Arizona Central: Plan On It

Chapter 6 Keywords from A to Z

AZ SPORTS SCHEDULE—Arizona Central: Plan On It
AZ STARDUST—Arizona Central: Stardust
AZ SUNS—Arizona Central: Sports
AZ THEATER—Arizona Central: Stardust
AZ THEATRE—Arizona Central: Stardust
AZ TRAVEL—Arizona Central: Destinations
AZ TRIPS—Arizona Central: Destinations
AZ TV—Arizona Central: Couching
AZ U OF A—Arizona Central: Sports
AZ VOLUNTEERS—Arizona Central: Volunteers
B&B—Bed & Breakfast U.S.A.
BA—Bank of America
BABY BOOMER—Baby Boomers Area
BABY BOOMERS—Baby Boomers Area
BABYLON—Babylon 5
BABYLON 5—Babylon 5
BACKCOUNTRY—Backpacker Magazine
BACKPACKER—Backpacker Magazine
BAHA'I—Religion & Ethics Forum
BALANCE SHEET—Disclosure's Financial Statements
BALI—One Hanes Place
BALKAN—Balkan Operation Joint Endeavor
BALLOON—800-Flowers
BALLOONS—800-Flowers
BALTIMORE ORIOLES—Major League Baseball Team: Baltimore Orioles
BANK AMERICA—Bank of America
BANK OF AMERICA—Bank of America
BARGAINS—Checkbook Bargains
BARRONS—Barrons Booknotes
BARTLETT—Bartlett's Quotations
BARTLETT'S—Bartlett's Quotations
BARTLETTS—Bartlett's Quotations
BASEBALL—MLB Baseball
BASEBALL DAILY—Baseball Daily by Extreme Fans
BASEBALL WORKSHOP—Motley Fool: The Fool Dome
BASELINE—Baseline Publishing
BASEVIEW—Baseview Products, Inc.

Chapter 6 Keywords from A to Z

BASIC—Development Forum [*Platform-dependent*]
BASKETBALL—NBA Basketball
BASKETBALL TRIVIA—NTN Basketball Trivia
BATBOY—Weekly World News
BATMAN—DC Comics Online
BAUMRUCKER—Baumrucker Conference [*May disappear without notice*]
BAY CITY—Digital Cities: Bay City MI
BAY CITY DC—Digital Cities: Bay City MI
BAY CITY DCITY—Digital Cities: Bay City MI
BAY CITY DIGC—Digital Cities: Bay City MI
BAY CITY MI—Digital Cities: Bay City MI
BBS—BBS Corner
BBS CORNER—BBS Corner
BC—Christian Books & Culture
BCS—Boston Computer Society
BEANIE—Pangea Toy Net
BEANIE BOY—Pangea Toy Net
BEATLES ANTHOLOGY—The ABC Rock & Road Beatles Anthology
BEATY—Company Research Message Boards
BEAUTY—Elle Magazine Online
BEAUTY 911—Style Channel
BED—Bed & Breakfast U.S.A.
BED & BREAKFAST—Bed & Breakfast U.S.A.
BEE—BeeSoft
BEEPER—Consumer Electronics
BEER—Food & Drink Network
BEESOFT—BeeSoft
BEGINNER—Help Desk [*Platform-dependent*]
BEGINNERS—Help Desk [*Platform-dependent*]
BELCH—AOL Plays With Sounds [*WAOL only*]
BELGIUM—Belgium
BERK SYS WIN—Berkeley Systems
BERKELEY—Berkeley Systems
BERKSYS—Berkeley Systems
BERNIE—Bernie Siegel Online
BEST OF AOL—Best of America Online Showcase

Chapter 6 Keywords from A to Z

BEST TIPS—Top Tips for AOL

BETA APPLY—Beta Test Application Area [*May disappear without notice*]

BETHEL—Bethel College and Seminary

BETHESDA—Bethesda Softworks, Inc.

BETHESDA SOFTWORKS—Bethesda Softworks, Inc.

BETHSEDA—Bethesda Softworks, Inc.

BETTER HEALTH—Better Health & Medical Forum

BETTER LIVING—Ideas for Better Living

BEVERAGES—Everything Edible!

BEVERLY HILLS—90210 Wednesdays

BEVERLY HILLS 90210—90210 Wednesdays

BEYOND—Beyond, Inc.

BI—Gay & Lesbian Community Forum

BI TEEN—Gay & Lesbian Community Forum Youth Area

BI YOUTH—Gay & Lesbian Community Forum Youth Area

BIC MAG—Bicycling Magazine

BICYCLE—The Bicycle Network

BICYCLING—Bicycling Magazine

BICYCLING MAGAZINE—Bicycling Magazine

BIG TWIN—Big Twin Online: The All-Harley Magazine

BIGFOOT—Weekly World News

BIKENET—The Bicycle Network

BILLING—Accounts and Billing*

BIOLOGY—Simon & Schuster Online: Biology Dept.

BIOSCAN—OPTIMAS Corporation

BIRDING—Birding Selections

BISEXUAL—Gay & Lesbian Community Forum

BISEXUAL TEEN—Gay & Lesbian Community Forum Youth Area

BISEXUAL TRIVIA—Gay & Lesbian Community Forum: Gaymeland

BISEXUAL YOUTH—Gay & Lesbian Community Forum Youth Area

BIT JUGGLERS—Bit Jugglers

BIZ WEEK—Business Week Online

BIZINSIDER—Herb Greenberg's Business Insider

BK—Burger King College Football

BKG—American Dialogue

BL—Buddy Lists

Chapter 6 Keywords from A to Z

BLACK AMERICAN—Afrocentric Culture

BLACK HERITAGE—Black History Month [*May disappear without notice*]

BLACK HISTORY—Black History Month [*May disappear without notice*]

BLACK VOICES—Orlando Sentinel Online: Black Voices

BLACK-AMERICAN—Afrocentric Culture

BLACK-VOICES—Orlando Sentinel Online: Black Voices

BLACKBERRY—Blackberry Creek

BLACKBERRY CREEK—Blackberry Creek

BLACKS—Afrocentric Culture

BLIND—DisABILITIES Forum

BLIZZARD—Blizzard Fun! [*May disappear without notice*]

BLIZZARD ENT—Blizzard Entertainment

BLOC DEVELOPMENT—TIGERDirect, Inc.

BLOCKBUSTER—Blockbuster Music's Online Store

BLUE JAYS—Major League Baseball Team: Toronto Blue Jays

BLUE RIBBON—Blue RIbbon Soundworks

BLUEPRINT—Graphsoft, Inc.

BLUES—House of Blues Online

BMUG—Berkeley Macintosh Users Group

BOARDSAILING—Sailing Forum

BOAT—Boating Online

BOATING—Boating Selections

BOATS—The Exchange

BOB BEATY—Company Research Message Boards

BOBB—Company Research Message Boards

BODY ELECTRIC—Style Channel

BOFA—Bank of America

BONK—60-Second Novelist: BOnKeRs Trivia

BONKERS—60-Second Novelist: BOnKeRs Trivia

BOOK—The Book Nook

BOOK BESTSELLERS—Books Area

BOOKNOOK—The Book Nook

BOOKNOTES—Barrons Booknotes

BOOKS—Book Areas

BOOKS & CULTURE—Christian Books & Culture

BOOKS ON BREAK—Just Books!

Chapter 6 Keywords from A to Z

BOOKSHOP—Mysteries from the Yard

BOOKSTORE—Online Bookstore

BOSNIA—Balkan Operation Joint Endeavor

BOSOX—Major League Baseball Team: Boston Red Sox

BOSTON—Digital City Boston

BOSTON BRUINS—NESN: New England Hockey

BOSTON CELTICS—NESN: New England Baskteball

BOSTON ONLINE—Digital City Boston MA

BOSTON RED SOX—Major League Baseball Team: Boston Red Sox

BOWERS—Bowers Development

BOWL—AOL Live!

BOWL GAME—Fool Bowl

BOWL GAMES—NCAA Football Bowl Info

BOWLING—The Grandstand: Other Sports

BOWLS—NCAA Football Bowl Info

BOXER—Boxer*Jam Gameshows [*WAOL only*]

BOXER JAM—Boxer*Jam Gameshows [*WAOL only*]

BOXER*JAM—Boxer*Jam Gameshows [*WAOL only*]

BOXING—Sports Channel

BOYS—Focus on Family: Breakaway Magazine

BP MARKETPLACE—Backpacker Online's Marketplace

BPS SOFTWARE—BPS Software

BRAINSTORM—Brainstorm Products

BRAINSTORMS—Brainstorms Store

BRATS—Overseas Brats

BRAVES—Major League Baseball Team: Atlanta Braves

BRAVOS—Major League Baseball Team: Atlanta Braves

BREAKAWAY—Focus on Family: Breakaway Magazine

BREAKFAST—Bed & Breakfast U.S.A.

BREW—Food & Drink Network

BREWERS—Major League Baseball Team: Milwaukee Brewers

BREWING—Food & Drink Network

BRIDGES—The Hub: Even More Bridges of Madison County

BRINKLEY—ABC News-On-Demand

BRIO—Focus on Family: Brio Magazine

BRITISH—Genealogy Forum

BROADBAND—AOL's Cable Center

Chapter 6 Keywords from A to Z

BROADCAST SOFTWARE—Software Unboxed
BROADWAY—Playbill Online
BRODERBUND—Brøderbund
BROKEN ARROW—Broken Arrow
BROWSER FIX—AOL 2.6 for Macintosh* [*MAOL only*]
BRUINS HOCKEY—NESN: New England Hockey
BRYAN—Digital Cities: Waco/Temple/Bryan TX
BRYAN DC—Digital Cities: Waco/Temple/Bryan TX
BRYAN DCITY—Digital Cities: Waco/Temple/Bryan TX
BRYAN DIGC—Digital Cities: Waco/Temple/Bryan TX
BRYAN DIGITAL CITY—Digital Cities: Waco/Temple/Bryan TX
BRYAN TX—Digital Cities: Waco/Temple/Bryan TX
BRYCE—MetaTools, Inc.
BS FORUM—Business Strategies Forum
BTS—Bethel Theological Seminary
BUCS—Major League Baseball Team: Pittsburgh Pirates
BUDDHISM—Religion & Ethics Forum
BUDDIES—Buddy Lists
BUDDY—Buddy Lists
BUDDY LIST—Buddy Lists
BUDDY LISTS—Buddy Lists
BUDDY MAIN—Buddy Lists
BUDDY VIEW—Buddy View
BUFFALO—Digital Cities: Buffalo NY
BUFFALO DC—Digital Cities: Buffalo NY
BUFFALO DCITY—Digital Cities: Buffalo NY
BUFFALO DIGC—Digital Cities: Buffalo NY
BUFFALO DIGITAL CITY—Digital Cities: Buffalo NY
BUFFALO NY—Digital Cities: Buffalo NY
BUILDING—HouseNet
BULGARIA—Bulgaria
BULL—Merrill Lynch
BULL MOOSE—Bull Moose Tavern
BUNGIE—Bungie Software
BURGER KING—Burger King College Football
BURP—AOL Plays With Sounds [*WAOL only*]
BUS—AOL Roadtrips [*WAOL only*]
BUSINESS—Business News Area

Chapter 6 Keywords from A to Z

BUSINESS CENTER—Your Business
BUSINESS FORUM—Applications/Business Forum [*Platform-dependent*]
BUSINESS INSIDER—The Business Insider
BUSINESS KNOW HOW—Business Strategies Forum
BUSINESS LUNCH—Your Business Lunch
BUSINESS NEWS—Business News Area
BUSINESS RANKINGS—Business Rankings
BUSINESS RESOURCES—Hoover's Business Resources
BUSINESS SCHOOL—Kaplan Online or The Princeton Review
BUSINESS SENSE—Business Sense
BUSINESS STRATEGIES—Business Strategies Forum
BUSINESS WEEK—Business Week Online
BV CHAT—Orlando Sentinel Online: Black Voices' Chat
BW—Business Week Online
BW ONLINE—Business Week Online
BW SEARCH—Business Week: Search
BWOL—Motley Fool: The Fool Dome
BYTE—ByteWorks
BYTE BY BYTE—Byte By Byte Corporation
BYTEWORKS—ByteWorks
C—Development Forum [*Platform-dependent*]
C!—Computers & Software Channel [*Platform-dependent*]
C&S—Computers & Software Channel [*Platform-dependent*]
CA—Crossword America
CABLE—AOL's Cable Center
CABLE MODEM—AOL's Cable Center
CABLE NEWS—New England Cable News
CAD—CAD Resource Center
CADILLAC—Cadillac WWW Home Page
CAFFE STARBUCKS—Caffe Starbucks
CALENDAR—What's Hot in Computing [*Platform-dependent*]
CALENDAR GIRLS—The Hub: Calendar Girls
CALIFORNIA ANGELS—Major League Baseball Team: California Angels
CALL—Accessing America Online*
CALLISTO—Callisto Corporation
CAMERA—Photography Selections

Chapter 6 Keywords from A to Z

CAMERAS—Popular Photography Online
CAMEROON—Cameroon
CAMPAIGN 96—The Campaign Trail
CAMPING—Backpacker Magazine
CAMPUS—Online Campus
CAMPUS LIFE—Campus Life Magazine
CAN'T SLEEP—The Late Night Survey
CANADA—AOL Canada
CANADA CHAT—AOL Canada: Chat
CANADIAN—AOL Canada
CANCEL—Cancel Account*
CANCELLED TV SHOWS—Lost & Found TV Shows
CANCER—Cancer Forum
CANCER J SCIAM—Cancer Journal from Scientific American
CANCER JOURNAL—Cancer Journal from Scientific American
CANNES—Cannes Film Festival
CANT SLEEP—The Late Night Survey
CANVAS—Deneba Software
CAPITAL—Politics
CAPITAL CONNECTION—Politics
CAPITALS—Washington Capitals
CAPS—Washington Capitals
CAPSTONE—Capstone Software
CAR—Car/Cycle Selections
CAR AND DRIVER—Car and Driver Magazine
CAR INFO—AutoVantage: New Car Summary
CAR PHOTOS—Wheels Exchange
CAR SUMMARY—AutoVantage: New Car Summary
CARDINAL—Cardinal Technologies, Inc.
CARDINALS—Major League Baseball Team: St. Louis Cardinals
CARDS—Hallmark Connections
CAREER—Career Selections
CAREER NEWS—USA Today Industry Watch section
CAREERS—Career Selections
CAROLE 2000—Astronet
CARPENTRY—HouseNet
CARS—Car/Cycle Selections
CARTOON NETWORK—Cartoon Network

Chapter 6 Keywords from A to Z

CARTOONS—The Cartoons Forum
CASADY—Casady & Greene
CASINO—RabbitJack's Casino
CASTING—The Casting Forum
CASTING FORUM—The Casting Forum
CATHOLIC—Catholic Community
CATHOLIC NEWS—Catholic News Service
CATHOLIC NEWS SERVICE—Catholic News Service
CATHOLIC REPORTER—National Catholic Reporter
CB—College Board
CBD—Commerce Business Daily
CC—Computing Company Connection
CC MAG—Christian Computing Magazine
CCB—Chicago Online: Crain's Chicago Business
CCC—Computing Company Connection
CCDA—Christian Community Development Association
CCE—Columbia Encyclopedia
CCG—Christian College Guide
CCGF—Collectible Card Games Forum
CCI—Christian Camping International
CD—Marketplace Gift Service
CDS—Stereo Review Online
CE—Consumer Electronics
CE SOFTWARE—CE Software
CEC—Christian Education Center
CELEBRITIES—Style Channel
CELEBRITY—The Hub: Celebrity Sightings
CELEBRITY CIRCLE—Oldsmobile/Celebrity Circle
CELEBRITY COOKBOOK—Celebrity Cookbook
CELLULAR—Consumer Electronics
CELLULAR PHONE—Consumer Electronics
CELTICS—NESN: New England Baskteball
CELTICS BASKETBALL—NESN: New England Baskteball
CENTER STAGE—AOL Live!
CENTRAL—Symantec
CENTRAL POINT—Symantec
CENTURY—Twentieth Century Mutual Funds
CENTURY FUNDS—Twentieth Century Mutual Funds

Chapter 6 Keywords from A to Z

CEP—Council on Economic Priorities
CEREBRAL PALSY—United Cerebral Palsy Association
CG—Computer Gaming World
CGW—Computer Gaming World
CH—Christian History Magazine
CH PRODUCTS—CH Products
CHALLENGER—Challenger Remembered
CHAMPION—One Hanes Place
CHANGE PASSWORD—Change your password*
CHANGE PROFILE—Edit your member profile
CHANNEL 1—Channel One Network Online
CHANNEL C—CNN Newsroom Online [*MAOL only*]
CHANNEL ONE—Channel One Network Online
CHANNEL ZERO—The Hub: Channel Zero
CHARITY—access.point
CHARTER—Charter Schools Forum
CHARTER SCHOOL—Charter Schools Forum
CHARTER SCHOOLS—Charter Schools Forum
CHAT—People Connection Channel
CHEESECAKE—Eli's Cheesecakes
CHEESECAKES—Eli's Cheesecakes
CHEF—Everything Edible!
CHEF'S CATALOG—Chef's Catalog
CHEFS—Everything Edible!
CHEFS CATALOG—Chef's Catalog
CHESS—Strategy & Wargaming Forum
CHICAGO—Chicago Online
CHICAGO CUBS—Major League Baseball Team: Chicago Cubs
CHICAGO ONLINE—Chicago Online
CHICAGO SYMPHONY—Chicago Symphony Orchestra Online
CHICAGO TRIBUNE—Chicago Tribune
CHICAGO WHITE SOX—Major League Baseball Team: Chicago White Sox
CHICO—California State University
CHILD SAFETY—Child Safety Brochure
CHILDREN'S HEALTH—Children's Health Forum
CHILDREN'S SOFTWARE—HomePC Magazine: Children's Software
CHINESE ASTROLOGY—Astronet

Chapter 6 Keywords from A to Z

CHIP—ChipNet Online
CHIPNET—ChipNet Online
CHISOX—Major League Baseball Team: Chicago White Sox
CHOCOLATE—The Health Zone
CHOOSE A SPORT—Choose a Sport on AOL
CHRIST—Christianity Online
CHRISTIAN—Religion & Ethics Forum
CHRISTIAN CAMPING—Christian Camping International
CHRISTIAN COLLEGES—Christian College Guide
CHRISTIAN COMPUTING—Christian Computing Magazine
CHRISTIAN CONNECTION—Christianity Online Chat & Live Events
CHRISTIAN EDUCATION—Christian Education Center
CHRISTIAN FAMILIES—Christianity Online: Marriage/Family Forum
CHRISTIAN FAMILY—Christianity Online: Marriage/Family Forum
CHRISTIAN HISTORY—Christian History Magazine
CHRISTIAN KID—Christianity Online: Kids
CHRISTIAN KIDS—Christianity Online: Kids
CHRISTIAN MAN—Christianity Online: Men
CHRISTIAN MEDIA—Christian Media Source
CHRISTIAN MEN—Christianity Online: Men
CHRISTIAN PRODUCTS—Christian Products Center
CHRISTIAN READER—Christian Reader
CHRISTIAN SINGLES—Christianity Online: Singles
CHRISTIAN STUDENT—Christianity Online: Campus Life's Student Hangout
CHRISTIAN STUDENTS—Christianity Online: Campus Life's Student Hangout
CHRISTIAN WOMAN—Christianity Online: Women
CHRISTIAN WOMEN—Christianity Online: Women
CHRISTIANITY—Christianity Online
CHRISTIANITY TODAY—Christianity Today
CHROL CHAT—Christianity Online Chat & Live Events
CHROL CLASSIFIEDS—Christianity Online Classifieds
CHROL RESOURCES—Christian Resource Center
CHURCH LEADERS—Christianity Online: Church Leaders Network
CHURCH LEADERS NETWORK—Christianity Online: Church Leaders Network

Chapter 6 Keywords from A to Z

CIGAR—Food & Drink Network
CIGARS—Food & Drink Network
CINCINNATI REDS—Major League Baseball Team: Cincinnati Reds
CINDY—Cindy Adams: Queen of Gourmet Gossip
CINDY ADAMS—Cindy Adams: Queen of Gourmet Gossip
CINEMA—@the.movies
CINEMAN—Movie Review Database
CINEMAN SYNDICATE—Movie Review Database
CINEMAPOV—CinemaPOV
CITIBANK—The Apple Citibank Visa Card
CITIZEN—access.point
CITY WEB—City Web
CIVIC—access.point
CIVIL LIBERTIES—American Civil Liberties Union
CIVIL WAR—The Civil War Forum
CJ CONTESTS—CyberJustice Contests
CL—Campus Life Magazine
CLARIS—Claris
CLASSES—Online Campus
CLASSICAL MUSIC—Saturday Review Online
CLASSIFIED—AOL Classifieds
CLASSIFIEDS—AOL Classifieds
CLASSIFIEDS ONLINE—AOL Classifieds
CLASSROOM—President's Day [*May disappear without notice*]
CLEARANCE—The Fragrance Counter: Clearance Counter
CLEVELAND INDIANS—Major League Baseball Team: Cleveland Indians
CLICK HERE—The Hub: Click Here
CLIFE—Computer Life Magazine
CLINTON—White House Forum
CLN—Christianity Online: Church Leaders Network
CLOCK—Time of day and length of time online
CLOTHES—Elle Magazine Online
CLOTHING—Elle Magazine Online
CLS—Christianity Online Classifieds
CLUB KIDSOFT—Club KidSoft
CLUBS—Life, Styles & Interests Channel

Chapter 6 Keywords from A to Z

CLUBS & INTERNET—Life, Styles & Interest's Top Internet Sites
CM—Christian Ministries Center
CMC—Creative Musician's Coalition
CMIL—University of California Extension
CMS—Christian Media Source
CMT—Coda Music Tech
CN—Christianity Online Newsstand
CNEWS—Christianity Online Newsstand
CNFA—The Grandstand's Simulation Football
CNN—CNN Newsroom Online
CNN GUIDES—CNN Newsroom Online
CNN NEWSROOM—CNN Newsroom Online
CNS—Catholic News Service
CO ASSOCIATIONS—Christianity Online: Associations & Interests
CO CLASSIFIEDS—Christianity Online Classifieds
CO CONTEST—Christianity Online: Contest
CO FAMILIES—Christianity Online: Marriage/Family Forum
CO FAMILY—Christianity Online: Marriage/Family Forum
CO HOLIDAY—Christianity Online: Holidays and Contests
CO HOLIDAYS—Christianity Online: Holidays and Contests
CO INTERESTS—Christianity Online: Associations & Interests
CO KIDS—Christianity Online: Kids
CO LIVE—Christianity Online Chat & Live Events
CO MAN—Christianity Online: Men
CO MEN—Christianity Online: Men
CO NEWS—Christianity Online Newsstand
CO SINGLE—Christianity Online: Singles
CO SINGLES—Christianity Online: Singles
CO STUDENT—Christianity Online: Campus Life's Student Hangout
CO STUDENTS—Christianity Online: Campus Life's Student Hangout
CO TEEN—Christianity Online: Campus Life's Student Hangout
CO TEENS—Christianity Online: Campus Life's Student Hangout
CO WOMAN—Christianity Online: Women
CO WOMEN—Christianity Online: Women
CO YOUTH—Christianity Online: Campus Life's Student Hangout
COBB—The Cobb Group Online

Chapter 6 Keywords from A to Z

COBB GROUP—The Cobb Group Online
CODA—Coda Music Tech
CODA MUSIC—Coda Music Tech
COINS—The Exchange
COL—Chicago Online
COL BUSINESS—Chicago Online: Business Guide
COL CALENDAR—Chicago Online: Calendar & Almanac
COL CHAT—Chicago Online: Chat
COL EDUCATE—Chicago Online: Education Guide
COL EDUCATION—Chicago Online: Education Guide
COL ENTERTAINMENT—Chicago Tribune: Local Entertainment Guide
COL FILES—Chicago Online: Libraries
COL GOVERNMENT—Chicago Tribune: Election '96
COL GOVT—Chicago Tribune: Election '96
COL LIFESTYLES—Chicago Online: Lifestyles
COL MALL—Chicago Online: Mall
COL MARKETPLACE—Chicago Online: Marketplace
COL MEDIA—Chicago Online: Media Guide
COL NEWS—Chicago Online: News, Business & Weather
COL PLANNER—Chicago Online: Planner
COL SPORTS—Chicago Online: Sports
COL TECH—Chicago Online: Technology Guide
COL TICKET—Chicago Online: Ticketmaster
COL TRAFFIC—Chicago Tribune: Traffic Updates
COL VISITOR—Chicago Online: Visitor Guide
COLISEUM—AOL Live!
COLLECT—Collectibles Online
COLLECT CARDS—Collectible Card Games Forum
COLLECTIBLES—Collectibles Online
COLLECTIBLES ONLINE—Collectibles Online
COLLECTING—Wizard World
COLLECTOR—The Exchange
COLLEGE—College Selections
COLLEGE BOARD—College Board
COLLEGE FOOTBALL—AOL Football
COLLEGE HOOPS—Extreme Fans: College Hoops
COLLEGE ONLINE—Simon & Schuster College Online

Chapter 6 Keywords from A to Z

COLLEGIATE—Merriam-Webster's Collegiate Dictionary
COLLEGIATE DICTIONARY—Merriam-Webster's Collegiate Dictionary
COLOGNE—The Fragrance Counter
COLOR IMAGING—Advanced Color Imaging Forum
COLOR WEATHERMAPS—Main Weather Area
COLORADO ROCKIES—Major League Baseball Team: Colorado Rockies
COLUMBIA—Columbia Encyclopedia
COLUMBIA.NET—Columbia's Health Today
COLUMBIA/HCA—Columbia's Health Today
COLUMBIANET—Columbia's Health Today
COLUMNISTS—Columnists & Features Online
COLUMNS—Columnists & Features Online
COMEDY—The Comedy Pub
COMEDY CENTRAL—Comedy Central
COMEDY PUB—The Comedy Pub
COMIC STRIP—Comic Strip Centennial
COMICS—Comics Selection
COMMANDO—Kim Komando's Komputer Clinic
COMMON GROUND—Common Ground Software
COMMONS—The Motley Fool
COMMUNICATIONS—Communications Forum [*Platform-dependent*]
COMMUNITIES—The Exchange: Communities Center
COMMUNITY—access.point
COMMUNITY CENTER—Life, Styles & Interests Channel
COMP SITES—Computing Internet Sites
COMPANIES—Computing Company Connection
COMPANY—Company Research
COMPANY 3DO—The 3DO Company
COMPANY PROFILES—Hoover's Handbook of Company Profiles
COMPANY RESEARCH—Company Research
COMPANY UPDATES—Hoover's Company Masterlist
COMPAQ—Compaq
COMPOSER—Composer's Coffeehouse
COMPOSER'S—Composer's Coffeehouse
COMPOSERS—Composer's Coffeehouse

Chapter 6 Keywords from A to Z

COMPTONS—Compton's NewMedia Forum

COMPTONS ENCYCLOPEDIA—Compton's Living Encyclopedia

COMPTONS SOFTWARE—Compton's Software Library

COMPUADD—CompuAdd

COMPUKIDS—Compukids

COMPUSERVE—Prodigy Refugees Forum

COMPUSTORE—Shopper's Advantage Online

COMPUTE—I-Wire Online

COMPUTER—Computers & Software Channel [*Platform-dependent*]

COMPUTER AMERICA—Craig Crossman's Computer America

COMPUTER BOWL—Computer Bowl

COMPUTER EXPRESS—Computer Express

COMPUTER FORUM—Computers & Software Channel [*Platform-dependent*]

COMPUTER GAMES—Hecklers Online

COMPUTER GAMING—Computer Gaming World

COMPUTER GAMING WORLD—Computer Gaming World

COMPUTER LAW—CyberLaw/Cyberlex

COMPUTER LIFE—Computer Life Magazine

COMPUTER NEWS—Newsbytes

COMPUTER PERIPHERALS—Computer Peripherals, Inc.

COMPUTER TERMS—Dictionary of Computer Terms

COMPUTING—Computers & Software Channel [*Platform-dependent*]

COMPUTING AND SOFTWARE—Computers & Software Channel [*Platform-dependent*]

COMPUTING DEPT—Computing & Software (Old Style) [*MAOL only*]

COMPUTING FORUMS—Computers & Software Channel [*Platform-dependent*]

COMPUTING LIFESTYLES—Family Computing Forum: Lifestyles & Computing

COMPUTING NEWS—Computing News [*MAOL only*]

COMPUTING SITES—Computing Internet Sites

COMPUTOON—CompuToon Area

CON—Christianity Online: Contest

CONFIG—Tune Up Your PC

CONGRESS—Politics Forum

Chapter 6 Keywords from A to Z

CONGRESSIONAL—Congressional Quarterly

CONNECTING—Accessing America Online*

CONNECTION—Intel Corporation

CONNECTIX—Connectix

CONSPIRACY—Parascope

CONSUMER—Consumer Reports

CONSUMER ELECTRONICS—Consumer Electronics

CONSUMER REPORTS—Consumer Reports

CONSUMERS—Consumer Reports

CONTACTS—Employer Contacts Database

CONTEST—AOL Contest Area

CONTEST AREA—AOL Contest Area

CONTEST CENTRAL—Family Computing Forum: Contest Central

CONTESTS—AOL Contest Area

COOK—Everything Edible!

COOKBOOK—Celebrity Cookbook

COOKIE—The Motley Fool

COOKING—Everything Edible!

COOKING CLUB—Cooking Club

COOKS—Everything Edible!

COOPER—JLCooper Electronics

CORBIS—Corbis Media

CORBIS MEDIA—Corbis Media

CORCORAN—Corcoran School of Art

COREL—Corel Special Interest Group

CORELDRAW—Corel Special Interest Group

CORKSCREWED—Corkscrewed Online

CORNER—Pro's Corner

CORPORATE PROFILES—Hoover's Handbook of Company Profiles

COSA—AfterEffects

COSTAR—CoStar

COSTARD—The Motley Fool

COUNTDOWN—NTN Trivia

COUNTRIES—The World

COURSES—Online Courses

COURSEWARE—Electronic Courseware

COURT TV—Court TV's Law Center

Chapter 6 Keywords from A to Z

COURTROOM TELEVISION—Court TV's Law Center
COURTS—CyberJustice's Courts of Karmic Justice
COW—Christianity Online: Women
COWLES—Cowles/SIMBA Media Information Network
COWLES SIMBA—Cowles/SIMBA Media Information Network
CP&B—Computing Print & Broadcast
CPB—Computing Print & Broadcast
CPC—Christian Products Center
CPI—Computer Peripherals, Inc.
CPOV—CinemaPOV
CPS—Symantec
CQ—Congressional Quarterly
CR—Christian Reader
CRAFTS—Craft Selections
CRAIG CROSSMAN—Craig Crossman's Computer America
CRAIN'S—Chicago Online: Crain's Chicago Business
CRAIN'S SMALL BIZ—Chicago Online: Crain's Small Business
CRAINS—Chicago Online: Crain's Chicago Business
CRASH—Flight Simulation Resource Center
CRAZY HORSE—Rockline Online
CRC—Family Computing: Maximum AOL
CREDIT—Credit Request Form for connect problems*
CREDIT REQUEST—Credit Request Form for connect problems*
CREED—Religion & Ethics Forum
CRIMINAL JUSTICE—Simon & Schuster Online: Criminal Justice Dept.
CRISPY—Pangea Toy Net
CRITIC—Critic's Choice
CRITICS—Critic's Choice
CRITICS CHOICE—Critic's Choice
CROATIA—Croatia
CROSSDRESSER—Transgender Community Forum
CROSSDRESSING—Transgender Community Forum
CROSSMAN—Craig Crossman's Computer America
CROSSWORD—The New York Times Crosswords
CROSSWORDS—The New York Times Crosswords
CRUISE—Cruise Critic
CRUISE CRITIC—Cruise Critic

Chapter 6 Keywords from A to Z

CRUISE CRITICS—Cruise Critic
CRUISES—Cruise Critic
CRUSADE—Avon's Breast Cancer Awareness Crusade Online
CRYSTAL—Crystal Dynamics
CRYSTAL BALL—The Crystal Ball Forum
CS—AOL Live!
CSB—Chicago Online: Crain's Small Business
CSLIVE—Member Services*
CSMITH—CyberSmith
CSPAN—C-SPAN
CSPAN BUS—C-SPAN in the Classroom
CSPAN CLASS—C-SPAN in the Classroom
CSPAN CLASSROOM—C-SPAN in the Classroom
CSPAN ONLINE—C-SPAN
CSPAN SCHOOLS—C-SPAN in the Classroom
CSUC—California State University
CT—Christianity Today
CUBBIES—Major League Baseball Team: Chicago Cubs
CUBS—Major League Baseball Team: Chicago Cubs
CURRICULUM—Assoc. for Supervisor & Curriculum Development
CUSTOMER SERVICE—Member Services*
CUTTING EDGE—NESN: New England Hockey
CWUG—ClarisWorks User Group
CYBER 24—24 Hours in Cyberspace
CYBERCAFE—CyberSmith
CYBERJUSTICE—CyberJustice
CYBERLAW—CyberLaw/CyberLex
CYBERLEX—CyberLaw/CyberLex
CYBERLOVE & LAUGHTER—Cyberlove & Laughter
CYBERSALON—Cybersalon
CYBERSERIALS—Cyberserials
CYBERSLEUTH—Murder Mysteries Online
CYBERSLIM—The Health Zone
CYBERSMITH—CyberSmith
CYBERSOAPS—Cyberserials
CYBERSPORTS—The Grandstand's Fantasy & Simulation Leagues
CYBERVIEW—This Week's Best Cyberviews
CYBERVIEWS—This Week's Best Cyberviews

Chapter 6 Keywords from A to Z

CYBERZINES—Digizine Sites on the Web
CYCLE—Cycle World Online
CYCLE WORLD—Cycle World Online
CYCLING—Cycle World Online
CYRANO—The Hub: Cyrano
CZECH REPUBLIC—Czech Republic
DACEASY—DacEasy, Inc.
DAD—AOL Families
DADS—AOL Families
DAILY—Reference Daily Dose
DAILY FIX—What's Hot in Entertainment
DAILY LIVING—Daily Living
DALAI LAMA—Dalai Lama Conference [*May disappear without notice*]
DALLAS—Digital Cities: Dallas - Ft. Worth TX
DALLAS DIGC—Digital Cities: Dallas - Ft. Worth TX
DALLAS DIGITAL CITY—Digital Cities: Dallas - Ft. Worth TX
DAN HURLEY—60-Second Novelist
DANCE—@times: Music & Dance
DANISH—Genealogy Forum
DATABASE—Database Support Special Interest Group
DATABASES—Database Support Special Interest Group
DATAPACK—DataPak Software
DATAPAK—DataPak Software
DATAWATCH—Datawatch
DATE—Love@AOL
DATING—Romance Connection
DATING SERVICE—Love@AOL
DATING SERVICES—Love@AOL
DAVIDSON—Davidson & Associates
DAY ONE—ABC News-On-Demand
DAYNA—Dayna Communications
DAYSTAR—Daystar Digital
DAYTIMER—DayTimer Technologies
DAYTON—Digital Cities: Dayton OH
DAYTON DC—Digital Cities: Dayton OH
DAYTON DCITY—Digital Cities: Dayton OH
DAYTON DIGC—Digital Cities: Dayton OH

Chapter 6 Keywords from A to Z

DAYTON DIGITAL CITY—Digital Cities: Dayton OH
DAYTON OH—Digital Cities: Dayton OH
DC—Digital City -or- DC Comics
DC ALASKA—Digital Cities: Alaska
DC ALBANY—Digital Cities: Albany NY
DC ALBUQUERQUE—Digital Cities: Albuquerque/Santa Fe NM
DC ATLANTA—Digital Cities: Atlanta GA
DC AUSTIN—Digital Cities: Austin TX
DC BAY CITY—Digital Cities: Bay City MI
DC BRYAN—Digital Cities: Waco/Temple/Bryan TX
DC BUFFALO—Digital Cities: Buffalo NY
DC CHAT—DC Comics Online: Chat Rooms
DC COMICS—DC Comics Online
DC COMICS ONLINE—DC Comics Online
DC DALLAS—Digital Cities: Dallas - Ft. Worth TX
DC DAYTON—Digital Cities: Dayton OH
DC DENVER—Digital Cities: Denver CO
DC DETROIT—Digital Cities: Detroit MI
DC EL PASO—Digital Cities: El Paso TX
DC EUGENE—Digital Cities: Eugene OR
DC EVENT—Digital City: The Event Source
DC FLINT—Digital Cities: Flint MI
DC FORT WORTH—Digital Cities: Dallas - Ft. Worth TX
DC FRESNO—Digital Cities: Fresno/Visalia CA
DC FT LAUDERDALE—Digital Cities: Miami - Ft Lauderdale FL
DC FT MYERS—Digital Cities: Ft. Myers/Naples FL
DC FUN—Digital City: Entertainment
DC HOTLANTA—Digital Cities: Atlanta GA
DC HOUSTON—Digital Cities: Houston TX
DC JOIN—Register as a Digital Citizen
DC LA—Digital Cities: Los Angeles CA
DC LOS ANGELES—Digital Cities: Los Angeles CA
DC MARKETPLACE—Digital City: Marketplace
DC MIDWEST—Digital Cities: Midwest
DC MINNEAPOLIS—Digital Cities: Minneapolis - St. Paul MN
DC NAPLES—Digital Cities: Ft. Myers/Naples FL
DC NEW BEDFORD—Digital Cities: New Bedford MA
DC NEW ORLEANS—Digital Cities: New Orleans LA

Chapter 6 Keywords from A to Z

DC NEWPORT NEWS—Digital Cities: Newport News and Norfolk VA
DC NEWS—Digital City: News/Weather
DC PEOPLE—Digital City: People
DC PHILA—Digital Cities: Philadelphia PA
DC PHILADELPHIA—Digital Cities: Philadelphia PA
DC PHILLY—Digital Cities: Philadelphia PA
DC RENO—Digital Cities: Reno NV
DC SAGINAW—Digital Cities: Saginaw MI
DC SAN DIEGO—Digital Cities: San Diego CA
DC SAN FRANCISCO—Digital Cities: San Francisco CA
DC SANTA FE—Digital Cities: Albuquerque/Santa Fe NM
DC SD—Digital Cities: San Diego CA
DC SEATTLE—Digital Cities: Seattle/Tacoma WA
DC SF—Digital Cities: San Francisco CA
DC SOUTH—Digital Cities: South
DC SPORTS—Digital City: Sports
DC ST PAUL—Digital Cities: Minneapolis - St. Paul MN
DC ST PETERSBURG—Ditial Cities: Tampa - St. Petersburg FL
DC TAMPA—Ditial Cities: Tampa - St. Petersburg FL
DC TEMPLE—Digital Cities: Waco/Temple/Bryan TX
DC TORONTO—Digital Cities: Toronto ON
DC TULSA—Digital Cities: Tulsa OK
DC VISALIA—Digital Cities: Fresno/Visalia CA
DC WACO—Digital Cities: Waco/Temple/Bryan TX
DC WEB—City Web
DC WEST—Digital Cities: West
DCI CHAT—The Discovery Channel: Chat
DCITY ALASKA—Digital Cities: Alaska
DCITY ALBANY—Digital Cities: Albany NY
DCITY ALBUQUERQUE—Digital Cities: Albuquerque/Santa Fe NM
DCITY AUSTIN—Digital Cities: Austin TX
DCITY BAY CITY—Digital Cities: Bay City MI
DCITY BRYAN—Digital Cities: Waco/Temple/Bryan TX
DCITY BUFFALO—Digital Cities: Buffalo NY
DCITY DAYTON—Digital Cities: Dayton OH
DCITY EL PASO—Digital Cities: El Paso TX
DCITY EUGENE—Digital Cities: Eugene OR

Chapter 6 Keywords from A to Z

DCITY FLINT—Digital Cities: Flint MI
DCITY FRESNO—Digital Cities: Fresno/Visalia CA
DCITY FT MYERS—Digital Cities: Ft. Myers/Naples FL
DCITY NAPLES—Digital Cities: Ft. Myers/Naples FL
DCITY NATIONAL—Digital City
DCITY NEW BEDFORD—Digital Cities: New Bedford MA
DCITY NEW ORLEANS—Digital Cities: New Orleans LA
DCITY NEWPORT NEWS—Digital Cities: Newport News and Norfolk VA
DCITY NORFOLK—Digital Cities: Newport News and Norfolk VA
DCITY RENO—Digital Cities: Reno NV
DCITY SAGINAW—Digital Cities: Saginaw MI
DCITY SANTA FE—Digital Cities: Albuquerque/Santa Fe NM
DCITY TEMPLE—Digital Cities: Waco/Temple/Bryan TX
DCITY TULSA—Digital Cities: Tulsa OK
DCITY VISALIA—Digital Cities: Fresno/Visalia CA
DCITY WACO—Digital Cities: Waco/Temple/Bryan TX
DCL—Dictionary of Cultural Literacy
DCN—Digital City
DCNATIONAL—Digital City
DD—Dial/Data
DEAD—Grateful Dead Forum
DEAD END—The Dead End of the Internet [*WAOL only*]
DEADLY—Deadly Games
DEAF—Deaf & Hard of Hearing Forum
DEAR DOTTI—Weekly World News
DEBATE—Politics
DEC—Digital Equipment Corporation
DECISION—Decision Point Forum
DECISION 94—The Campaign Trail
DECISION POINT—Decision Point Forum
DECORATING—Home Magazine Online
DEFENSE—Military City Online
DELL—Dell Computer Corporation
DELRINA—Symantec
DELTA—Delta Tao
DELTA POINT—Delta Point
DELTA TAO—Delta Tao

Chapter 6 Keywords from A to Z

DEMOCRACY—CNN Newsroom Online
DENEBA—Deneba Software
DENMARK—Denmark
DENOMINATION—Religion & Ethics Forum
DENVER—Digital Cities: Denver CO
DENVER DIGC—Digital Cities: Denver CO
DENVER DIGITAL CITY—Digital Cities: Denver CO
DEPARTMENT 56—Department 56 Collecting
DEPENDENCY—Dependency and Recovery Issues
DEPIXION—InToon with the News
DEPT 56—Department 56 Collecting
DES—DeskMate
DESIGN—Elle Magazine Online
DESIGN SIG—Design Special Interest Group
DESIGNER—Design Special Interest Group
DESIGNER STUDIO—Style Channel
DESIGNERS—Elle Magazine Online
DESK REFERENCE—NY Public Library Desk Reference
DESKMATE—DeskMate
DESKTOP CINEMA—Desktop Cinema*
DESKTOP PUBLISHING—Desktop and Web Publishing Area [*Platform-dependent*]
DETROIT—Digital Cities: Detroit MI
DETROIT DIGC—Digital Cities: Detroit MI
DETROIT DIGITAL CITY—Digital Cities: Detroit MI
DETROIT TIGERS—Major League Baseball Team: Detroit Tigers
DEV—Development Forum [*Platform-dependent*]
DEVELOPER—Development Forum [*Platform-dependent*]
DEVELOPMENT—Development Forum [*Platform-dependent*]
DEVELOPMENT FORUM—Development Forum [*Platform-dependent*]
DF FOOD—Destination Florida: Restaurants and Nightlife
DF OUT—Destination Florida: Outdoors
DF PARKS—Destination Florida: Attractions
DF ROOMS—Destination Florida: Places to Stay
DF SHOP—Destination Florida: Shopping
DF SPACE—Destination Florida: Kennedy Space Center
DF SPORTS—Destination Florida: Sports

Chapter 6 Keywords from A to Z

DF TICKET—Destination Florida: Ticketmaster

DI—Disney Interactive

DIABETES—American Diabetes Association

DIAL—Dial/Data

DIALOGUE—American Dialogue

DIAMOND—Diamond Computer Systems

DIAMOND COMPUTERS—Diamond Computer Systems

DICTIONARY—Dictionary Selections

DIG CITY—Digital City

DIG CITY NATIONAL—Digital City

DIG CITY PHILLY—Digital Cities: Philadelphia PA

DIG CITY USA—Digital City

DIGC—Digital City

DIGC ALASKA—Digital Cities: Alaska

DIGC ALBANY—Digital Cities: Albany NY

DIGC ALBUQUERQUE—Digital Cities: Albuquerque/Santa Fe NM

DIGC ATLANTA—Digital Cities: Atlanta GA

DIGC AUSTIN—Digital Cities: Austin TX

DIGC BAY CITY—Digital Cities: Bay City MI

DIGC BRYAN—Digital Cities: Waco/Temple/Bryan TX

DIGC BUFFALO—Digital Cities: Buffalo NY

DIGC DAYTON—Digital Cities: Dayton OH

DIGC DENVER—Digital Cities: Denver CO

DIGC DETROIT—Digital Cities: Detroit MI

DIGC EL PASO—Digital Cities: El Paso TX

DIGC EUGENE—Digital Cities: Eugene OR

DIGC FLINT—Digital Cities: Flint MI

DIGC FRESNO—Digital Cities: Fresno/Visalia CA

DIGC FT LAUDERDALE—Digital Cities: Miami - Ft Lauderdale FL

DIGC FT MYERS—Digital Cities: Ft. Myers/Naples FL

DIGC FT WORTH—Digital Cities: Dallas - Ft. Worth TX

DIGC HOTLANTA—Digital Cities: Atlanta GA

DIGC HOUSTON—Digital Cities: Houston TX

DIGC LA—Digital Cities: Los Angeles CA

DIGC LOS ANGELES—Digital Cities: Los Angeles CA

DIGC MIAMI—Digital Cities: Miami - Ft Lauderdale FL

DIGC MIDWEST—Digital Cities: Midwest

DIGC MINNEAPOLIS—Digital Cities: Minneapolis - St. Paul MN

Chapter 6 Keywords from A to Z

DIGC NAPLES—Digital Cities: Ft. Myers/Naples FL
DIGC NEW BEDFORD—Digital Cities: New Bedford MA
DIGC NEW ORLEANS—Digital Cities: New Orleans LA
DIGC NEWPORT NEWS—Digital Cities: Newport News and Norfolk VA
DIGC PHILA—Digital Cities: Philadelphia PA
DIGC PHILADELPHIA—Digital Cities: Philadelphia PA
DIGC PHILLY—Digital Cities: Philadelphia PA
DIGC RENO—Digital Cities: Reno NV
DIGC SAGINAW—Digital Cities: Saginaw MI
DIGC SAN DIEGO—Digital Cities: San Diego CA
DIGC SAN FRANCISCO—Digital Cities: San Francisco CA
DIGC SANTA FE—Digital Cities: Albuquerque/Santa Fe NM
DIGC SD—Digital Cities: San Diego CA
DIGC SEATTLE—Digital Cities: Seattle/Tacoma WA
DIGC SF—Digital Cities: San Francisco CA
DIGC SOUTH—Digital Cities: South
DIGC ST PAUL—Digital Cities: Minneapolis - St. Paul MN
DIGC ST PETERSBURG—Ditial Cities: Tampa - St. Petersburg FL
DIGC TACOMA—Digital Cities: Seattle/Tacoma WA
DIGC TAMPA—Ditial Cities: Tampa - St. Petersburg FL
DIGC TEMPLE—Digital Cities: Waco/Temple/Bryan TX
DIGC TORONTO—Digital Cities: Toronto ON
DIGC TULSA—Digital Cities: Tulsa OK
DIGC VISALIA—Digital Cities: Fresno/Visalia CA
DIGC WACO—Digital Cities: Waco/Temple/Bryan TX
DIGC WEST—Digital Cities: West
DIGITAL—Digital Menu
DIGITAL CITIES—Digital City
DIGITAL CITY—Digital City
DIGITAL CITY ALASKA—Digital Cities: Alaska
DIGITAL CITY ALBANY—Digital Cities: Albany NY
DIGITAL CITY ATLANTA—Digital Cities: Atlanta GA
DIGITAL CITY AUSTIN—Digital Cities: Austin TX
DIGITAL CITY BRYAN—Digital Cities: Waco/Temple/Bryan TX
DIGITAL CITY BUFFALO—Digital Cities: Buffalo NY
DIGITAL CITY DALLAS—Digital Cities: Dallas - Ft. Worth TX
DIGITAL CITY DAYTON—Digital Cities: Dayton OH

Chapter 6 Keywords from A to Z

DIGITAL CITY DENVER—Digital Cities: Denver CO
DIGITAL CITY DETROIT—Digital Cities: Detroit MI
DIGITAL CITY EL PASO—Digital Cities: El Paso TX
DIGITAL CITY EUGENE—Digital Cities: Eugene OR
DIGITAL CITY FLINT—Digital Cities: Flint MI
DIGITAL CITY FRESNO—Digital Cities: Fresno/Visalia CA
DIGITAL CITY FT WORTH—Digital Cities: Dallas - Ft. Worth TX
DIGITAL CITY HOUSTON—Digital Cities: Houston TX
DIGITAL CITY JOIN—Register as a Digital Citizen
DIGITAL CITY LA—Digital Cities: Los Angeles CA
DIGITAL CITY MIAMI—Digital Cities: Miami - Ft Lauderdale FL
DIGITAL CITY MIDWEST—Digital Cities: Midwest
DIGITAL CITY NAPLES—Digital Cities: Ft. Myers/Naples FL
DIGITAL CITY NATIONAL—Digital City
DIGITAL CITY PHILLY—Digital Cities: Philadelphia PA
DIGITAL CITY RENO—Digital Cities: Reno NV
DIGITAL CITY SANTA FE—Digital Cities: Albuquerque/Santa Fe NM
DIGITAL CITY SD—Digital Cities: San Diego CA
DIGITAL CITY SEATTLE—Digital Cities: Seattle/Tacoma WA
DIGITAL CITY SF—Digital Cities: San Francisco CA
DIGITAL CITY SOUTH—Digital Cities: South
DIGITAL CITY ST PAUL—Digital Cities: Minneapolis - St. Paul MN
DIGITAL CITY TACOMA—Digital Cities: Seattle/Tacoma WA
DIGITAL CITY TAMPA—Ditial Cities: Tampa - St. Petersburg FL
DIGITAL CITY TORONTO—Digital Cities: Toronto ON
DIGITAL CITY TULSA—Digital Cities: Tulsa OK
DIGITAL CITY US—Digital City
DIGITAL CITY VISALIA—Digital Cities: Fresno/Visalia CA
DIGITAL CITY WACO—Digital Cities: Waco/Temple/Bryan TX
DIGITAL CITY WEST—Digital Cities: West
DIGITAL ECLIPSE—Digital Eclipse
DIGITAL IMAGING—Digital Imaging Resource Center
DIGITAL RESEARCH—Novell Desktop Systems
DIGITAL RESEARCH INC—Novell Desktop Systems
DIGITAL TECH—Digital Technologies
DIGITAL USA—Digital City
DIGIZINES—Digizine Sites on the Web

Chapter 6 Keywords from A to Z

DILBERT—Dilbert Comics
DILBERT COMICS—Dilbert Comics
DILBOARD—Dilbert Comics
DINE—Everything Edible!
DINE OUT—Dinner On Us Club
DINER—The Web Diner
DINER CREW—The Web Diner
DINING—Everything Edible!
DIR OF SERVICES—Directory of Services
DIR OF SVCS—Directory of Services
DIRECTORY—Member Directory
DIRECTORY OF SERVICES—Directory of Services
DIS—DisABILITIES Forum
DISABILITIES—DisABILITIES Forum
DISABILITY—DisABILITIES Forum
DISCLOSURE—Disclosure Incorporated
DISCOVER—Discover America Online
DISCOVER AOL—Discover America Online
DISCOVERY—The Discovery Channel
DISCOVERY CHAT—The Discovery Channel: Chat
DISCOVERY ED—The Discovery Channel: Education
DISNEY—Disney Services
DISNEY ADVENTURES—Disney Adventures Magazine
DISNEY INTERACTIVE—Disney Interactive
DISNEY JOBS—Disney Jobs
DISNEY MAGAZINE—Disney Adventures Magazine
DISNEY SOFT—Disney Interactive
DISNEY SOFTWARE—Disney Interactive
DIVA—Soap Opera Digest
DIVA LA DISH—Soap Opera Digest
DJ—Don Johnston, Inc.
DL—Dalai Lama [*May disappear without notice*]
DO SOMETHING—Do Something!
DOBSON—Focus on the Family
DOCL—Dictionary of Cultural Literacy
DOCTOR WHO—Doctor Who Online
DODGERS—Major League Baseball Team: Los Angeles Dodgers
DOGERS—Major League Baseball Team: Los Angeles Dodgers

Chapter 6 Keywords from A to Z

DOMARK—Domark Software, Inc.

DON JOHNSTON—Don Johnston, Inc.

DON'T CLICK HERE—Don't Click Here [*WAOL only*]

DONATION—access.point

DONATIONS—access.point

DONT MISS—Directory of Services

DOROTHY—CyberJustice's Oasis of Xaiz

DOS 6—MS-DOS 6.0 Resource Center

DOS 60—MS-DOS 6.0 Resource Center

DOWNLOAD—Software Center [*Platform-dependent*]

DOWNLOAD 101—Download Help*

DOWNLOAD CREDIT—Credit Request Form for connect problems*

DOWNLOAD GAMES—Download Online Games* [*WAOL and GAOL only*]

DOWNLOAD HELP—Download Help*

DOWNLOADING—Software Center [*Platform-dependent*]

DOWNTOWN—Downtown AOL

DOWNTOWN AOL—Downtown AOL

DOWNTOWN MSG—Downtown AOL Message Boards

DP—Decision Point Forum

DPA—Decision Point Forum

DR GAMEWIZ—Dr Gamewiz Online

DR WHO—Doctor Who Online

DRAGONREALMS—DragonRealms

DREALMS—DragonRealms

DRESSAGE—Horse Forum's Dressage MiniForum

DRI—Novell Desktop Systems

DRIVING—Car and Driver Magazine

DRUG REFERENCE—Consumer Reports Complete Drug Reference Search

DRUM—Drum Magazine

DS—Do Something!

DSC—The Discovery Channel

DSC ED—The Discovery Channel: Education

DSC-ED—The Discovery Channel: Education

DT—Downtown AOL

DT AOL—Downtown AOL

Chapter 6 Keywords from A to Z

DTP—Desktop and Web Publishing Area [*Platform-dependent*]

DTV—Motley Fool: Desktop Video

DUBLCLICK—Dubl-Click Software

DUTCH—Genealogy Forum

DVORAK—Software Hardtalk with John C. Dvorak

DWP—Desktop & Web Publishing [*Platform-dependent*]

DYNAMIX—Sierra On-Line

DYNAWARE—Dynaware USA

DYNAWARE USA—Dynaware USA

E!—E! Entertainment Television

E—Entertainment Channel

E-ZONE—Your Business

EAASY SABRE—EAASY SABRE Travel Service

EAGLE—Eagle Home Page

EARL'S GARAGE—Pro's Corner

EARLS GARAGE—Pro's Corner

EARLY ED—Preschool/Early Childhood Special Interest Group

EARLY EDUCATION—Preschool/Early Childhood Special Interest Group

EARTH—Environmental Forum

EARTHLINK—TBS Network Earth/IBM Project [*MAOL and GAOL only*]

EASTER—AOL's Easter Area [*May disappear without notice*]

EASTERN EUROPEAN—Genealogy Forum

EASY—EAASY SABRE

EASY SABRE—EAASY SABRE Travel Service

EAT—Dinner On Us Club

EAT OUT—Dinner On Us Club

EATS—Good Morning America Recipes

ECCLESIASTICAL—Religion & Ethics Forum

ECHAT—Entertainment Chat

ECOTOURISM—Backpacker Magazine

ECS—Electronic Courseware

ED ADVISORY—Education Advisory Council Online

ED ANGER—Weekly World News

EDA—Education Advisory Council Online

EDDIE BAUER—Eddie Bauer

EDELSTEIN—Fred Edelstein's Pro Football Insider

Chapter 6 Keywords from A to Z

EDGAR—Disclosure's EdgarPlus
EDIT PROFILE—Edit your member profile
EDITOR'S CHOICE—Pictures of the Week
EDITORIAL CARTOONS—InToon with the News
EDITORS CHOICE—Pictures of the Week
EDMARK—Edmark Technologies
EDTECH—Association for Supervisor & Curriculum Development
EDUCATION—Learning & Culture Channel
EDUCATION CONNECTION—Compton's Education Connection
EFORUM—Environmental Forum
EGG—Electronic Gourmet Guide
EGG BASKET—Electronic Gourmet Guide
EGYPT—Egypt
EL PASO—Digital Cities: El Paso TX
EL PASO DC—Digital Cities: El Paso TX
EL PASO DCITY—Digital Cities: El Paso TX
EL PASO DIGC—Digital Cities: El Paso TX
EL PASO DIGITAL CITY—Digital Cities: El Paso TX
EL PASO TX—Digital Cities: El Paso TX
ELECTION HANDBOOK—Student's Election Handbook
ELECTRIC—Electric Image
ELECTRIC IMAGE—Electric Image
ELECTRONIC PUBLISHING—Desktop & Web Publishing [*Platform-dependent*]
ELECTRONICS—Andy Pargh/The Gadget Guru
ELI—Eli's Cheesecakes
ELI CONTEST—Elie's Cheesecakes Contest
ELI'S—Eli's Cheesecakes
ELI'S CHEESECAKES—Eli's Cheesecakes
ELIS CHEESECAKES—Eli's Cheesecakes
ELLE—Elle Magazine Online
ELVIS—Weekly World News
EMAIL—Post Office
EMALL—Orlando Sentinel Online: E-Mall
EMERALD COAST—Emerald Coast
EMERGENCY—Public Safety Center
EMERGENCY RESPONSE—Public Safety Center

125

Chapter 6 Keywords from A to Z

EMIGRE—Emigre Fonts
EMPOWERMENT—Personal Empowerment Network
ENCYCLOPEDIA—Enclopedias
ENDER—Hatrack River Town Meeting
ENDNOTE—Niles and Associates
ENGINEERING—NAS Online
ENGLISH—Simon & Schuster Online: English Department
ENT SPOT—What's Hot in Entertainment
ENTERPRISE—AOL Enterprise
ENTERPRISES—AOL Enterprise
ENTERTAINMENT—Entertainment Channel
ENTERTAINMENT CHAT—Entertainment Chat
ENTERTAINMENT NEWS—Entertainment News
ENTERTAINMENT WEEKLY—Entertainment Weekly
ENTREPRENEUR ZONE—Your Business
ENVIRONMENT—Environment Forum
ENVIRONMENTAL ED—Earth Day / Environment
ENVOY—Motorola
EPARTNERS—Electronic Partnerships
EPSCONVERTER—Art Age Software
EPUB—Desktop & Web Publishing [*Platform-dependent*]
EPUBS—Desktop & Web Publishing [*Platform-dependent*]
EQUIBASE—Horse Racing
EQUIS—Equis International
ERC—Public Safety Center
ERIC—AskERIC
ESH—Electronic Schoolhouse
ESPOT—What's Hot in Entertainment
ETEXT—PDA's Palmtop Paperbacks!
ETHICS—Religion & Ethics Forum
ETRADE—How to use StockLink & Gateway Host
EUGENE—Digital Cities: Eugene OR
EUGENE DC—Digital Cities: Eugene OR
EUGENE DCITY—Digital Cities: Eugene OR
EUGENE DIGC—Digital Cities: Eugene OR
EUGENE DIGITAL CITY—Digital Cities: Eugene OR
EUGENE OR—Digital Cities: Eugene OR
EUN—Electronic University Network

Chapter 6 Keywords from A to Z

EVENT—Today's Events in AOL Live!
EVENTS—Today's Events in AOL Live!
EVERYTHING EDIBLE—Everything Edible!
EW—Entertainment Weekly
EWORLD—Apple Aloha for eWorld Alumni
EXAM PREP—Exam Prep Center
EXCELLENCE—Access Excellence
EXCHANGE—The Exchange
EXERCISE—Fitness Forum
EXPERT—Expert Software, Inc.
EXPERT PAD—PDA/Palmtop Forum
EXPERT SOFT—Expert Software, Inc.
EXPOS—Major League Baseball Team: Montreal Expos
EXPRESS NET—ExpressNet (American Express)
EXPRESSNET ART—ExpressNet Art Download*
EXTENSIS—Extensis Corporation
EXTRA—EXTRA Online
EXTREME FANS—Extreme Fans: College Hoops
EZ—Your Business
EZINE—PDA's Palmtop Paperbacks!
EZINES—Digizine Sites on the Web
EZONE—Your Business
F2M—Transgender Community Forum
FABFACTS—Fabulous Facts
FACE—Style Channel
FALL TV—Lost & Found TV Shows
FALL TV SHOWS—Lost & Found TV Shows
FAM HOT—What's Hot in AOL Families
FAMILY—Family Areas
FAMILY ALBUM—Family Computing Forum: The Family Room
FAMILY COMPUTING—Family Computing Resource Center
FAMILY FINANCES—Real Life Financial Tips
FAMILY GAMES—Family Computing Forum: Family Games
FAMILY LIFE—Family Life Magazine Online
FAMILY NEWS—Family Computing Forum: News & Reviews
FAMILY PC—FamilyPC Online
FAMILY RESOURCE—Family Computing Forum: Maximum AOL
FAMILY ROOM—Family Computing Forum: Family Room

Chapter 6 Keywords from A to Z

FAMILY SHOWCASE—Family Product Showcase
FAMILY TRAVEL—Family Travel Selections
FAMILY TRAVEL NETWORK—Family Travel Network
FANS—Extreme Fans: College Hoops
FANTASY—Science Fiction & Fantasy
FANTASY BASEBALL—The Grandstand's Fantasy Baseball
FANTASY BASKETBALL—The Grandstand's Fantasy Basketball
FANTASY FOOTBALL—The Grandstand's Fantasy Football
FANTASY HOCKEY—The Grandstand's Fantasy Hockey
FANTASY LEAGUE—The Grandstand's Fantasy & Simulation Leagues
FANTASY LEAGUES—The Grandstand's Fantasy & Simulation Leagues
FAO—F.A.O. Schwarz
FAO SCHWARZ—F.A.O. Schwarz
FARALLON—Farallon
FASHION—Elle Magazine Online
FATHER—AOL Families
FATHERS—AOL Families
FAVE FLICKS—Favorite Flicks!
FAVORITE FLICKS—Favorite Flicks!
FAX—Fax/Paper Mail
FC—Family Computing Forum
FC TIPS—Family Computing Forum: Tip of the Day
FCF—Family Computing Forum
FCRC—Family Computing Forum: Maximum AOL
FD—AOL's Full Disclosure for Investors
FDN—Food & Drink Network
FEATURES—Columnists & Features Online
FED—Federation
FEDERATION—Federation
FEDEX—Federal Express Online
FEEDBACK—Member Services*
FELISSIMO—Felissimo
FELLOWSHIP—Fellowship of Online Gamers/RPGA Network
FELLOWSHIP HALL—Christianity Online Chat & Live Events
FERNDALE—Ferndale [*WAOL only*]
FESTE—The Motley Fool

Chapter 6 Keywords from A to Z

FFGF—Free-Form Gaming Forum
FICTION—The Atlantic Monthly Online
FID—Fidelity Online Investments Center
FID AT WORK—Fidelity Online's Working Area
FID BROKER—Fidelity Online's Funds Area
FID FUNDS—Fidelity Online's Funds Area
FID GUIDE—Fidelity Online's Guide Area
FID NEWS—Fidelity Online's Newsworthy Area
FID PLAN—Fidelity Online's Planning Area
FIDELITY—Fidelity Online Investments Center
FIESTA BOWL—Fool Bowl
FIFTH—Symantec
FIGURE SKATING—ABC Sports Figure Skating
FILE—Software Center [*Platform-dependent*]
FILE SEARCH—Search database of files [*Platform-dependent*]
FILEMAKER—The Filemaker Pro Resource Center
FILES—Software Center [*Platform-dependent*]
FILM REVIEW DATABASE—Movie Review Database
FILM REVIEW DB—Movie Review Database
FILM REVIEWS DATABASE—Movie Review Database
FILM STUDIOS—MovieVisions
FILMBALL—Follywood Games
FINANCE—Personal Finance Channel
FINANCIAL ASTROLOGY—Astronet
FINANCIAL PLANNING—Real Life Financial Tips
FINANCIAL STATEMENT—Disclosure's Financial Statements
FINANCIALS—Disclosure's Financial Statements
FIND—Directory of Services
FINLAND—Finland
FIREBALL—Flight Simulation Resource Center
FIRST—First Look at Hot New Products
FIRST BYTE—Baumrucker Conference [*May disappear without notice*]
FIRST CHICAGO ONLINE—First Chicago Online
FIRST LADY—Hillary Rodham Clinton
FIRST LOOK—First Look at Hot New Products
FISH—Boating Online
FISHING—Boating Online

Chapter 6 Keywords from A to Z

FITNESS—Fitness Forum
FIX—What's Hot in Entertainment
FLASH—Mad About Music
FLASHCARDS—MarketMaster
FLIGHT—Flight Simulator Resource Center
FLIGHT CENTER—Flight Simulation Resource Center
FLIGHT SIM—Flight Simulation Resource Center
FLIGHT SIMS—Flight Simulation Resource Center
FLIGHT SIMULATIONS—Flight Simulation Resource Center
FLINT—Digital Cities: Flint MI
FLINT DC—Digital Cities: Flint MI
FLINT DCITY—Digital Cities: Flint MI
FLINT DIGC—Digital Cities: Flint MI
FLINT DIGITAL CITY—Digital Cities: Flint MI
FLINT MI—Digital Cities: Flint MI
FLORIDA—Destination Florida
FLORIDA KEYS—The Florida Keys
FLORIDA MARLINS—Major League Baseball Team: Florida Marlins
FLOWERS—800-Flowers
FLY—Aviation Forum
FLYING—Flying Magazine
FLYING MAG—Flying Magazine
FLYING MAGAZINE—Flying Magazine
FOCUS—Focus Enhancements
FOCUS ENHANCEMENTS—Focus Enhancements
FOF—Focus on the Family
FOG—Fellowship of Online Gamers/RPGA Network
FOLKWAYS—Folklife & Folkways
FOLLYWOOD—Follywood
FONTBANK—FontBank
FOOD—Everything Edible!
FOOD & DRINK—Food & Drink Network
FOOL—The Motley Fool
FOOL AERO—Motley Fool: Aero
FOOL AIR—Motley Fool: Airlines
FOOL BIO—Motley Fool: Biotechnology
FOOL BOWL—Fool Bowl

Chapter 6 Keywords from A to Z

FOOL CHEM—Motley Fool: Chemicals
FOOL CHIPS—Motley Fool: Semiconductors
FOOL DOME—Motley Fool: The Fool Dome
FOOL DTV—Motley Fool: Desktop Video
FOOL FOOD—Motley Fool: Food
FOOL HARD—Motley Fool: Hardware
FOOL HEALTH—Motley Fool: Health
FOOL MART—Motley Fool: FoolMart
FOOL NET—Motley Fool: Networking
FOOL OIL—Motley Fool: Oilfield Services
FOOL PAPER—Motley Fool: Paper & Trees
FOOL RAILS—Motley Fool: Railroads
FOOL REIT—Motley Fool: Real Estate
FOOL REITTO—Motley Fool: Real Estate
FOOL SEM—Motley Fool: Semiconductors
FOOL SOFT—Motley Fool: Software
FOOL SPORTS—Motley Fool: The Fool Dome
FOOL STORE—Motley Fool: FoolMart
FOOL TECH—Motley Fool: Storage Tech
FOOL UTIL—Motley Fool: Utilities
FOOL VID—Motley Fool: Desktop Video
FOOLBALL—Motley Fool: The Fool Dome
FOOLISH—The Motley Fool
FOOTBALL—AOL Football
FOREIGN—International Cafe
FORMZ—auto*des*sys, Inc.
FORTE—Forte Technologies
FORTNER—Fortner Research
FORTRAN—Fortner Research
FORUM—Computers & Software Channel [*Platform-dependent*]
FORUM AUD—The Computing Rotunda
FORUM AUDITORIUM—The Computing Rotunda
FORUM ROT—The Computing Rotunda
FORUMS—Computers & Software Channel [*Platform-dependent*]
FOSSIL—Fossil Watches and More
FOSSIL WATCHES—Fossil Watches and More

Chapter 6 Keywords from A to Z

FOTF—Focus on the Family
FOUND TV—Lost & Found TV Shows
FOUR RESOURCES—AT&T Home Business Resources
FRACTAL—Fractal Design
FRACTAL DESIGN—Fractal Design
FRAGRANCE—The Fragrance Counter
FRANCE—International Channel
FRANCE & ASSOCIATES—France & Associates
FRANKLIN—Franklin Quest
FRASIER—Fraiser Tuesdays
FRASIER TUESDAYS—Fraiser Tuesdays
FREE—Member Services*
FREELANCE—Freelance Artists Special Interest Group
FREEMAIL—FreeMail, Inc.
FREESHOP—The FreeShop Online
FREESHOP ONLINE—The FreeShop Online
FREETHOUGHT—Freethought Forum
FRENCH OPEN—French Open [*May disappear without notice*]
FRENCH TEST—France Beta Test* [*May disappear without notice*]
FREQUENT FLYER—Inside Flyer
FRESNO—Digital Cities: Fresno/Visalia CA
FRESNO CA—Digital Cities: Fresno/Visalia CA
FRESNO DC—Digital Cities: Fresno/Visalia CA
FRESNO DCITY—Digital Cities: Fresno/Visalia CA
FRESNO DIGC—Digital Cities: Fresno/Visalia CA
FRESNO DIGITAL CITY—Digital Cities: Fresno/Visalia CA
FRIDAY AT 4—ABC Online Auditorium
FRIEND—Sign on a friend to AOL*
FRIEND IN FRANCE—France Beta Test* [*May disappear without notice*]
FROG—The WB Network
FROMMER—Frommer's City Guides
FROMMER'S—Frommer's City Guides
FROMMER'S CITY GUIDES—Frommer's City Guides
FROMMERS—Frommer's City Guides
FROMMERS CITY GUIDES—Frommer's City Guides
FRONTIERS—Scientific American Frontiers

Chapter 6 Keywords from A to Z

FSRC—Flight Simulation Resource Center
FT LAUDERDALE DIGC—Digital Cities: Miami - Ft Lauderdale FL
FT MYERS—Digital Cities: Ft. Myers/Naples FL
FT MYERS DC—Digital Cities: Ft. Myers/Naples FL
FT MYERS DCITY—Digital Cities: Ft. Myers/Naples FL
FT MYERS FL—Digital Cities: Ft. Myers/Naples FL
FT MYRES DIGC—Digital Cities: Ft. Myers/Naples FL
FT WORTH—Digital Cities: Dallas - Ft. Worth TX
FT WORTH DIGC—Digital Cities: Dallas - Ft. Worth TX
FT WORTH DIGITAL CITY—Digital Cities: Dallas - Ft. Worth TX
FTN—Family Travel Network
FTP—Internet FTP
FULL DISCLOSURE—AOL's Full Disclosure for Investors
FULLD—AOL's Full Disclosure for Investors
FULLWRITE—FullWrite
FUND—Morningstar Mutual Funds
FUNDS—Morningstar Mutual Funds
FUNDWORKS—Fundworks Investors' Center
FUNNIES—The Funny Pages
FURNISHINGS—Home Magazine Online
FURNITURE—Home Magazine Online
FUTURE LABS—Future Labs, Inc.
FUZZY—The Hub: Fuzzy Memories
GADGET—Andy Pargh/The Gadget Guru
GADGET GURU—Andy Pargh/The Gadget Guru
GALACTICOMM—Galacticomm
GALILEO—Galileo Mission to Jupiter [*May disappear without notice*]
GALLERY—Portrait Gallery
GAME—Games Channel
GAME BASE—Game Base
GAME DESIGN—Game Designers Forum
GAME DESIGNER—Game Designers Forum
GAME DESIGNERS—Game Designers Forum
GAME ROOMS—Games Parlor
GAME SITES—WWW Game Sites
GAMEPRO—GamePro Online
GAMES—Games Channel

Chapter 6 Keywords from A to Z

GAMES CHANNEL—Games Channel

GAMES DOWNLOAD—Download Online Games* [*WAOL and GAOL only*]

GAMES & ENTERTAINMENT—Games Channel

GAMES FORUM—Games Forum [*Platform-dependent*]

GAMES PARLOR—Games Parlor

GAMESTER—FamilyPC Online

GAMETEK—Gametek

GAMEWIZ—Dr. Gamewiz Online

GAMEWIZ INC—Dr Gamewiz Online

GAMING—Online Gaming Forums

GARAGE—Pro's Corner

GARDEN—Gardening Online Selections

GARDENING—Gardening Online Selections

GATEWAY—Gateway 2000, Inc.

GATEWAY 2000—Gateway 2000, Inc.

GAY—Gay & Lesbian Community Forum

GAY BOARDS—Gay & Lesbian Community Forum Boards

GAY BOOKS—Lambda Rising Bookstore Online

GAY CHAT—Gay & Lesbian Community Forum Events and Conferences

GAY MESSAGE—Gay & Lesbian Community Forum Boards

GAY NEWS—Gay & Lesbian Community Forum News

GAY ORG—Gay & Lesbian Community Forum Organizations

GAY ORGS—Gay & Lesbian Community Forum Organizations

GAY POLITICS—Gay & Lesbian Community Forum News

GAY SOFTWARE—Gay & Lesbian Community Forum Libraries

GAY TRAVEL—Gay & Lesbian Community Forum Travel

GAY TRIVIA—Gay & Lesbian Community Forum: Gaymeland

GAY YOUTH—Gay & Lesbian Community Forum Youth Area

GAYME—Gay & Lesbian Community Forum: Gaymeland

GAYMELAND—Gay & Lesbian Community Forum: Gaymeland

GAYMES—Gay & Lesbian Community Forum: Gaymeland

GAZETTE—CyberJustice's Gazette Online/Email

GBL—The Grandstand's Simulation Baseball

GC ACTION—Games Channel: Action

GC CLASSIC—Games Channel: Classic Games

GC CONTESTS—Games Channel: Contests

Chapter 6 Keywords from A to Z

GC HOT—What's Hot in AOL Games
GC INFO—Games Channel: Gaming Information
GC KNOWLEDGE—Games Channel: Knowledge Games
GC NEWS—Games Channel: News [*WAOL only*]
GC PERSONA—Games Channel: Persona Games
GC RPG—Games Channel: Role Playing Games
GC SIMULATION—Games Channel: Simulation Games
GC SPORTS—Games Channel: Sports Games
GC STRATEGY—Games Channel: Strategy Games
GCC—GCC Technologies
GCFL—The Grandstand's Simulation Football
GCS—Gaming Company Support
GD STORE—Grateful Dead Forum Store
GDT—GDT Softworks, Inc.
GDT SOFTWORKS—GDT Softworks, Inc.
GEMSTONE—GemStone III
GEMSTONE III—GemStone III
GEN NEXT—Generation Next
GENDER—Transgender Community Forum
GENDER TRIVIA—Gay & Lesbian Community Forum: Gaymeland
GENEALOGY—Genealogy Forum
GENEALOGY CLUB—Genealogy Forum
GENERAL AVIATION—Aviation Forum
GENERAL HOSPITAL—ABC Daytime/Soapline
GENERAL MAGIC—General Magic
GENERATION NEXT—Generation Next
GENERATIONS—Generations
GENESIS—Video Games Area
GENIE EASY—Astronet
GEO SDK—Geoworks Development
GEOGRAPHIC—Odyssey Project
GEOGRAPHY—Simon & Schuster Online: Geography Deptartment
GEOWORKS—Geoworks
GERALDO—The Geraldo Show
GERALDO SHOW—The Geraldo Show
GERMANY—International Channel
GERTIE—Mercury Center Trivia
GET A LIFE—The Hub: Get A Life

Chapter 6 Keywords from A to Z

GETTING STARTED—Help Desk [*Platform-dependent*]
GGL—The Grandstand's Simulation Golf
GH—ABC Daytime/Soapline
GIANTS—Major League Baseball Team: San Francisco Giants
GIF CONVERTER—GIF Converter
GIFT CERTIFICATE—AOL Gift Certificates
GIFT SERVICES—Marketplace Gift Services
GIFTED—Gifted Online
GIFTS—800-Flowers
GIGABRAIN—FamilyPC Online
GIGABYTES—The Hub: Gigabytes Island
GIRL STUFF—Style Channel
GIRLS—Focus on Family: Brio Magazine
GIX—Gaming Information Exchange
GLCF—Gay & Lesbian Community Forum
GLCF BOARDS—Gay & Lesbian Community Forum Boards
GLCF CHAT—Gay & Lesbian Community Forum Events and Conferences
GLCF EVENT—Gay & Lesbian Community Forum Events and Conferences
GLCF EVENTS—Gay & Lesbian Community Forum Events and Conferences
GLCF H2H—Gay & Lesbian Community Forum Heart to Heart
GLCF HEART—Gay & Lesbian Community Forum Heart to Heart
GLCF HEART TO HEART—Gay & Lesbian Community Forum Heart to Heart
GLCF LIBRARY—Gay & Lesbian Community Forum Libraries
GLCF NEWS—Gay & Lesbian Community Forum News
GLCF ORG—Gay & Lesbian Community Forum Organizations
GLCF ORGANIZATIONS—Gay & Lesbian Community Forum Organizations
GLCF ORGS—Gay & Lesbian Community Forum Organizations
GLCF QUILT—Gay & Lesbian Community Forum Aids Scrapbook
GLCF SOFTWARE—Gay & Lesbian Community Forum Libraries
GLCF TCF—Transgender Community Forum
GLCF TEEN—Gay & Lesbian Community Forum Youth Area
GLCF TRAVEL—Gay & Lesbian Community Forum Travel
GLCF WOMAN—Gay & Lesbian Community Forum: Women's Space

Chapter 6 Keywords from A to Z

GLCF WOMEN—Gay & Lesbian Community Forum: Women's Space

GLCF YOUTH—Gay & Lesbian Community Forum Youth Area

GLOBAL—Global Village Communication

GLOBAL PLAZA—Global Plaza

GLOBAL VILLAGE—Global Village Communication

GLOBALNET—AOLGLOBALnet International Access*

GLOBE—AOL Live

GLOSSARY—America Online Glossary*

GM—General Motors Web Site

GM'S CORNER—The GM's Corner

GMA—ABC Good Morning America

GMAT—Kaplan Online or The Princeton Review

GMFL—The Grandstand's Simulation Football

GMME—Grolier's Encyclopeda

GMS CORNER—The GM's Corner

GNN—GNN Best of the Net

GO SCUBA—Scuba Club

GOALS 200—Goals 2000: National Education Act

GODIVA—Godiva Chocolatiers

GOLF—AOL Golf Area

GOLF AMERICA—Golfis Forum

GOLF COURSES—Golfis Forum

GOLF DATA—GolfCentral

GOLF INFORMATION—Golfis Forum

GOLF RESORTS—Golfis Forum

GOLFIS—Golfis Forum

GONER TV—Lost & Found TV Shows

GOOD LIFE—Your Good Life

GOOD MORNING AMERICA—ABC Good Morning America

GOPHER—Internet Gopher

GOSSIP—Entertainment Channel

GOURMET—Everything Edible!

GOVERNING—Governing Magazine

GOVERNMENT—AOL Politics

GOVERNMENT RESOURCES—Your Government Resources

GPF—GPF Help* [*WAOL only*]

GPFL—The Grandstand's Simulation Football

Chapter 6 Keywords from A to Z

GPS—Trimble Navigation, Ltd.
GRADUATE SCHOOL—Kaplan Online or The Princeton Review
GRANDSTAND—The Grandstand
GRANDSTAND TRIVIA—The Grandstand's Sports Trivia
GRAPH SIM—Graphic Simulations
GRAPHIC—Graphic Simulations
GRAPHIC ARTS—Graphic Arts & CAD Forum [*Platform-dependent*]
GRAPHIC DESIGN—Design Special Interest Group
GRAPHIC SIMULATIONS—Graphic Simulations
GRAPHICS—Graphic Arts & CAD Forum [*Platform-dependent*]
GRAPHICS FORUM—Graphic Arts & CAD Forum [*Platform-dependent*]
GRAPHISOFT—Graphisoft
GRAPHSOFT—Graphsoft, Inc.
GRATEFUL DEAD—Grateful Dead Forum
GRAVIS—Advanced Gravis
GRE—Kaplan Online or The Princeton Review
GREECE—Greece
GREEK—Genealogy Forum
GREENBERG—Kaplan Online
GREENHOUSE—AOL Greenhouse
GREET ST—Greet Street Greeting Cards
GREET STREET—Greet Street Greeting Cards
GROLIER—Grolier's Encyclopeda
GROLIER'S—Grolier's Encyclopeda
GROLIERS—Grolier's Encyclopeda
GROUP—McLaughlin Group
GROUPWARE—GroupWare Special Interest Group
GRYPHON—Gryphon Software
GRYPHON SOFTWARE—Gryphon Software
GS—WWW Game Sites
GS ARTS—The Grandstand's Martial Arts (The Dojo)
GS AUTO—The Grandstand's Motor Sports (In The Pits)
GS BASEBALL—The Grandstand's Baseball (Dugout)
GS BASKETBALL—The Grandstand's Basketball (Off the Glass)
GS BOXING—The Grandstand's Boxing (Squared Circle)
GS COLLECTING—The Grandstand's Collecting (Sports Cards)

Chapter 6 Keywords from A to Z

GS FOOTBALL—The Grandstand's Football (50 Yard Line)
GS GOLF—The Grandstand's Golf (On The Green)
GS HOCKEY—The Grandstand's Hockey (Blue Line)
GS HORSE—The Grandstand's Horse Sports & Racing Forum
GS MAG—GS+ Magazine
GS OTHER—The Grandstand's Other Sports (Whole 9 Yards)
GS SIDELINE—The Grandstand's Sideline
GS SOCCER—The Grandstand's Soccer (The Kop)
GS SOFTWARE—The Grandstand's Sports Software Headquarters
GS SPORTS TRIVIA—The Grandstand's Sports Trivia
GS SPORTSMART—The Grandstand's Sports Products (Sportsmart)
GS TRIVIA—The Grandstand's Sports Trivia
GS WINTER—The Grandstand's Winter Sports (The Chalet)
GS WRESTLING—The Grandstand's Wrestling (Squared Circle)
GSC—Graphic Simulations
GSDL—The Grandstand's Simulation Basketball
GSFL—The Grandstand's Simulation Football
GSHL—The Grandstand's Simulation Hockey
GSS—Global Software Suport
GTR—America Online Guitar Special Interest Group
GUAM—Guam
GUCCI—Gucci Parfums Counter
GUESS—Guess, Inc.
GUFL—The Grandstand's Simulation Football
GUIDE PAGE—Guide Pager
GUIDE PAGER—Guide Pager
GUITAR—America Online Guitar Special Interest Group
GUITAR SIG—America Online Guitar Special Interest Group
GUNS—The Exchange: Interests & Hobbies
GURU—Andy Pargh/The Gadget Guru
GUY STUFF—Style Channel
GVC—MaxTech Corporation
GWA—The Grandstand's Simulation Wrestling
GWALTNEY—Gwaltney Hams & Turkeys
GWF—The Grandstand's Simulation Wrestling
GWPI—The Hub: Global Worldwide Pictures International, Ltd.
GWU—George Washington University

Chapter 6 Keywords from A to Z

H&C—The Exchange: Home & Careers
H&H—Christianity Online: Holidays and Contests
H2H—Gay & Lesbian Community Forum Heart to Heart
HACHETTE—Hachette Filipacchi Magazines
HACIENDA—Channel One Network Online
HACK—MacHack
HACKER—MacHack
HACKERS—"Hackers" movie Area
HALL OF FAME—Downloading Hall of Fame
HALLMARK—Hallmark Connections
HALLMARK CONNECTIONS—Hallmark Connections
HAM—Ham Radio Club
HAM RADIO—Ham Radio Club
HAMMACHER—Hammacher Schlemmer
HAMMACHER SCHLEMMER—Hammacher Schlemmer
HAMS—Gwaltney Hams & Turkeys
HANDLE—Add, change or delete screen names
HANES—One Hanes Place
HAPPY NEW YEAR—Happy New Year Area [*May disappear without notice*]
HAPPY NEW YEARS DAY—Happy New Year Area [*May disappear without notice*]
HARDBALL—Baseball Daily by Extreme Fans
HARDWARE—Hardware Forum [*Platform-dependent*]
HARDWARE FORUM—Hardware Forum [*Platform-dependent*]
HARLEY—Big Twin Online: The All-Harley Magazine
HARLEY DAVIDSON—Big Twin Online: The All-Harley Magazine
HASH—Hash, Inc.
HATRACK—Hatrack River Town Meeting
HATRACK RIVER TOWN—Hatrack River Town Meeting
HBS PUB—Harvard Business School Publishing
HDC—hDC Corporation
HDC CORPORATION—hDC Corporation
HEADHUNTER—Motley Fool: Ask the Headhunter
HEADLINES—Today's News Channel
HEALTH—Health Channel
HEALTH EXP—Health and Vitamin Express
HEALTH EXPRESS—Health and Vitamin Express

Chapter 6 Keywords from A to Z

HEALTH FOCUS—Health Focus
HEALTH LIVE—Health Speakers and Support Groups
HEALTH MAGAZINE—Health Magazine
HEALTH MAGAZINES—Health Resources
HEALTH REFERENCE—Health Resources
HEALTH RESOURCES—Health Resources
HEALTH TODAY—Columbia's Health Today
HEALTH WEB—Health Web Sites
HEALTH ZONE—The Health Zone
HEART TO HEART—Gay & Lesbian Community Forum Heart to Heart
HEAVEN—The Hub: Heaven
HECKLE—Hecklers Online
HECKLER—Hecklers Online
HECKLER ONLINE—Hecklers Online
HECKLER'S ONLINE—Hecklers Online
HECKLERS—Hecklers Online
HECKLERS CLUBS—Hecklers Online: Clubs
HECKLERS ONLINE—Hecklers Online
HECKLING CLUBS—Hecklers Online: Clubs
HELMETS—Cycle World Online
HELP—Member Services*
HELP DESK—Help Desk [*Platform-dependent*]
HELP OKC—Help Heal Oklahoma City
HELP WANTED—Help Wanted Ads
HEM—Home Education Magazine
HERBS—Longevity Magazine Online
HERITAGE—Heritage Foundation
HERITAGE FOUNDATION—Heritage Foundation Area
HFC—Highlights for Children
HFC CATALOG—Highlights for Children Catalog
HFC STORE—Highlights for Children Catalog
HFM MAGNET WORK—Hachette Filipacchi Magazines
HFS—WHFS 99.1 FM
HH KIDS—Homework Help
HIGH SPEED—High Speed Access*
HIGHLIGHTS—Highlights for Children
HIGHLIGHTS CATALOG—Highlights for Children Catalog

Chapter 6 Keywords from A to Z

HIGHLITES—Highlights for Children
HIGHLITES CATALOG—Highlights for Children Catalog
HIGHTS ONLINE—Highlights for Children
HIKER—Backpacker Magazine
HIKING—Backpacker Magazine
HILLARY—Hillary Rodham Clinton
HINDUISM—Religion & Ethics Forum
HISPANIC—Hispanic Selections
HISPANIC MAGAZINE—HISPANIC Online
HISPANIC ONLINE—HISPANIC Online
HISTORICAL QUOTES—Historical Stock & Fund Quotes
HITCHHIKER—The Hub: John the Hitchhiker
HITCHIKER—The Hub: John the Hitchhiker
HITS—Rockline Online
HIV—AIDS and HIV Resource Center
HMCURRENT—Health Magazine's Current Area
HMFITNESS—Health Magazine's Fitness Area
HMFOOD—Health Magazine's Food Area
HMRELATIONSHIPS—Health Magazine's Relationships Area
HMREMEDIES—Health Magazine's Remedies Area
HO—Hecklers Online
HO CLUBS—Hecklers Online: Clubs
HOB—House of Blues Online
HOBBIES—Life, Styles & Interests Channel
HOBBY—Hobby Central
HOBBY CENTRAL—Hobby Central
HOC—Home Office Computing Magazine
HOCKEY—NHL Hockey
HOCKEY TRIVIA—ABC Hockey Trivia
HOF—Downloading Hall of Fame
HOL—Hecklers Online
HOL PRO—The Biz!
HOLI—Christianity Online: Holidays and Contests
HOLIDAY—AOL Holiday Central [*May disappear without notice*]
HOLIDAYS—AOL Holiday Central [*May disappear without notice*]
HOLIDAYS & HAPPENINGS—Christianity Online: Holidays and Contests

Chapter 6 Keywords from A to Z

HOLLYWOOD—Hollywood Online
HOLLYWOOD ONLINE—Hollywood Online
HOLLYWOOD PRO—The Biz!
HOLMES—Mysteries from the Yard
HOME—House & Home Area
HOME AUDIO—Consumer Electronics
HOME BANKING—Bank of America
HOME BREW—Food & Drink Network
HOME BREWING—Food & Drink Network
HOME DESIGN—Home Magazine Online
HOME EQUITY LOANS—AOL's Real Estate Center
HOME OFFICE—Home Office Computing Magazine
HOME OWNER—Homeowner's Forum
HOME OWNERS—Homeowner's Forum
HOME PAGE—Personal WWW Publishing Area
HOME PC—HomePC Magazine
HOME REFINANCING—AOL's Real Estate Center
HOME THEATER—Stereo Review Online
HOME VIDEO—Home Video
HOMEOPATHIC REMEDIES—Longevity Magazine Online
HOMER—Homer's Page at The Odyssey Project
HOMESCHOOL—Homeschooling Forum
HOMESCHOOLING—Homeschooling Forum
HOMEWORK—Homework Area
HOMEWORK HELP—Homework Area
HONG KONG—Hong Kong
HOOPS—NCAA Hoops [*May disappear without notice*]
HOOPS BOARDS—Extreme Fans: Message Boards
HOOPS TRIVIA—NTN Basketball Trivia
HOOVER—Hoover's Business Resources
HOOVER'S—Hoover's Business Resources
HOOVERS—Hoover's Business Resources
HOOVERS UPDATES—Hoover's Company Masterlist
HOROSCOPE—Horoscopes
HOROSCOPES—Horoscopes
HORROR—Science Fiction & Fantasy
HORSE—The Horse Forum
HORSE RACING—The Grandstand: Horse Sports & Racing Forum

Chapter 6 Keywords from A to Z

HORSE SPORTS—The Grandstand: Horse Sports & Racing Forum
HORSES—The Horse Forum
HOT—What's Hot This Month Showcase
HOT AIR—Global Challenger Balloon Race
HOT BUTTON—The Hub: The Hot Button
HOT CHAT—Entertainment Chat
HOT ENT—What's Hot in Entertainment
HOT ENTERTAINMENT—What's Hot in Entertainment
HOT GAMES—What's Hot in AOL Games
HOT HEALTH—What's Hot in Health
HOT MAC—What's Hot in Mac Computing
HOT NEWS—Hot News
HOT PC—What's Hot in PC Computing
HOT REF—Hot Reference
HOT REFERENCE—Hot Reference
HOT SPORTS—What's Hot in Sports
HOT SPOT—MTV Online: Hot Spot
HOT TODAY—What's Hot Today!
HOT TOPICS—Hot Topics
HOT TRAVEL—What's Hot in Travel
HOTLANTA—Digital Cities Atlanta GA
HOTLINE—Member Services*
HOUSE—Home Magazine Online
HOUSE OF BLUES—House of Blues Online
HOUSENET—HouseNet
HOUSTON—Digital Cities: Houston TX
HOUSTON ASTROS—Major League Baseball Team: Houston Astros
HOUSTON DIGC—Digital Cities: Houston TX
HOUSTON DIGITAL CITY—Digital Cities: Houston TX
HOW TO—Top Tips for AOL
HP—Hewlett-Packard
HP FAX—Hewlett-Packard: Fax Products
HP FILES—Hewlett-Packard: Support Information Files
HP HOME—Hewlett-Packard: Home Products Information
HP MULTI—Hewlett-Packard: Multifunction Products
HP PLOT—Hewlett-Packard: Plotter Products

Chapter 6 Keywords from A to Z

HP SCAN—Hewlett-Packard: Scanner Products
HP SCSI—Hewlett-Packard: SCSI Products
HP SERVER—Hewlett-Packard: Server Products
HP STORE—Hewlett-Packard: Information Storage Products
HP VECTRA—Hewlett-Packard: Vectra Products
HPPRN—Hewlett-Packard: Printer Products
HQ—Company Research
HRS—Better Health & Medical Forum
HSC—MetaTools, Inc.
HSC SOFTWARE—MetaTools, Inc.
HTML—Web Page Toolkit
HTML HELP—The Web Diner
HTS—Home Team Sports
HTTP—What is http?
HUB—The Hub
HUB CONTENTS—The Hub: Index
HUB INDEX—The Hub: Index
HUM—Virtual Christian Humor
HUMAN SEXUALITY—Simon & Schuster Online: Human Sexuality Department
HUMOR—The Comedy Pub
HUNGARY—Hungary
HUNT—AOL Treasure Hunt
HURLEY—60-Second Novelist
HURRICANE—Tropical Storm and Hurricane Info
HYPERCARD—Mac HyperCard & Scripting Forum
HYPERSTUDIO—Roger Wagner Publishing
HYPR—Hypractv8 with Thomas Dolby
HZ—The Health Zone
I FORSOOTH—Murder Mysteries Online
I-WIRE—I-Wire Online
IA—Print Artist Special Interest Group
IBD—Investor's Business Daily
IBIZ—InBusiness
IBM—IBM Forum
IBM OS2—OS/2 Forum
IBVA—IBVA Technologies
IBVA TECH—IBVA Technologies

Chapter 6 Keywords from A to Z

IC—Computing Company Connection
IC HILITES—IC Hilites
IC STORE—Internet Connection Store
ICELAND—Iceland
ICF—Investors' Exchange
ICS—Internet Connection Store
IDEAS—The Atlantic Monthly Online
IDEAS FOR BETTER LIVING—Ideas for Better Living
IDITAROD—Iditarod Trail Sled Dog Race
IE—Investors' Exchange
IES—Online Campus
IFR—Flying Magazine
IG—Intelligent Gamer Online
IG ONLINE—Intelligent Gamer Online
IGOLF—iGolf
IGOLF HISTORY—iGolf History
IGS—Internet Graphics
IHRSA—The Health Zone
IIN—New Product Showcase
ILLUSTRATOR—Mac Graphics Illustrator Special Interest Group
IMAGE—Image Exchange
IMAGE EXCHANGE—Image Exchange
IMAGING—Advanced Color Imaging Forum
IMH—Issues in Mental Health
IMMIGRATION—Genealogy Forum
IMPROV—The IMPROVisation Online
IMPROVISATION—The IMPROVisation Online
IN—Investors' Network
INBIZ—InBusiness
INBOARD—Boating Online
INBUSINESS—InBusiness
INC—Inc. Magazine
INC.—Inc. Magazine
INC MAGAZINE—Inc. Magazine
INC. MAGAZINE—Inc. Magazine
INC ONLINE—Inc. Magazine
INC. ONLINE—Inc. Magazine
INCOME STATEMENT—Disclosure's Financial Statements

Chapter 6 Keywords from A to Z

INDIANS—Major League Baseball Team: Cleveland Indians
INDUSTRIES—Your Industry
INDUSTRY CONNECTION—Computing Company Connection
INDUSTRY PROFILES—Hoover's Industry Profiles
INDY—Indianapolis 500
INDY 500—Indianapolis 500
INET CHAT—Internet Chat
INET EMAIL—Internet E-Mail
INET EXCHANGE—Internet Exchange
INET MAGAZINES—Internet Computing Magazines
INET MAGS—Internet Computing Magazines
INET ORGS—Internet Organizations
INFINITI—Infiniti Online
INFINITI ONLINE—Infiniti Online
INFORMATION—Member Services*
INFORMATION PROVIDER—Information Provider Resource Center
INFORMATION PROVIDERS—Information Provider Resource Center
INFORMED PARENT—Princeton Review Informed Parent
INLINE—Inline Design
INLINE SOFTWARE—Inline Design
INNOSYS—InnoSys, Inc.
INSIDE—Industry Insider or The Cobb Group Online
INSIDE FLYER—Inside Flyer
INSIDE MEDIA—Cowles/SIMBA Media Information Network
INSIDER—Industry Insider
INSIGNIA—Insignia Solutions
INSIGNIA SOLUTION—Insignia Solutions
INSTANT ARTIST—Print Artist Special Interest Group
INSTANT ARTIST1—Print Artist Special Interest Group
INSURANCE—Real Life Financial Tips
INTEL—Intel Corporation
INTEL INSIDE—Intel Corporation
INTELLIGENT GAMER—Intelligent Gamer Online
INTERACTIVE ASTROLOGY—Astronet
INTERACTIVE ED—Online Courses
INTERACTIVE EDUCATION—Online Courses

Chapter 6 Keywords from A to Z

INTERCON—InterCon Systems Corporation
INTEREST—Life, Styles & Interests Channel
INTERIOR DESIGN—Home Magazine Online
INTERNATIONAL—International Channel
INTERNATIONAL CAFE—International Cafe
INTERNATIONAL US—International Channel
INTERNET—Internet Connection Channel
INTERNET BIZ—InBusiness
INTERNET CENTER—Internet Connection Channel
INTERNET CHAT—Internet Chat
INTERNET CONNECTION—Internet Connection Channel
INTERNET EMAIL—Internet E-Mail
INTERNET EXCHANGE—Internet Exchange
INTERNET GRAPHICS—Internet Graphic Sites [*WAOL 2.5 and MAOL 2.6 only*]
INTERNET GRAPHICS—Internet Graphics
INTERNET MAGAZINES—Internet Computing Magazines
INTERNET MAGS—Internet Computing Magazines
INTERNET NEWS—Internet Newsstand
INTERNET NEWSSTAND—Internet Newsstand
INTERNET ORGS—Internet Organizations
INTERNET.ORGS—Internet Organizations
INTERNET QUESTIONS—Internet Questions*
INTERNET SOFTWARE—Internet Software
INTERNET STORE—Internet Connection Store
INTERPLAY—Interplay
INTL—International Channel
INTOON—InToon with the News
INTREK—InTrek
INTUIT—Intuit, Inc.
INVEST—Investors' Network
INVESTING—Investors' Network
INVESTMENT—Investors' Network
INVESTMENT LINGO—Investment Lingo
INVESTMENTS—Investors' Network
INVESTOR—Investors' Network
INVESTOR RELATIONS—AOL's Full Disclosure for Investors
INVESTOR'S BUSINESS—Investor's Business Daily

Chapter 6 Keywords from A to Z

INVESTOR'S DAILY—Investor's Business Daily
INVESTOR'S NETWORK—Investors' Network
INVESTORS—Investors' Network
INVESTORS BUSINESS—Investor's Business Daily
INVESTORS DAILY—Investor's Business Daily
INVESTORS NETWORK—Investors' Network
IOMEGA—Iomega Corporation
IOTW—Pictures of the Week
IP—Information Provider Resource Center
IPA—Advanced Color Imaging Forum
IQ—Wizard World
IR—AOL's Full Disclosure for Investors
IRELAND—Ireland
IRISH—Genealogy Forum
ISCNI—Institute for the Study of Contact with Non-Human Intelligence
ISDN—ISDN Special Interest Group
ISIS—ISIS International
ISIS INTERNATIONAL—ISIS International
ISKI—iSKI
ISLAM—Religion & Ethics Forum
ISLAND—Island Graphics Corporation
ISLAND GRAPHICS—Island Graphics Corporation
ISRAEL—Israel
ISREAL—Israel
ISREAL ELECTIONS—Jewish Israeli Elections
ISSUES—AOL Politics
ITALIAN—Genealogy Forum
ITALIAN FOOD—Mama's Cucina by Ragu
ITALY—Italy
IVILLAGE—Parent Soup
IWIRE—I-Wire Online
JAPAN—International Channel
JASC—JASC, Inc.
JAYS—Major League Baseball Team: Toronto Blue Jays
JAZZFEST—House of Blues Online
JCOL—Jewish.COMMunity
JCPENNEY—JCPenney

Chapter 6 Keywords from A to Z

JENNY FLAME—The Comedy Pub
JET—Aviation Forum
JEWISH—Jewish.COMMunity
JEWISH ARTS—Jewish Arts
JEWISH BOARDS—Jewish Message Boards
JEWISH CHAT—Jewish Chat Room
JEWISH COMMUNITY—Jewish.COMMunity
JEWISH DOWNLOADS—Jewish File Downloads
JEWISH EDUCATION—Jewish Education
JEWISH ELECTIONS—Jewish Isreali Elections
JEWISH FOOD—Jewish Food
JEWISH HOLIDAY—Jewish Holidays
JEWISH HOLIDAYS—Jewish Holidays
JEWISH MATCHMAKER—Jewish Singles
JEWISH NEWS—Jewish News
JEWISH SINGLES—Jewish Singles
JEWISH STORE—Jewish Store
JEWISH YOUTH—Jewish Youth
JIM'S BRAIN—Motley Fool's Rogue
JL COOPER—JLCooper Electronics
JOB—Real Life Financial Tips
JOBS—Help Wanted Ads
JOEL SIEGEL—ABC Good Morning America
JOHN GRAY—Men Are From Mars
JOHN NABER—John Naber [*May disappear without notice*]
JOIN DC—Register as a Digital Citizen
JOIN DIGITAL CITY· —Register as a Digital Citizen
JOKES—Jokes! Etc.
JORDAN—Michael Jordan Area
JPEGVIEW—JPEGView
JUDAISM—Religion & Beliefs: Judaism
JUDGMENT—CyberJustice's Record Your Judgment
JUPITER—Galileo Mission to Jupiter [*May disappear without notice*]
JUST DO IT—Computer Life Magazine
KAAL TV—ABC Online: KAAL-TV in Rochester, MN
KABC TV—ABC Online: KABC-TV in Los Angeles, CA
KAIT TV—ABC Online: KAIT-TV in Jonesboro AR

Chapter 6 Keywords from A to Z

KAKE TV—ABC Online: KAKE-TV in Wichita, KS
KANSAS CITY ROYALS—Major League Baseball Team: Kansas City Royals
KAPLAN—Kaplan Online
KARATE—The Grandstand's Martial Arts (The Dojo)
KARROS—Eric Karros Kronikles
KASAN—Kasanjian Research
KASANJIAN—Kasanjian Research
KAUFMANN—The Kaufmann Fund
KAZAKHSTAN—Kazakhstan
KEEFE—InToon with the News
KEEPER—Internet Usenet Newsgroup Area
KENNEDY SPACE—Challenger Remembered
KENNEDY SPACE CENTER—Challenger Remembered
KENNEHORA—CyberJustice's Kennehora Junction
KENNEHORA JUNCTION—CyberJustice's Kennehora Junction
KENS GUIDE—The Hub: Ken's Guide to the Bible
KENSINGTON—Kensington Microware, Ltd.
KENT MARSH—Kent*Marsh
KESMAI—Air Warrior
KESQ TV—ABC Online: KESQ-TV in Palm Springs, CA
KEYWORD—Keyword List Area
KEYWORD LIST—Keyword List Area
KEYWORDS—Keyword List Area
KEZI TV—ABC Online: KEZI-TV in Eugene, OR
KFSN TV—ABC Online: KFSN-TV in Fresno, CA
KGO—KGO—San Francisco Newstalk AM 810
KGO TV—ABC Online: KGO-TV in San Francisco, CA
KGTV TV—ABC Online: KGTV-TV in San Diego, CA
KGUN TV—ABC Online: KGUN-TV in Tucson, AZ
KHBS TV—ABC Online: KHBS/KHOG-TV in Fort Smith, AR
KID DESK—Edmark Technologies
KID SPORTS—New England Cable Network: Sports for Kids
KID TRAVEL—Family Travel Network
KIDCARE—KidCare
KIDS—Kids Only Channel
KIDS CHOICE—Nickelodeon: Kids' Choice Awards
KIDS DICTIONARY—Merriam-Webster's Kids Dictionary

Chapter 6 Keywords from A to Z

KIDS ONLY—Kids Only Channel
KIDS OUT—Kids Out: London's Family Events Guide
KIDS QUEST—The Quest CD-ROM Companion to AOL's Kids Only Channel
KIDS WB—Kids' Warner Brothers Online
KIDS' WB—Kids' Warner Brothers Online
KIDS WEB—Kid's Top Internet Sites
KIDSBIZ—KidsBiz
KIDSOFT—Club KidSoft
KIDSOFT STORE—KidSoft Superstore
KIDZINE—ABC Kidzine
KIFI TV—ABC Online: KIFI-TV in Idaho Falls, ID
KING—Martin Luther King
KING OF THE BEACH—AVP Pro Beach Volleyball
KIP—Block Financial Software Support
KIPLINGER—Block Financial Software Support
KIRSHNER—Simon & Schuster College Online
KITCHEN—Everything Edible!
KIVETCH—CyberJustice's Worry, Complain & Sob
KIVI TV—ABC Online: KIVI-TV in Boise, ID
KMBC TV—ABC Online: KMBC-TV in Kansas City, MO
KMGH TV—ABC Online: KMGH-TV in Denver, CO
KMIZ TV—ABC Online: KMIZ-TV in Columbia, MO
KNITTING—Needlecrafts/Sewing Center
KNOWLEDGE BASE—Microsoft Knowledge Base
KNTV TV—ABC Online: KNTV-TV in San Jose, CA
KNXV TV—ABC Online: KNXV-TV in Phoenix, AZ
KO—Kids Out: London's Family Events Guide
KO HELP—Kids' Guide Pager
KOAT TV—ABC Online: KOAT-TV in Albuquerque, NM
KOB—AVP Pro Beach Volleyball
KOCO TV—ABC Online: KOCO-TV in Oklahoma, OK
KODAK—Kodak Photography Forum
KODAK WEB—Kodak Web Site
KODE TV—ABC Online: KODE-TV in Joplin, MO
KOMANDO—Kim Komando's Komputer Clinic
KOMPUTER CLINIC—Kim Komando's Komputer Clinic
KOMPUTER TUTOR—Kim Komando's Komputer Clinic

Chapter 6 Keywords from A to Z

KONSPIRACY—The Hub: Konspiracy Korner
KOREA—Korea
KPT—MetaTools, Inc.
KPT BRYCE—MetaTools, Inc.
KQTV TV—ABC Online: KQTV-TV in St. Joseph, MO
KR—Kasanjian Research
KRAMER—Astronet
KRANK—MTV Online: Krank
KTBS TV—ABC Online: KTBS-TV in Shreveport, LA
KTKA TV—ABC Online: KTKA-TV in Topeka, KS
KTRK TV—ABC Online: KTRK-TV in Houston, TX
KTVX TV—ABC Online: KTVX-TV in Salt Lake City, UT
KTXS TV—ABC Online: KTXS-TV in Abilene, TX
KURZWEIL—Kurzweil Music Systems
KVIA TV—ABC Online: KVIA-TV in El Paso, TX
KVUE TV—ABC Online: KVUE-TV in Austin, TX
KWM WEB—Korean War Memorial Home Page
L AND C—Lois & Clark
L & C—Lois & Clark
L&C HOT—What's Hot in Learning & Culture
L&C STORE—Learning & Culture Store
L'EGGS—One Hanes Place
LA COMM—Digital City Los Angeles: Community
LA DIGC—Digital Cities: Los Angeles CA
LA DIGITAL CITY—Digital Cities: Los Angeles CA
LA NEWS—Digital City Los Angeles: News & Weather
LA PEOPLE—Digital City Los Angeles: People
LA TOUR—Digital City Los Angeles: City Tour
LA WEATHER—Digital City Los Angeles: News & Weather
LACROSSE—The Lacrosse Forum
LAMBDA—Lambda Rising Bookstore Online
LAMBDA RISING—Lambda Rising Bookstore Online
LAMDA—Gay & Lesbian Community Forum
LANDSCAPING—Home Magazine Online
LANGUAGE—International Languages
LANGUAGE SYS—Fortner Research
LANGUAGES—International Cafe
LANIER—Lanier Family Travel Guides

Chapter 6 Keywords from A to Z

LANIER FAMILY TRAVEL—Lanier Family Travel Guides
LAPIS—Focus Enhancements
LAPTOP—PowerBook Resource Center
LAPUB—LaPub
LATE NIGHT SURVEY—The Late Night Survey
LATINA—HISPANIC Online
LATINO—HISPANIC Online
LATINONET—LatinoNet Registration
LATVIA—Latvia
LAUNCE—The Motley Fool
LAVATCH—The Motley Fool
LAW—Court TV's Law Center
LAW CENTER—Court TV's Law Center
LAW SCHOOL—Kaplan Online or The Princeton Review
LAWRENCE—Lawrence Productions
LAX—The Lacrosse Forum
LC HOT—What's Hot in Learning & Culture
LEADER—Leader Technologies
LEADER TECH—Leader Technologies
LEADER TECHNOLOGIES—Leader Technologies
LEADERS NETWORK—Christianity Online: Church Leaders Network
LEADERSHIP—Leadership Journal
LEADERSHIP JOURNAL—Leadership Journal
LEADING EDGE—Leading Edge
LEARN—Learning & Culture Channel
LEARNING—Learning & Culture Channel
LEARNING AND REFERENCE—Learning & Culture Channel
LEARNING CENTER—Learning & Culture Channel
LEARNING & CULTURE HOT—What's Hot in Learning & Culture
LEARNING & REFERENCE—Learning & Culture Channel
LEGAL—Online Legal Areas
LEGAL PAD—The Legal Pad
LEGAL SIG—Legal Information Network
LEISURE—@times: Leisure Guide
LENS—Lens Express
LENS EXPRESS—Lens Express
LESBIAN—Gay & Lesbian Community Forum

Chapter 6 Keywords from A to Z

LESBIAN BOARDS—Gay & Lesbian Community Forum Boards
LESBIAN CHAT—Gay & Lesbian Community Forum Events and Conferences
LESBIAN LIBRARY—Gay & Lesbian Community Forum Libraries
LESBIAN MESSAGE—Gay & Lesbian Community Forum Boards
LESBIAN NEWS—Gay & Lesbian Community Forum News
LESBIAN ORG—Gay & Lesbian Community Forum Organizations
LESBIAN ORGS—Gay & Lesbian Community Forum Organizations
LESBIAN POLITICS—Gay & Lesbian Community Forum News
LESBIAN SOFTWARE—Gay & Lesbian Community Forum Libraries
LESBIAN TEEN—Gay & Lesbian Community Forum Youth Area
LESBIAN TRAVEL—Gay & Lesbian Community Forum Travel
LESBIAN TRIVIA—Gay & Lesbian Community Forum: Gaymeland
LESBIAN YOUTH—Gay & Lesbian Community Forum Youth Area
LETTER—Community Updates From Steve Case*
LETTER2—Community Updates From Steve Case*
LIBERTARIAN—Libertarian Party Forum
LIBERTARIAN PARTY—Libertarian Party Forum
LIBERTARIANS—Libertarian Party Forum
LIBRARIES—Software Center [*Platform-dependent*]
LIBS—Software Center [*Platform-dependent*]
LIFE—Computer Life Magazine
LIFE STYLES & INTEREST—Life, Styles & Interests Channel
LIFE STYLES & INTERESTS—Life, Styles & Interests Channel
LIFESTYLES—Life, Styles & Interests Channel
LIFESTYLES & HOBBIES—Life, Styles & Interests Channel
LIFETIME—Lifetime Television
LIFETIME TELEVISION—Lifetime Television
LIFETIME TV—Lifetime Television
LIGHT WAVE—New Tek
LILLIAN—Lillian Vernon
LILLIAN VERNON—Lillian Vernon
LIMERICK—Hecklers Online
LIN—Legal Information Network
LIND—Lind Portable Power
LINGO—Investment Lingo
LINKS—Access Software

Chapter 6 Keywords from A to Z

LINKSWARE—LinksWare, Inc.
LINN SOFTWARE—Linn Software
LINN SOFT—Linn Software
LISTINGS—TV Quest
LISTSERV—Internet Mailing Lists
LITERACY—Adult Literacy & Education Forum
LITERATURE—Saturday Review Online
LIVE—AOL Live!
LIVE!—AOL Live!
LIVE PICTURE—Live Picture, Inc.
LIVE SPORTS—AOL Sports Live
LIVE TONIGHT—AOL Live!
LJ—Leadership Journal
LOCAL NEWSPAPERS—Newspapers Selection
LOCALNEWS—Newspapers Selection
LOCALS—CyberJustice's Meet The Locals
LOGICODE—Logicode Technology, Inc.
LOIS AND CLARK—Lois & Clark
LOIS & CLARK—Lois & Clark
LOL—The Comedy Pub
LONGEVITY—Longevity Magazine Online
LOOKING GLASS—Looking Glass
LOS ANGELES—Digital Cities: Los Angeles CA
LOS ANGELES DIGC—Digital Cities: Los Angeles CA
LOS ANGELES DODGERS—Major League Baseball Team: Los Angeles Dodgers
LOST TV—Lost & Found TV Shows
LOST TV SHOWS—Lost & Found TV Shows
LOTTERY—Lotteries
LOVE—Love@AOL
LOVE@AOL—Love@AOL
LOVE AT AOL—Love@AOL
LOVE MOM—I Love My Mom Because... [*May disappear without notice*]
LOVE ONLINE—ABC Love Online
LOVE SHACK—The Love Shack
LOVER—Love@AOL
LSAT—Kaplan Online or The Princeton Review

Chapter 6 Keywords from A to Z

LUCAS—LucasArts Games
LUCAS ARTS—LucasArts Games
LUNCH—Your Business Lunch
LUST—Love@AOL
LUV—ABC Love Online
LUV—Love@AOL
LUXEMBOURG—Luxembourg
LYNCH—Merrill Lynch
LYNX—Virtual Airlines
LYNX AIRWAYS—Virtual Airlines
M'S—Major League Baseball Team: Seattle Mariners
M2F—Transgender Community Forum
MAC—Apple/Macintosh Forums
MAC ALPT—The Grandstand's Simulation Golf
MAC ART—Graphic Art & CAD Forum [*MAOL only*]
MAC BIBLE—The Macintosh Bible/Peachpit Forum
MAC BUSINESS—Macintosh Business & Home Office Forum
MAC COMMUNICATION—Mac Communications and Networking Forum
MAC COMMUNICATIONS—Mac Communications and Networking Forum
MAC COMPUTING—Apple/Macintosh Forums
MAC CONFERENCE—Mac Computing Conference Center
MAC DESKTOP—Mac Desktop Publishing/WP Forum
MAC DEVELOPMENT—Macintosh Developers Forum
MAC DOWNLOADING—Mac Software Center
MAC DTP—Mac Desktop Publishing/WP Forum
MAC EDUCATION—Mac Education & Technology Forum
MAC ESSENTIALS—Macintosh Essential Utilities
MAC GAME—Mac Games Forum
MAC GAMES—Mac Games Forum
MAC GRAPHICS—Mac Graphic Art & CAD Forum
MAC HARDWARE—Mac Hardware Forum
MAC HELP—Help Desk [*Platform-dependent*]
MAC HOME—Mac Home Journal
MAC HOME JOURNAL—Mac Home Journal
MAC HOT—What's Hot in Mac Computing
MAC HYPERCARD—Mac HyperCard & Scripting Forum

Chapter 6 Keywords from A to Z

MAC KIDS—Mac Kids World

MAC LIBRARIES—Mac Software Center

MAC MULTIMEDIA—Mac Desktop Video & Multimedia Forum

MAC MUSIC—Mac Music & Sound Forum

MAC NEWS—Mac Computing News & Newsletters

MAC O/S—Mac Operating Systems Forum

MAC OPERATING SYSTEMS—Mac Operating Systems Forum

MAC OS—Mac Operating Systems Forum

MAC PROGRAMMING—Macintosh Developers Forum

MAC SOFTWARE—Mac Software Center

MAC SOFTWARE CENTER—Mac Software Center

MAC SOUND—Mac Music & Sound Forum

MAC SPEAKERZ—True Image Audio

MAC TELECOM—Mac Communications and Networking Forum

MAC TELECOMM—Mac Communications and Networking Forum

MAC TIPS—Family Computing Forum: Tip of the Day

MAC TODAY—Mac Today Magazine

MAC UTILITIES—Mac Utilities Forum

MAC VIRUS—Mac Virus Information Center

MAC WORD PROCESSING—Mac Desktop Publishing/WP Forum

MACHACK—MacHack

MACHINERY—American Woodworker: Tool Reviews

MACINTOSH—Apple/Macintosh Forums

MACINTOSH BIBLE—The Macintosh Bible/Peachpit Forum

MACMILLAN—MacMillan Information SuperLibrary

MACRO—Affinity Microsystems

MACROMEDIA—MacroMedia, Inc.

MACROMIND—MacroMedia, Inc.

MACROS—Affinity Microsystems

MACSCITECH—MacSciTech Special Interest Group

MACTIVITY—Mactivity '95 Forum

MACWORLD—MacWorld Magazine

MAD—DC Comics Online

MAD ABOUT—Mad About You Fan Forum

MAD ABOUT YOU—Mad About You Fan Forum

MAD ABOUT YOU SUNDAYS—Mad About You Fan Forum

MAD MAGAZINE—DC Comics Online

Chapter 6 Keywords from A to Z

MAD WORLD—Today's News: It's a Mad, Mad World...Dispatches from the Wires
MADA—MacApp Developers Association
MAGAZINES—The Newsstand
MAGIC LINK—Sony Magic Link
MAGICK—Pagan Religions & Occult Sciences
MAGICKAL—Pagan Religions & Occult Sciences
MAGNET—Hachette Filipacchi Magazines
MAGNETO—Hachette Filipacchi Magazines
MAIL—Post Office
MAIL GATEWAY—Mail Gateway
MAILING LIST—Business Yellow Pages
MAILING LISTS—Internet Mailing Lists
MAINSTAY—Mainstay
MAKEOVER—Style Channel
MAKEUP—Style Channel
MALAWI—Malawi
MALL—Marketplace Channel
MALTA—City Guide to Malta
MAM—Mad About Music
MAMA—Mama's Cucina by Ragu
MAMA'S CUCINA—Mama's Cucina by Ragu
MANAGER—Manager's Network
MANAGER'S NETWORK—Manager's Network
MANAGERS—Manager's Network
MANAGING—Manager's Network
MANGA—Wizard World
MANHATTAN GRAPHICS—Manhattan Graphics
MANTICORE—Image Exchange: Gallery of the Mousepad
MARCO—Motorola
MARINE—Boating Online
MARINERS—Major League Baseball Team: Seattle Mariners
MARKET—MarketMaster
MARKET NEWS—Market News Area
MARKET PLACE—Markeplace Department
MARKETING PREFERENCES—Marketing Preferences*
MARKETING PREFS—Marketing Preferences*
MARKETPLACE—Marketplace Channel

Chapter 6 Keywords from A to Z

MARKETS—Market News Area
MARLINS—Major League Baseball Team: Florida Marlins
MARRIAGE—Marriage Partnership Magazine
MARRIAGE PARTNERSHIP—Marriage Partnership Magazine
MARS—Men Are From Mars
MARTIAL ARTS—The Grandstand's Martial Arts (The Dojo)
MARTIN—Martin Luther King
MARTIN LUTHER—Martin Luther King
MARTIN LUTHER KING—Martin Luther King
MARTINSEN—Martinsen's Software
MASS—Massachusetts Governor's Forum
MASS.—Massachusetts Governor's Forum
MASSACHUSETTS—Massachusetts Governor's Forum
MASSAGE—Longevity Magazine Online
MASTERLIST—Hoover's Company MasterList
MATCHMAKER—Love@AOL
MATCHMAKING—Love@AOL
MATH—NAS Online
MATHEMATICS—Simon & Schuster Online: Mathematics Department
MATT—Matt Williams' Hot Corner
MATT WILLIAMS—Matt Williams' Hot Corner
MAX AOL—Family Computing Forum: Maximum AOL
MAXIMUM AOL—Family Computing Forum: Maximum AOL
MAXIS—Maxis
MAXTECH—MaxTech Corporation
MAY—Mad About You Fan Forum
MBS—Macintosh Business & Home Office Forum
MC—Military City Online
MC ADS—Mercury Center Advertising
MC BUSINESS—Mercury Center Business & Technology Area
MC COMMUNICATION—Mercury Center Communication
MC ENTERTAINMENT—Mercury Center Entertainment Area
MC LIBRARY—Mercury Center Newspaper Library
MC LIVING—Mercury Center Bay Area Living Area
MC MARKET—Mercury Center Advertising
MC NEW—San Jose Mercury News [*GAOL only*]
MC NEWS—Mercury Center In the News Area

Chapter 6 Keywords from A to Z

MC PR—Mercury Center Newshound
MC SPORTS—Mercury Center Sports Area
MC TALK—Mercury Center Communication
MC TRIVIA—Mercury Center Trivia
MCAFEE—McAfee Associates
MCAT—Kaplan Online or The Princeton Review
MCDONALD'S—McFamily Community
MCFAMILY—McFamily Community
MCINTIRE—University of Virginia Alumni/McIntire School of Commerce
MCINTIRE ALUMNI—University of Virginia Alumni/McIntire School of Commerce
MCL—McLaughlin Group
MCLAUGHLIN—The McLaughlin Group
MCLAUGHLIN GROUP—The McLaughlin Group
MCM—Mac Communications and Networking Forum
MCO—Military City Online
MCO BASES—Military City Online Worldwide Military Installations Database
MCO COMM—Military City Online Communications
MCO HQ—Military City Online Headquarters
MCO SHOP—Military City Online Shop
MCO TOUR—Military City Online Tour
MDP—Mac Desktop Publishing/WP Forum
MDV—Macintosh Developers Forum
MEANWHILE—The Hub: Meanwhile
MECC—MECC
MED—Mac Education & Technology Forum
MEDIA—Cowles/SIMBA Media Information Network
MEDIA CENTER—Library Media Center Special Interest Group
MEDIA INFORMATION—Cowles/SIMBA Media Information Network
MEDICAL DICTIONARY—Merriam-Webster's Medical Dictionary
MEDICAL SCHOOL—Kaplan Online or The Princeton Review
MEDICINE—Health Channel
MEDLINE—Medline
MEGA NEWS—FamilyPC Online
MEGAZINE—FamilyPC Online
MEGAZONE—FamilyPC Online

Chapter 6 Keywords from A to Z

MELROSE—Melrose Mondays
MELROSE MONDAYS—Melrose Mondays
MEMBER DIRECTORY—Member Directory
MEMBER PROFILE—Edit your member profile
MEMBER SURVEY—Member Survey
MEMBERS—Member Directory
MEMBERS' RIDES—Wheels Exchange
MEMBERS RIDES—Wheels Exchange
MEMORIAL DAY—Memorial Day 1996 [*May disappear without notice*]
MEN—The Exchange: Communities Center
MEN ARE FROM MARS—Men Are From Mars
MEN'S HEALTH—Men's Health Forum
MENS' HEALTH WEB—Men's Health Internet Sites
MENTAL HEALTH—Mental Health Forum
MENTAL HEALTH WEB—Mental Health Web Sites
MER—Merrill Lynch
MERCPR—Mercury Center Newshound
MERCURY—Mercury Center
MERCURY CENTER—Mercury Center
MERRIAM—Merriam-Webster Dictionary
MERRIAM-WEBSTER—Merriam-Webster Dictionary
MERRILL—Merrill Lynch
MERRILL LYNCH—Merrill Lynch
MES—Messiah College
MESSAGE PAD—Newton Resource Center
MESSIAH—Messiah College
MET HOME—Metropolitan Home
METAPHYSICS—Religion & Ethics Forum
METATOOLS—MetaTools, Inc.
METRICOM—Metricom, Inc.
METROPOLITAN HOME—Metropolitan Home
METROWERKS—Metrowerks
METS—Major League Baseball Team: New York Mets
METZ—Metz
MEXICO—Mexico
MFC—AOL Mutual Fund Center
MFC 95—AOL Mutual Fund Center

Chapter 6 Keywords from A to Z

MFOOL—The Motley Fool
MFTY—Mysteries from the Yard
MGM—Mac Games Forum
MGR—Mac Graphic Art & CAD Forum
MGX—Micrografx, Inc.
MHC—Mac HyperCard & Scripting Forum
MHJ—Mac Home Journal
MHM—Members Helping Members message board*
MHS—Mac HyperCard & Scripting Forum
MHW—Mac Hardware Forum
MIAMI—Digital Cities: Miami - Ft Lauderdale FL
MIAMI COMM—Digital City Miami: Community
MIAMI DIGC—Digital Cities: Miami - Ft Lauderdale FL
MIAMI DIGITAL CITY—Digital Cities: Miami - Ft Lauderdale FL
MIAMI NEWS—Digital City Miami: News & Weather
MIAMI PEOPLE—Digital City Miami: People
MIAMI TOUR—Digital City Miami: City Tour
MIAMI WEATHER—Digital City Miami: News & Weather
MICHAEL JORDAN—Michael Jordan Area
MICHIGAN—Michigan Governor's Forum
MICHIGAN GOVERNOR—Michigan Governor's Forum
MICHIGAN J FROG—The WB Network
MICRO J—Micro J Systems, Inc.
MICROFRONTIER—MicroFrontier, Ltd.
MICROGRAFX—Micrografx, Inc.
MICROMAT—MicroMat Computer Systems
MICROPROSE—MicroProse
MICROSEEDS—Microseeds Publishing, Inc.
MICROSOFT—Microsoft Resource Center
MIDI—Music & Sound Forum [*Platform-dependent*]
MIDWEST—Digital Cities: Midwest
MIDWEST DIGC—Digital Cities: Midwest
MIDWEST DIGITAL CITY—Digital Cities: Midwest
MIKE KEEFE—InToon with the News
MILESTONE—DC Comics Online
MILITARY—Military and Vets Club
MILITARY CITY—Military City Online
MILITARY CITY ONLINE—Military City Online

Chapter 6 Keywords from A to Z

MILWAUKEE BREWERS—Major League Baseball Team: Milwaukee Brewers
MIN—Minirth Meier New Life Clinics
MIND AND BODY—Your Mind & Body Online
MIND & BODY—Your Mind & Body Online
MINDSCAPE—Mindscape
MINICAD—Graphsoft, Inc.
MINIRTH MEIER—Minirth Meier New Life Clinics
MINNEAPOLIS—Digital Cities: Minneapolis - St. Paul MN
MINNEAPOLIS DIGC—Digital Cities: Minneapolis - St. Paul MN
MINNESOTA TWINS—Major League Baseball Team: Minnesota Twins
MIRABELLA—Mirabella Magazine
MIRABELLA ONLINE—Mirabella Magazine
MIRROR—Mirror Technologies
MISST-U—CyberJustice: Misst-U & The 7 Pillars of Wisdom
MIX CITICORP—Citicorp Mortgage
MIX CMBA—California Mortgage Bankers Association
MIX DATA TRACK—Data Track Systems, Inc.
MIX GENESIS—Genesis 2000 [*WAOL only*]
MIXSTAR—Mixstar Mortgage Information Exchange
MJ—Michael Jordan Area
ML—Merrill Lynch
MLB—ABC Sports Major League Baseball
MLK—Martin Luther King
MLPF&S—Merrill Lynch
MLS—AOL's Real Estate Center
MLS LIVE—The Grandstand's Major League Soccer
MM—PC Multimedia Forum
MM SHOWCASE—Multimedia Showcase*
MMC—Music Message Center
MME—Grolier's Encycloped
MMM—Mac Desktop Video & Multimedia Forum
MMNLC—Minirth Meier New Life Clinics
MMO—Murder Mysteries Online
MMS—Mac Music & Sound Forum
MMS TOOL—Sound & Midi Resource Center
MMW—Multimedia World Online

Chapter 6 Keywords from A to Z

MMW CLINIC—Multimedia World Online's Clinic
MMW LIBRARY—Multimedia World Online's Library
MMW NEWS—Multimedia World Online
MMW OFFICE—Multimedia World Online's Office
MMW PAVILION—Multimedia World Online's Pavilion
MMW TEST TRACK—Multimedia World Online's Test Track
MMW WELCOME—Multimedia World Online's Welcome Area
MOBILE—Mobile Office Online
MOBILEMEDIA—MobileMedia
MODELS—Elle Magazine Online
MODELS! MODELS!—Style Channel
MODEM—High Speed Access*
MODEM HELP—High Speed Access*
MODERN LIVES—The Hub: Modern Lives
MODERN ROCK—WHFS 99.1 FM
MODUS—Modus Operandi
MODUS OPERANDI—Modus Operandi
MOM—AOL Families
MOMS—AOL Families
MOMS ONLINE—Moms Online
MONEY—Personal Finance Channel
MONOLITH—The Hub: Monolith
MONSTER ISLAND—Adventures by Mail
MONTESSORI—Montessori Schools
MONTESSORI SCHOOLS—Montessori Schools
MONTREAL EXPOS—Major League Baseball Team: Montreal Expos
MOO—Gateway 2000, Inc.
MOONSTONE—Moonstone Mountaineering
MORGAN DAVIS—Morgan Davis Group
MORNINGSTAR—Morningstar Mutual Funds
MORPH—Gryphon Software
MORTGAGE—AOL's Real Estate Center
MORTGAGE RATES—AOL's Real Estate Center
MORTGAGES—AOL's Real Estate Center
MOS—Mac Operating Systems Forum
MOS UPDATE—Apple System 7.5 Update
MOSIAC—Spiritual Mosiac

Chapter 6 Keywords from A to Z

MOTHER—AOL Families
MOTHER'S DAY—Mother's Day Area [*May disappear without notice*]
MOTHERS—AOL Families
MOTHERS DAY—Mother's Day Area [*May disappear without notice*]
MOTLEY—The Motley Fool
MOTLEY FOOL—The Motley Fool
MOTORCYCLE—Car/Cycle Selections
MOTORCYCLES—Car/Cycle Selections
MOTORCYCLING—Cycle World Online
MOTOROLA—Motorola
MOTORSPORT—Motorsport '95 Online
MOTORSPORTS—Motorsport '95 Online
MOTU—Mark of the Unicorn
MOUNTAIN—iSKI
MOUNTAIN BIKE—Bicycling Magazine
MOUSEPAD—Image Exchange: Gallery of the Mousepad
MOVIE—@the.movies
MOVIE FORUMS—Movie Forums Area
MOVIE REVIEW DATABASE—Movie Review Database
MOVIE REVIEW DB—Movie Review Database
MOVIE REVIEWS—Movie Reviews
MOVIE REVIEWS DATABASE—Movie Review Database
MOVIELINK—MovieLink
MOVIES—@the.movies
MOVIES WEB—Movies on the Web
MOVIEVISIONS—MovieVisions
MP—Multimedia Preferences
MR SCIENCE—Kim Komando's Komputer Clinic
MRD—Movie Review Database
MS BIZ—Your Business
MS DOS 6—MS-DOS 6.0 Resource Center
MS DOS 60—MS-DOS 6.0 Resource Center
MS SUPPORT—Microsoft Resource Center
MS WORKS—Microsoft Works Resource Center
MSA—Management Science Associates
MSBC—Your Business

Chapter 6 Keywords from A to Z

MSCOPE—Standard & Poor's Marketscope

MSKB—Microsoft Knowledge Base

MSTATION—Bentley Systems, Inc.

MT—iSKI

MTC—Mac Communications and Networking Forum

MTV—MTV Online

MTV NEWS—MTV News

MU—CyberJustice: Misst-U & The 7 Pillars of Wisdom

MUCHMUSIC—MuchMusic Online

MUCHMUSIC ONLINE—MuchMusic Online

MUG—America Online Store

MULTIMEDIA—Multimedia Menu

MULTIMEDIA PREFS—Multimedia Preferences

MULTIMEDIA WORLD—Multimedia World Online

MULTIPLE SCLEROSIS—Multiple Sclerosis Forum

MURDER—Murder Mysteries Online

MURDER MYSTERIES—Murder Mysteries Online

MURDER MYSTERY—Murder Mysteries Online

MUSEUM—Smithsonian Online

MUSEUMS—Smithsonian Online

MUSIC—MusicSpace

MUSIC AND SOUND FORUM—Music and Sound Forum [*Platform-dependent*]

MUSIC FORUM—Music and Sound Forum [*Platform-dependent*]

MUSIC MEDIA—Music Media

MUSIC NEWS—MTV Online: News

MUSIC PROMO—MusicSpace Events

MUSIC & SOUND—Music and Sound Forum [*Platform-dependent*]

MUSIC TALK—MusicSpace Communications

MUSIC WEB—MusicSpace WEB TopStops

MUSICSPACE—MusicSpace

MUSTANG—Mustang Software

MUSTANG SOFTWARE—Mustang Software

MUT—Mac Utilities Forum

MUT AWARD—Mac Shareware Awards [*MAOL only*]

MUT AWARDS—Mac Shareware Awards [*MAOL only*]

Chapter 6 Keywords from A to Z

MUTUAL FUND—AOL Mutual Fund Center
MUTUAL FUND 95—AOL Mutual Fund Center
MUTUAL FUND CENTER—AOL Mutual Fund Center
MUTUAL FUNDS—AOL Mutual Fund Center
MVD—Mac Desktop Video & Multimedia Forum
MVT—Mac Utilities Forum
MW DICTIONARY—Merriam-Webster's Collegiate Dictionary
MY PLACE—My Place (for FTP sites)
MYOB—Best! Ware
MYSTERIES—Mysteries from the Yard
MYSTERIES FROM THE YARD—Mysteries from the Yard
MYSTERY—Science Fiction & Fantasy
N MARIANA ISLANDS—Northern Mariana Islands
N&V—USA Weekend: News & Views
NAA—Newspaper Association of America
NABER—John Naber [*May disappear without notice*]
NAEA—NAEA Tax Channel
NAESP—NAESP Web Link
NAGF—Non-Affiliated Gamers Forum
NAME—Add, change or delete screen names
NAMES—Add, change or delete screen names
NAMI—National Alliance of Mentally Ill
NAN—Nick at Nite
NAPC—Employment Agency Database
NAPLES—Digital Cities: Ft. Myers/Naples FL
NAPLES DC—Digital Cities: Ft. Myers/Naples FL
NAPLES DCITY—Digital Cities: Ft. Myers/Naples FL
NAPLES DIGC—Digital Cities: Ft. Myers/Naples FL
NAPLES DIGITAL CITY—Digital Cities: Ft. Myers/Naples FL
NAPLES FL—Digital Cities: Ft. Myers/Naples FL
NAQP—National Association of Quick Printers Area
NAREE—AOL's Real Estate Center
NAS—NAS Online
NASA—Galileo Mission to Jupiter [*May disappear without notice*]
NASCAR—AOL Auto Racing
NATIONAL DEBT—U.S. Treasury Securities
NATIONAL GEOGRAPHIC—Odyssey Project

Chapter 6 Keywords from A to Z

NATIONAL PARENTING—The National Parenting Center
NATIVE AMERICAN—The Exchange: Communities Center
NATURE—The Nature Conservancy
NAVIGATE—Top Tips for AOL
NAVISOFT—Navisoft
NBA DRAFT—1995 NBA Draft
NBC—NBC...NOT!
NBR—The Nightly Business Report: Making $ense of It All
NBR REPORT—The Nightly Business Report: NBR Online Report
NC8—News Channel 8
NCAA—NCAA Hoops [*May disappear without notice*]
NCLEX—Kaplan Online
NCPA—America's National Parks
NCR—National Catholic Reporter
NCT—Next Century Technologies
NEA—Accessing the NEA Public Forum*
NEA ONLINE—Accessing the NEA Public Forum*
NEA PUBLIC—National Education Association Public Forum
NEC—NEC Technologies
NEC TECH—NEC Technologies
NECN—New England Cable News
NEIGHBORHOODS—Neighborhoods, USA
NEIGHBORHOODS, USA—Neighborhoods, USA
NEOLOGIC—NeoLogic
NESN—New England Sports Network
NESN BASEBALL—NESN: New England Baseball
NESN BASKETBALL—NESN: New England Basketball
NESN FOOTBALL—NESN: New England Football
NESN HOCKEY—NESN: New England Hockey
NESN OUTDOORS—NESN: New England Outdoors
NESN SPORT CIRCUIT—New England Sports Network
NESN SPORTS—New England Sports Network
NESSIE—Weekly World News
NET BOOKS—Internet Connection Store
NET CHAT—Internet Chat
NET EXCHANGE—Internet Exchange
NET EXPERT—Pro's Corner
NET HEAD JED—CyberSmith

Chapter 6 Keywords from A to Z

NET HEAD RED—CyberSmith

NET LIBRARY—Internet Software

NET NEWS—Internet Newsstand

'NET NEWS—Internet Newsstand

NET_NOIR—NetNoir

NET_NOIRE—NetNoir

NET ORGS—Internet Organizations

NET SOFTWARE—Internet Software

NET STORE—Internet Connection Store

NET SUGGESTIONS—Internet Suggestions

NETGIRL—NetGirl

NETGIRL PERSONALS—NetGirl: Personals

NETHERLANDS—Netherlands

NETNOIR—NetNoir

NETNOIRE—NetNoir

NETORGS—Net.Orgs

NETSCAPE—Netscape

NETWORKING—Communications/Telecom/Networking Forum [*Platform-dependent*]

NETWORKING FORUM—Communications/Telecom/Networking Forum [*Platform-dependent*]

NETWORKS EXPO—New Product Showcase

NEVERWINTER—AD&D Neverwinter Nights

NEW—New Features & Services

NEW AGE—Religion & Ethics Forum

NEW AOL—Newest Version of AOL Software [*Platform-dependent*]

NEW AUTO—AutoVantage: New Car Summary

NEW BEDFORD—Digital Cities: New Bedford MA

NEW BEDFORD DC—Digital Cities: New Bedford MA

NEW BEDFORD DCITY—Digital Cities: New Bedford MA

NEW BEDFORD DIGC—Digital Cities: New Bedford MA

NEW BEDFORD MA—Digital Cities: New Bedford MA

NEW CAR—AutoVantage: New Car Summary

NEW ENGLAND—Genealogy Forum

NEW ENGLAND BASEBALL—NESN: New England Baseball

NEW ENGLAND CABLE—New England Cable News

NEW ENGLAND CABLE NEWS—New England Cable News

Chapter 6 Keywords from A to Z

NEW ENGLAND FOOTBALL—NESN: New England Football
NEW ENGLAND HOCKEY—NESN: New England Hockey
NEW ENGLAND NEWS—New England Cable News
NEW ENGLAND OUTDOORS—NESN: New England Outdoors
NEW ENGLAND PATRIOTS—NESN: New England Football
NEW ENGLAND SPORTS—New England Sports Network
NEW ERA—Tactic Software
NEW FILM—New Movie Releases
NEW FILMS—New Movie Releases
NEW GUINEA—Papua New Guinea
NEW INTERESTS—New Interests
NEW LIFE—Minirth Meier New Life Clinics
NEW MEMBER—Discover America Online (New Member Area)
NEW MEMBERS—Discover America Online (New Member Area)
NEW MOVIE—New Movie Releases
NEW MOVIE RELEASES—New Movie Releases
NEW MOVIES—New Movie Releases
NEW ORLEANS—Digital Cities: New Orleans LA
NEW ORLEANS DC—Digital Cities: New Orleans LA
NEW ORLEANS DCITY—Digital Cities: New Orleans LA
NEW ORLEANS DIGC—Digital Cities: New Orleans LA
NEW ORLEANS LA—Digital Cities: New Orleans LA
NEW PRODUCT—New Product News
NEW PRODUCT SHOWCASE—New Product Showcase
NEW PRODUCTS—New Product News
NEW RELEASES—New Movie Releases
NEW REPUBLIC—The New Republic Magazine
NEW TEK—New Tek
NEW TV SEASON—Lost & Found TV Shows
NEW WORLD—New World Computing
NEW YEAR—Have a Healthy New Year!
NEW YEAR DAY—Happy New Year Area [*May disappear without notice*]
NEW YEARS—Happy New Year Area [*May disappear without notice*]
NEW YORK—@times/The New York Times Online
NEW YORK CITY—@times/The New York Times Online

Chapter 6 Keywords from A to Z

NEW YORK METS—Major League Baseball Team: New York Mets

NEW YORK TIMES—@times/The New York Times Online

NEW YORK YANKEES—Major League Baseball Team: New York Yankees

NEW ZEALAND—New Zealand

NEWBIE—Discover America Online (New Member Area)

NEWPORT NEWS DC—Digital Cities: Newport News and Norfolk VA

NEWPORT NEWS DCITY—Digital Cities: Newport News and Norfolk VA

NEWPORT NEWS DIGC—Digital Cities: Newport News and Norfolk VA

NEWPORT NEWS VA—Digital Cities: Newport News and Norfolk VA

NEWS—Today's News Channel

NEWS 8—News Channel 8

NEWS AND FINANCE—Today's News Channel

NEWS CHANNEL—News Channel 8

NEWS CHANNEL 8—News Channel 8

NEWS & FINANCE—Today's News Channel

NEWS LIBRARY—Mercury Center Newspaper Library

NEWS QUIZ—Chicago Tribune: News Quiz

NEWS & REVIEWS—Family Computing Forum: News & Reviews

NEWS ROOM—Today's News Channel

NEWS SEARCH—Search News Articles

NEWS TEXT—Today's News Channel

NEWS VIEWS—ABC Online: News Views

NEWS & VIEWS—USA Weekend: News & Views

NEWS WATCH—Search News Articles

NEWS/SPORTS/MONEY—Today's News Channel

NEWSBYTES—Newsbytes

NEWSGRIEF—NewsGrief

NEWSGROUP—Internet Usenet Newsgroup Area

NEWSGROUPS—Internet Usenet Newsgroup Area

NEWSHOUND—Mercury Center Newshound

NEWSLETTER—Games & Entertainment Newsletter

NEWSLETTERS—Genealogy Forum

NEWSLINK—Today's News Channel

Chapter 6 Keywords from A to Z

NEWSPAPER—Newspapers Selection
NEWSPAPER LIBRARY—Mercury Center Newspaper Library
NEWSPAPERS—Newspapers Selection
NEWSSTAND—The Newsstand
NEWSWEEK—Newsweek Magazine
NEWSWIRE—Newswire [*WAOL only*]
NEWTON—Newton Resource Center
NEWTON BOOK—PDA/Palmtop Forum
NEXT—Generation Next
NFL DRAFT—NFL Draft
NG—Newsgrief
NGLTF—Nation Gay & Lesbian Task Force
NGS—Odyssey Project
NGUIDES—CNN Newsroom Online
NHL—NHL Online
NICK—Nickelodeon Selections
NICK AT NITE—Nick at Nite
NICK @ NITE—Nick at Nite
NICKELODEON—Nickelodeon Online
NIGERIA—Nigeria
NIGHTLINE—ABC News-On-Demand
NIKON—Nikon Electronic Imaging
NILES—Niles and Associates
NINTENDO—Nintendo Power Source
NINTENDO POWER SOURCE—Nintendo Power Source
NISSAN—Nissan Online
NISUS—Nisus Software
NMAA—National Museum of American Art
NMAH—National Museum of American History
NMSS—National Multiple Sclerosis Society
NNFY—National Network for Youth
NNY—National Network for Youth
NO HANDS—Common Ground Software
NO HANDS SOFTWARE—Common Ground Software
NOA—Nintendo Power Source
NOIR-NET—NetNoir
NOIRE_NET—NetNoir
NOIRENET—NetNoir

Chapter 6 Keywords from A to Z

NOLO—Nolo Press' Self-Help Law Center
NOLO PRESS—Nolo Press' Self-Help Law Center
NOMADIC—Nomadic Computing Discussion Special Interest Group
NON PROFIT NETWORK—access.point: Nonprofit Professionals Network
NONPROFIT—access.point: Nonprofit Professionals Network
NORFOLK—Digital Cities: Newport News and Norfolk VA
NORFOLK DCITY—Digital Cities: Newport News and Norfolk VA
NORFOLK DIGC—Digital Cities: Newport News and Norfolk VA
NORTON—Symantec
NORWAY—Norway
NORWEGIAN—Genealogy Forum
NOT NBC—NBC... NOT!
NOT-FOR-PROFIT—access.point
NOTEBOOK—PowerBook Resource Center
NOVEL—60-Second Novelist
NOVELIST—60-Second Novelist
NOVELL—Novell Desktop Systems
NOW—Now Software
NOW PLAYING—Directory of Services
NPC—The National Parenting Center
NPN—access.point: Nonprofit Professionals Network
NPR—National Public Radio Outreach
NPS—New Product Showcase
NSS—National Space Society
NTN—NTN Trivia
NTN BASKETBALL TRIVIA—NTN Basketball Trivia
NTN HOCKEY TRIVIA—ABC Hockey Trivia
NTN HOOPS TRIVIA—NTN Basketball Trivia
NTN PLAYBOOK—NTN Playbook
NTN TRIVIA—NTN Trivia
NUBASE—Tactic Software
NUL—National Urban League
NUMBERS—Accessing America Online*
NURSING—Kaplan Online
NUTRITION—Nutrition Forum
NVN—Newspaper Association of America

Chapter 6 Keywords from A to Z

NWFL—The Grandstand's Simulation Football

NWN—AD&D Neverwinter Nights

NY PUBLIC LIBRARY—NY Public Library Desk Reference

NY TIMES—@times/The New York Times Online

NYC—@times/The New York Times Online

NYNEX—@times/The New York Times Online

NYT—@times/The New York Times Online

NYT CROSSWORD—The New York Times Crosswords

NYT CROSSWORDS—The New York Times Crosswords

NYT STORE—@times Store

O.J.—O.J. Simpson Trial [*May disappear without notice*]

O.J. SIMPSON—O.J. Simpson Trial [*May disappear without notice*]

O'S—Major League Baseball Team: Baltimore Orioles

OADD—AD&D Neverwinter Nights

OAKLAND A'S—Major League Baseball Team: Oakland Athletics

OAKLAND ATHLETICS—Major League Baseball Team: Oakland Athletics

OAO—Outdoor Adventures Online

OBJECT FACTORY—Object Factory

OC—Owens Corning

ODEON—AOL Live!

ODY—The Odyssey Project

ODYSSEY—The Odyssey Project

ODYSSEY PROJECT—The Odyssey Project

OFFICE—OfficeMax Online

OFFICEMAX—OfficeMax Online

OFL—The Grandstand's Simulation Football

OGF—Online Gaming Forums

OJ—Court TV's Law Center

OKC—Help Heal Oklahoma City

OLD DOMINION—Virginia Forum

OLD FAVES—Favorite Flicks

OLDS—Oldsmobile/Celebrity Circle

OLDSMOBILE—Oldsmobile/Celebrity Circle

OLDUVAI—Olduvai Software, Inc.

OLTL—ABC Daytime/Soapline

OLYMPIC—Olympic Festival Online

Chapter 6 Keywords from A to Z

OLYMPIC FESTIVAL—Olympic Festival Online
OLYMPIC SHOP—The Olympic Shop
OLYMPIC STORE—The Olympic Shop
OLYMPICS—Olympic Festival Online
OMAHA—Omaha Steaks
OMAHA STEAKS—Omaha Steaks
OMEGA—Omega Research
OMNI—OMNI Magazine Online
OMNI GO—Hewlett-Packard Omni Go 100
OMNI MAGAZINE—OMNI Magazine Online
OMNI ONLINE—OMNI Magazine Online
ON—ON Technology
ON HOOPS—On Hoops Basketball (Web Page)
ONE LIFE TO LIVE—ABC Daytime/Soapline
ONE SOURCE—Columbia's Health Today
ONE WORLD—One World Travel
ONE WORLD TRAVEL—One World Travel
ONLINE CLOCK—Time of day and length of time online
ONLINE GAMING—Online Gaming Forums
ONLINE PSYCH—Psych Online
ONYX—Onyx Technology
OPCODE—Opcode Systems, Inc.
OPCODE SYSTEMS—Opcode Systems, Inc.
OPERA—Afterwards Cafe
OPRAH—Get Movin' With Oprah
OPTIMA—Optima Technology
OPTIMAGE—Philips Media OptImage
OPTIMAS—OPTIMAS Corporation
ORANGE—Nickelodeon Online
ORANGE BOWL—Fool Bowl
ORGANIZATIONS—The Exchange: Communities Center
ORIENTATION—Discover America Online (New Member Area)
ORIENTATION EXPRESS—Discover America Online (New Member Area)
ORIGIN—Origin Systems
ORIGIN SYSTEMS—Origin Systems
ORIOLES—Major League Baseball Team: Baltimore Orioles
ORLANDO—Orlando Sentinel Online

Chapter 6 Keywords from A to Z

ORLANDO SENTINEL—Orlando Sentinel Online
ORSON SCOTT CARD—Hatrack River Town Meeting
OS TWO—OS/2 Forum
OS2—OS/2 Forum
OSCAR—Academy Awards
OSCARS—Academy Awards
OSKAR'S—Oskar's Magazine
OSKARS—Oskar's Magazine
OSO—Orlando Sentinel Online
OSO AUTO—Orlando Sentinel Online: Autos
OSO BASEBALL—Orlando Sentinel Online: Baseball
OSO BEACH—Orlando Sentinel Online: Beach
OSO BEACHES—Orlando Sentinel Online: Beach
OSO BLACK—Orlando Sentinel Online: Black Voices
OSO BUSINESS—Orlando Sentinel Online: Business
OSO CHAT—Orlando Sentinel Online: Chat
OSO CLASSIFIED—Orlando Sentinel Online: Classified Ads
OSO CLASSIFIEDS—Orlando Sentinel Online: Classified Ads
OSO COLLEGE FB—Orlando Sentinel Online: College Football
OSO COLLEGE FOOTBALL—Orlando Sentinel Online: College Football
OSO DOWNLOAD—Orlando Sentinel Online: Download Libraries
OSO E-MALL—Orlando Sentinel Online: E-Mall
OSO EMALL—Orlando Sentinel Online: E-Mall
OSO ENTERTAIN—Orlando Sentinel Online: Entertainment
OSO GOVERNMENT—Orlando Sentinel Online: Government
OSO HOMES—Orlando Sentinel Online: Homes
OSO JOBS—Orlando Sentinel Online: Jobs
OSO LIVING—Orlando Sentinel Online: Living
OSO MAGIC—Orlando Sentinel Online: Magic
OSO MAGIC MAG—Orlando Sentinel Online: Magic
OSO MALL—Orlando Sentinel Online: E-Mall
OSO MERCHANDISE—Orlando Sentinel Online: Merchandise
OSO MOVIES—Orlando Sentinel Online: Movies
OSO NET—Orlando Sentinel Online: OSOnet
OSO PHOTOS—Orlando Sentinel Online: Photos
OSO POLITICS—Orlando Sentinel Online: Government
OSO PREDATORS—Orlando Sentinel Online: Predators

Chapter 6 Keywords from A to Z

OSO REAL ESTATE—Orlando Sentinel Online: Classified Real Estate

OSO RELIGION—Orlando Sentinel Online: Religion News

OSO SERVICE—Orlando Sentinel Online: Services

OSO SERVICES—Orlando Sentinel Online: Services

OSO SOUND OFF—Orlando Sentinel Online: Sound Off

OSO SPACE—Orlando Sentinel Online: Space

OSO SPORTS—Orlando Sentinel Online: Sports

OSO STORM—Orlando Sentinel Online: Hurricane Survival Guide

OSO THEME PARK—Orlando Sentinel Online: Theme Parks

OSO TO DO—Orlando Sentinel Online: Things To Do

OSO TOP—Orlando Sentinel Online: Top Stories

OSO TRANS—Orlando Sentinel Online: Transportation

OSO WANT ADS—Orlando Sentinel Online: Jobs

OSO WEATHER—Orlando Sentinel Online: Weather

OTHER NEWS—The Hub: The Other News

OUR WORLD—Today's News Channel

OUTBOARD—Boating Online

OUTDOOR—Outdoor Adventures Online

OUTDOOR ADVENTURE—Outdoor Adventures Online

OUTDOOR FUN—The Exchange: Outdoor Fun

OUTDOOR GEAR—Backpacker Magazine

OUTDOORS—The Exchange

P6—Intel Corporation

PACEMARK—PaceMark Technologies, Inc.

PACKER—Packer Software

PADRES—Major League Baseball Team: San Diego Padres

PAGAN—Pagan Religions & Occult Sciences

PAGE—Page Sender

PAGER—Consumer Electronics

PALM—Palm Computing

PALM COMPUTING—Palm Computing

PALMTOP—PDA/Palmtop Forum

PANASONIC—Andy Pargh/The Gadget Guru

PANGEA—Pangea Toy Net

PANGEA TOY NET—Pangea Toy Net

PAP—Applications Forum

Chapter 6 Keywords from A to Z

PAPER MAIL—Fax/Paper Mail
PAPERPORT—Visioneer
PAPUA—Papua New Guinea
PAPUA NEW GUINEA—Papua New Guinea
PAPYRUS—Sierra On-line
PARADOX—DC Comics Online
PARASCOPE—Parascope
PARENT—AOL Families
PARENT ADVICE—Princeton Review Informed Parent
PARENT SOUP—Parent Soup
PARENT SOUP CHAT—Parent Soup: Chat
PARENT SOUP LOCAL INFO—Parent Soup: Local Information
PARENT'S SOUP—Parent Soup
PARENTAL CONTROL—Parental Controls*
PARENTAL GUIDANCE—Princeton Review Informed Parent
PARENTING—AOL Families
PARENTS—AOL Families
PARENTS SOUP—Parent Soup
PARGH—Andy Pargh/The Gadget Guru
PARKS—America's National Parks
PARLOR—Games Parlor
PARSONS—Parsons Technology
PARTY GIRL—Style Channel
PASSION—Love@AOL
PASSOVER—Jewish Holidays
PASSPORT—Passport Designs
PASSWORD—Change your password*
PASTA—Mama's Cucina by Ragu
PAT O—The Pat O'Brien Report
PAT O'BRIEN—The Pat O'Brien Report
PAT OBRIEN—The Pat O'Brien Report
PAUL FREDERICK—Paul Frederick MenStyle
PAUL HARVEY—ABC Radio
PBM—Play-By-Mail Forum
PBM CLUBS—Play-By-Mail Clubs & Messaging
PC—People Connection Channel
PC ANIMATION—PC Graphics Forum
PC APPLICATIONS—PC Applications Forum

Chapter 6 Keywords from A to Z

PC APPLICATIONS FORUM—PC Applications Forum
PC APS—PC Applications Forum
PC AUD—AOL Live
PC BEGINNERS—PC Help Desk
PC BG—PC Help Desk
PC CATALOG—PC Today
PC DATA—PC Data
PC DESKMATE—DeskMate
PC DEV—Developers Forum [*Platform-dependent*]
PC DEVELOPMENT—Developers Forum [*Platform-dependent*]
PC DEVELOPMENT FORUM—Developers Forum [*Platform-dependent*]
PC DM—DeskMate
PC FINANCIAL—PC Financial Network
PC FINANCIAL NETWORK—PC Financial Network
PC FORUMS—Computers & Software Channel [*Platform-dependent*]
PC FORUMS HOT—What's Hot in PC Computing
PC GAMES—PC Games Forum
PC GRAPHICS—PC Graphics Forum
PC GRAPHICS FORUM—PC Graphics Forum
PC HARDWARE—PC Hardware Forum
PC HARDWARE FORUM—PC Hardware Forum
PC HELP—PC Help Desk
PC HOT—What's Hot in PC Computing
PC MUSIC FORUM—PC Music and Sound Forum
PC PC—Personal Computer Peripherals
PC PLAZA—People Connection Plaza
PC SECURITY—Computers & Software Channel [*Platform-dependent*]
PC SOFTWARE—PC Software Center
PC SOUND—PC Music and Sound Forum
PC SOUND FORUM—PC Music and Sound Forum
PC STUDIO—PC Studio
PC TELECOM—PC Telecom/Networking Forum
PC TELECOM FORUM—PC Telecom/Networking Forum
PC TODAY—PC Today
PC TOOL—PC Virtual Toolbox

Chapter 6 Keywords from A to Z

PC WORLD—PCWorld Online
PC WORLD ONLINE—PCWorld Online
PC-LINK HOTLINE—Credit Request Form for connect problems
PCFN—PC Financial Network
PCM—PC Telecom/Networking Forum
PCMU—PC Music and Sound Forum
PCMUSIC—PC Music and Sound Forum
PCS—MobileMedia
PCW ONLINE—PCWorld Online
PCW NETSCAPE—PC World: Netscape [*WAOL only*]
PD—Dinner On Us Club
PDA—PDA/Palmtop Forum
PDA DEV—PDA Development Special Interest Group
PDA DEV SIG—PDA Development Special Interest Group
PDA FORUM—PDA/Palmtop Forum
PDA SHOP—PDA Forum: PDA Shop
PDV—Developers Forum [*Platform-dependent*]
PEACHPIT—The Macintosh Bible/Peachpit Forum
PEACHTREE—Peachtree Software
PEANUTS—Virgin's Virtual Valley
PEAPOD—Peapod Online
PEN—Personal Empowerment Network
PEN PAL—Edmark Technologies
PENTIUM—Intel Corporation
PEOPLE—People Connection Channel
PEOPLE CONNECTION—People Connection Channel
PEREGRINE—Pictorius, Inc.
PERFUME—The Fragrance Counter
PERISCOPE—Parascope
PERSON OF THE WEEK—ABC News-On-Demand
PERSONAL CHOICES—Personal Choices Area
PERSONAL FINANCE—Personal Finance Channel
PERSONAL REPORTER—Mercury Center Newshound
PERSUASION—Religion & Ethics Forum
PET—Pet Care Forum
PET CARE—Pet Care Forum
PETER JENNINGS—ABC News-On-Demand
PETER NORTON—Symantec

Chapter 6 Keywords from A to Z

PETITIONS—Accessing America Online*
PETS—Pet Care Forum
PF—Personal Finance Channel
PF SOFTWARE—Personal Finance Software Center
PFSS—Personal Finance Software Support
PGM—PC Games Forum
PGR—PC Graphics Forum
PH—Simon & Schuster College Online
PHIL MARKET—Digital City Philadelphia: Classifieds
PHIL TOUR—Digital City Philadelphia: City Tour
PHILA DIGITAL CITY—Digital Cities: Philadelphia PA
PHILADELPHIA—Digital Cities: Philadelphia PA
PHILADELPHIA DIGC—Digital Cities: Philadelphia PA
PHILANTHROPY—access.point
PHILIPPINES—Philippines
PHILLIES—Major League Baseball Team: Philadelphia Phillies
PHILLY DIG CITY—Digital Cities: Philadelphia PA
PHILLY DIGITAJ CITY—Digital Cities: Philadelphia PA
PHILOSOPHY—Religion & Ethics Forum
PHOENIX—Arizona Central
PHONE BOOK—Phone Directories
PHONE DIRECTORY—Phone Directories
PHONE HELP—Local access numbers*
PHONE NUMBER—Accessing America Online*
PHONE NUMBERS—Accessing America Online*
PHONES—Accessing America Online*
PHOTO—Photography Area
PHOTO FOCUS—Graphics and Photo Focus Area
PHOTODEX—Photodex
PHOTOGRAPHY—Photography Area
PHOTOS—Popular Photography Online
PHOTOSHOP—Photoshop Special Interest Group
PHS—Practical Homeschooling
PHW—PC Hardware Forum
PHYS ED—Simon & Schuster Online: Health, Physical Education & Recreation Department
PHYSICALLY DISABLED—DisABILITIES Forum
PIC—PictureWeb & PicturePlace

Chapter 6 Keywords from A to Z

PICTORIUS—Pictorius, Inc.
PICTUREPLACE—PictureWeb & PicturePlace
PICTURES—Pictures of the World
PICTUREWEB—PictureWeb & PicturePlace
PIERIAN—Pierian Spring Software
PIERIAN SP—Pierian Spring Software
PILOTS—Flying Magazine
PIN—AOL Families
PINK TRIANGLE—Gay & Lesbian Community Forum
PIPE—Food & Drink Network
PIPES—Food & Drink Network
PIRATES—Major League Baseball Team: Pittsburgh Pirates
PITTSBURGH PIRATES—Major League Baseball Team: Pittsburgh Pirates
PIXEL—Pixel Resources
PIXEL RESOURCES—Pixel Resources
PKWARE—PKWare, Inc.
PLACES—P.L.A.C.E.S. Interest Group
PLACES RATED—Places Rated Almanac
PLACES RATED ALMANAC—Places Rated Almanac
PLANET EALING—Planet Ealing [*WAOL only*]
PLANETOUT—PlanetOut
PLANNING—Real Life Financial Tips
PLANS—American Woodworker
PLANTS—800-Flowers
PLASTIC SURGERY—Longevity Magazine Online
PLAY—Entertainment Channel
PLAY KEYWORD—Preview Vacations' Travel Update
PLAY-BY-MAIL—Play-By-Mail Forum
PLAYBILL—Playbill Online
PLAYER—Viewer Resource Center
PLAYERS—Viewer Resource Center
PLAYMATES—Pangea Toy Network: ToyBuzz
PLAYTEX—One Hanes Place
PLAYWELL—U.S. Golf Society Online
PLF—The Positive Living Forum
PLF QUILT—Gay & Lesbian Community Forum Aids Scrapbook
PLUS—Plus ATM Network

183

Chapter 6 Keywords from A to Z

PMM—PC Multimedia Forum
PMU—PC Music and Sound Forum
PNO—PlanetOut
POETRY—Afterwards Cafe
POG—KidzBiz' POG Area
POGS—KidzBiz' POG Area
POLAND—Poland
POLICY REVIEW—Heritage Foundation Area
POLITICAL SCIENCE—Simon & Schuster Online: Political Science Dept.
POLITICS—Politics Area
POLLS—CyberJustice's Arch of Public Opinion Polls
POP PHOTO—Popular Photography Online
POPE—Catholic Community
POPULAR PHOTOGRAPHY—Popular Photography Online
PORK—Pork Online
PORT FOLLY—The Motley Fool
PORTABLE—Mobile Office Online
PORTABLE COMPUTING—Mobile Office Online
PORTFOLIO—Your Stock Portfolio
PORTUGAL—Portugal
POSITIVE LIVING—The Positive Living Forum
POST OFFICE—Post Office
POSTAL STAMPS—Comic Strip Centennial
POSTCARDS—Virtual Post Card Center
POV—3D Forum
POWER BOATS—Boating Online
POWER EQUIPMENT—American Woodworker: Tool Reviews
POWERBOOK—PowerBook Resource Center
POWERMAC—PowerMac Resource Center
POWERPC—PowerMac Resource Center
POWERTOOL—American Woodworker: Tool Reviews
POWERTOOLS—American Woodworker: Tool Reviews
PP—Personal WWW Publishing Area [*WAOL only*]
PPI—Practical Peripherals, Inc.
PR—The Princeton Review Online
PRACTICAL PERIPHERALS—Practical Peripherals, Inc.
PRAIRIE—Prairie Group

PRAIRIE SOFT—Prairie Group
PRAYER NET—The Prayer Network
PREMIER—Dinner On Us Club
PREMIER DINING—Dinner On Us Club
PRENTICE HALL—Simon & Schuster College Online
PRESCHOOL—Preschool/Early Childhood Special Interest Group
PRESIDENT—President's Day [*May disappear without notice*]
PRESIDENT 96—President '96
PRESIDENTIAL—President's Day [*May disappear without notice*]
PRESS—AOL Press Release Library
PRESS RELEASE—AOL Press Release Library
PREVIEW VACATIONS—Preview Vacations
PRICE—Price Online
PRICE ONLINE—Price Online
PRIDE—Gay & Lesbian Community Forum
PRIMESTAR—Andy Pargh/The Gadget Guru
PRIN—Principians Online
PRINCETON—The Princeton Review Online
PRINCETON REVIEW—The Princeton Review Online
PRINCIPALS—National Principals Center Web link
PRINO—Principians Online
PRINT ARTIST—Print Artist Special Interest Group
PRO BOWL—1996 Pro Bowl
PRO'S—Pro's Corner
PRO'S CORNER—Pro's Corner
PROCD—ProCD National Telephone Directory Search
PRODIGY—Prodigy Refugees Forum
PRODIGY REFUGEES—Prodigy Refugees Forum
PRODUCT REVIEWS—Family Computing Forum: News & Reviews
PRODUCTIVITY—Applications/Business/Productivity Forum [*Platform-dependent*]
PRODUCTIVITY FORUM—Applications/Business/Productivity Forum [*Platform-dependent*]
PROFILE—Edit your member profile
PROGRAMMER U—Programmer University
PROGRAMMING—Development Forum [*Platform-dependent*]
PROGRAPH—Pictorius, Inc.

Chapter 6 Keywords from A to Z

PROS—Pro's Corner
PROS CORNER—Pro's Corner
PROUD—Gay & Lesbian Community Forum
PROVUE—ProVUE Development
PS—Parascope
PSC—Public Safety Center
PSCP—Parascope
PSION—Psion
PSP—JASC, Inc.
PSYCH ONLINE—Psych Online
PSYCHOLOGY—Psychology Forum
PTC—PC Telecom/Networking Forum
PU—Programmer University
PUB—The Comedy Pub
PUBLIC DEBT—U.S. Treasury Securities
PUBLIC POLICY—Politics Area
PUBLIC RADIO—National Public Radio Outreach
PUBLIC SAFETY—Public Safety Center
PUBLISHERS—Computing Company Connection
PUERTO RICO—Puerto Rico
PUR—PUR Drinking Water Systems
QB1—NTN's QB1
QMMS—Mac Music & Sound Forum
QMODEM—Mustang Software
QOTD—Grandstand's Sport Trivia Question of the Day
QQP—Quantum Quality Productions
QUALITAS—Qualitas
QUALITY—The Health Zone
QUARK—Quark, Inc.
QUE—PC Studio
QUEER—Gay & Lesbian Community Forum
QUES DICTIONARY—Computer and Internet Dictionary
QUEST—Adventures by Mail
QUESTION—One Stop Infoshop*
QUESTIONS—One Stop Infoshop*
QUICK FIND—Search database of files [*Platform-dependent*]
QUICK FINDER—Search database of files [*Platform-dependent*]
QUICK PRINTERS—National Association of Quick Printers Area

Chapter 6 Keywords from A to Z

QUICKTIME—Mac Desktop Video & Multimedia Forum
QUIKJUSTICE—CyberJustice's Reward & Punishment
QUILT—Quilting Forum
QUILTERS—Quilting Forum
QUILTING—Quilting Forum
QUOTATION—Bartlett's Quotations
QUOTATIONS—Bartlett's Quotations
QUOTE—StockLink: Quotes & Portfolios Area
QUOTES—StockLink: Quotes & Portfolios Area
QUOTES PLUS—Quotes Plus
R&R—ABC Online: Rock & Road
R&T—Road & Track Magazine
RABBITJACK'S CASINO—RabbitJack's Casino
RABBITJACKS CASINO—RabbitJack's Casino
RACING—Wheels
RADIO—Entertainment's Radio Forum
RADIO FORUM—Entertainment's Radio Forum
RADIUS—Radius, Inc.
RAGU—Mama's Cucina by Ragu
RAILROADING—The Exchange
RALPH Z—UniverseCentral.Com
RALPH ZERBONIA—UniverseCentral.Com
RAM DOUBLER—Connectix Corporation
RANGERS—Major League Baseball Team: Texas Rangers
RANKINGS—Business Rankings
RASTEROPS—Truevision
RAW—World Wrestling Federation
RAY—Ray Dream
RAY DREAM—Ray Dream
RAY TRACE—3D Forum
RBO—Ringling Online
RC—Christian Resource Center
RCA—Andy Pargh/The Gadget Guru
RDI—Free-Form Gaming Forum
REACTOR—Reactor
READ—Adult Literacy & Education Forum
READ USA—Online Bookstore
READING—Saturday Review Online

Chapter 6 Keywords from A to Z

READING ROOM—The Reading Room
REAL ESTATE—Real Estate Selections
REAL LIFE—Real Life Financial Tips
REC CENTER—Entertainment Channel
RECIPES—Woman's Day Online
RECORD—Tower Records
RECORDS—Tower Records
RECREATION—Entertainment Channel
RECREATION CENTER—Entertainment Channel
RED SOX—NESN: New England Baseball
RED SOX BASEBALL—NESN: New England Baseball
RED ZONE—NESN: New England Football
REDGATE—New Product Showcase
REDS—Major League Baseball Team: Cincinnati Reds
REF HOT—Hot Reference
REFERENCE—Reference Desk Channel
REFERENCE DESK—Reference Desk Channel
REFERENCE HELP—Reference Desk: Help
REGISTER—Online Campus
REI—REI Recreation Equipment, Inc.
REIT—Motley Fool: Real Estate
RELIGION NEWS—Religion News Update
RELIGIONS—Religion & Ethics Forum
REMODELING—Home Magazine Online
RENDERING—3D Forum
RENO—Digital Cities: Reno NV
RENO DC—Digital Cities: Reno NV
RENO DCITY—Digital Cities: Reno NV
RENO DIGC—Digital Cities: Reno NV
RENO DIGITAL CITY—Digital Cities: Reno NV
RENO NV—Digital Cities: Reno NV
REPRISE—Warner/Reprise Records Online
RESEARCH—Academic Assistance Center
RESERVATION—One World Travel
RESERVATIONS—One World Travel
RESNOVA—ResNova Software
RESNOVA SOFTWARE—ResNova Software
RESTAURANT—Everything Edible!

Chapter 6 Keywords from A to Z

RESTAURANTS—Everything Edible!
RETIREMENT—Real Life Financial Tips
REV—ABC Sports' REV Speedway
REV SPEEDWAY—ABC Sports' REV Speedway
REVIEW—1995: The Year in Review
REVIEWS—Family Computing Forum: News & Reviews
RICKI LAKE—The Ricki Lake Show
RICOCHET—Metricom, Inc.
RINGLING—Ringling Online
RINGLING BROS—Ringling Online
RINGLING ONLINE—Ringling Online
RL—Real Life Financial Tips
RNU—Religion News Update
ROAD—Road & Track Magazine
ROAD & TRACK—Road & Track Magazine
ROADTRIP—AOL Roadtrips [*WAOL only*]
ROADTRIPS—AOL Roadtrips [*WAOL only*]
ROCK AND ROLL—Rock and Roll Hall of Fame
ROCK N ROLL—Rock and Roll Hall of Fame
ROCK & ROAD—ABC Online: Rock & Road
ROCK & ROLL—Rock and Roll Hall of Fame
ROCKIES—Major League Baseball Team: Colorado Rockies
ROCKLINE—Rockline Online
ROCKLINK—RockNet Information & Web Link
ROCKNET—RockNet Information & Web Link
ROGER CLEMENS—Roger Clemens' Playoff Baseball Journal
ROGER WAGNER—Roger Wagner Publishing
ROGUE—Motley Fool's Rogue
ROLAND—Roland Corporation U.S.
ROLE PLAYING—Role-Playing Forum
ROLLERSKATING—The Grandstand: Other Sports
ROMANCE—Romance Channel
ROMANCE GROUP—Writer's Club: Romance Writers & Readers
ROMANCE STORE—Romance Store
ROOTS—Genealogy Forum
ROSE BOWL—Fool Bowl
ROSES—800-Flowers
ROSH HASHANA—Jewish New Year Area

Chapter 6 Keywords from A to Z

ROTUNDA—The Computing Rotunda
ROYALS—Major League Baseball Team: Kansas City Royals
RPG—Role-Playing Forum
RPGA—Fellowship of Online Gamers/RPGA Network
RPGA NETWORK—Fellowship of Online Gamers/RPGA Network
RPM—RPM Worldwide Entertainment & Travel
RPM TRAVEL—RPM Worldwide Entertainment & Travel
RR—ABC Online: Rock & Road
RSFL—The Grandstand's Simulation Football
RSG—Manhattan Graphics
RSP—RSP Funding Focus
RT—AOL Roadtrips [*WAOL only*]
RUBBERMAID—Andy Pargh/The Gadget Guru
RUNNING—AOL Sports: Running
RUSSIA—Russia
RX—Health and Vitamin Express
RYOBI—Ryobi
S.F. GIANTS—Major League Baseball Team: San Francisco Giants
S&S—Simon & Schuster College Online
SA—Shopper's Advantage Online
SA MED—Scientific American Medical Publications
SABRE—EAASY SABRE Travel Service
SAF—Scientific American Frontiers
SAFETY—Public Safety Center
SAGINAW—Digital Cities: Saginaw MI
SAGINAW DC—Digital Cities: Saginaw MI
SAGINAW DCITY—Digital Cities: Saginaw MI
SAGINAW DIGC—Digital Cities: Saginaw MI
SAGINAW MI—Digital Cities: Saginaw MI
SAILING—Boating Selections
SAN DIEGO—Digital Cities: San Diego CA
SAN DIEGO DIGC—Digital Cities: San Diego CA
SAN DIEGO PADRES—Major League Baseball Team: San Diego Padres
SAN FRAN—Major League Baseball Team: San Francisco Giants
SAN FRANCISCO—Digital Cities: San Francisco CA
SAN FRANCISCO DIGC—Digital Cities: San Francisco CA
SAN JOSE—Mercury Center

Chapter 6 Keywords from A to Z

SANTA FE—Digital Cities: Albuquerque/Santa Fe NM
SANTA FE DC—Digital Cities: Albuquerque/Santa Fe NM
SANTA FE DCITY—Digital Cities: Albuquerque/Santa Fe NM
SANTA FE DIGC—Digital Cities: Albuquerque/Santa Fe NM
SANTA FE DIGITAL CITY—Digital Cities: Albuquerque/Santa Fe NM
SAT—Kaplan Online or The Princeton Review
SAT REVIEW—Saturday Review Online
SATAN—Weekly World News
SATELLITES—Entertainment's Radio Forum
SATIRE—Soundbites Online
SATURDAY—Saturday Review Online
SATURDAY REVIEW—Saturday Review Online
SAUCE—Mama's Cucina by Ragu
SAVINGS BONDS—U.S. Treasury Securities
SBA—Small Business Administration
SBC—Your Business
SCANDINAVIAN—Genealogy Forum
SCANNERS—Digital Imaging Resource Center
SCENTS—Style Channel
SCHEDULE—What's Hot in Computing [*Platform-dependent*]
SCHOLAR'S HALL—Scholars' Hall
SCHOLARS—Scholars' Hall
SCHOLARS HALL—Scholars' Hall
SCHOLARS' HALL—Scholars' Hall
SCHOLARSHIP—RSP Funding Focus
SCHOLARSHIPS—RSP Funding Focus
SCHOLASTIC—Scholastic Network Preview Area
SCHOOLHOUSE—Electronic Schoolhouse
SCI AM—Scientific American
SCI FI—Science Fiction & Fantasy
SCI-FI—Science Fiction & Fantasy
SCIENCE—Scientific American
SCIENCE FICTION—Science Fiction & Fantasy
SCIENTIFIC—Scientific American
SCIENTIFIC AMERICAN—Scientific American
SCIFI CHANNEL—The Sci-Fi Channel
SCOOP—Newsgroup Scoop

Chapter 6 Keywords from A to Z

SCOPE—Parascope
SCORPIA—Scorpia's Lair
SCORPIA'S LAIR—Scorpia's Lair
SCORPIAS LAIR—Scorpia's Lair
SCOT—Genealogy Forum
SCOTCH—Genealogy Forum
SCOUNDREL—Military City Online: Villains of Fact & Fiction
SCOUNDRELS—Military City Online: Villains of Fact & Fiction
SCOUTING—Scouting Forum
SCOUTS—Scouting Forum
SCRAPBOOK—Member Scrapbook
SCREAM—MusicSpace Events
SCREEN NAME—Add, change or delete screen names
SCREEN NAMES—Add, change or delete screen names
SCRIPT—Affinity Microsystems
SCRIPTING—Affinity Microsystems
SCRIPTS—Affinity Microsystems
SCUBA—Scuba Club
SD—Digital Cities: San Diego CA
SD COMM—Digital City San Diego: Community
SD DIGC—Digital Cities: San Diego CA
SD DIGITAL CITY—Digital Cities: San Diego CA
SD NEWS—Digital City San Diego: News & Weather
SD PEOPLE—Digital City San Diego: People
SD TOUR—Digital City San Diego: City Tour
SD WEATHER—Digital City San Diego: News & Weather
SEARCH—Software Center [*Platform-dependent*]
SEARCH NEWS—Search News articles
SEATTLE—Digital Cities: Seattle/Tacoma WA
SEATTLE DIGC—Digital Cities: Seattle/Tacoma WA
SEATTLE DIGITAL CITY—Digital Cities: Seattle/Tacoma WA
SEATTLE MARINERS—Major League Baseball Team: Seattle Mariners
SECRET BARGAINS—Arthur Frommer's Secret Bargains
SECT—Religion & Ethics Forum
SECURITY—Consumer Electronics
SEGA—Video Games Area
SELF HELP—Self-Help Area

CHAPTER 6 KEYWORDS FROM A TO Z

SELF-HELP—Self-Help Area
SEM—Motley Fool: Semiconductors
SEND PAGE—Page Sender
SENIOR—SeniorNet
SENIOR FRIENDS—Columbia's Health Today
SERIALS—Cyberserials
SERIUS—Serius
SERVENET—SERVEnet
SERVICE—Member Services*
SERVICES—Directory of Services
SERVICES DIRECTORY—Directory of Services
SEVEN WONDERS—Seven Wonders of the Web
SEVENTEEN—Seventeen Magazine Online
SEVENTH—Seventh Level Software
SEW—Needlecrafts/Sewing Center
SEWING—Woman's Day Online
SEX—Entertainment (just try it)
SF—Science Fiction & Fantasy
SF COMM—Digital City San Francisco: Community
SF DIGC—Digital Cities: San Francisco CA
SF DIGITAL CITY—Digital Cities: San Francisco CA
SF NEWS—Digital City San Francisco: News & Weather
SF PEOPLE—Digital City San Francisco: People
SF TOUR—Digital City San Francisco: City Tour
SF WEATHER—Digital City San Francisco: News & Weather
SHADOW—Traffic Center
SHADOW BROADCASTING—Traffic Center
SHADOW TRAFFIC—Traffic Center
SHAREWARE SOLUTIONS—Shareware Solutions
SHARPER IMAGE—The Sharper Image
SHERLOCK—Mysteries from the Yard
SHERLOCK HOLMES—Mysteries from the Yard
SHIP CRITIC—Cruise Critic
SHIP CRITICS—Cruise Critic
SHOPPERS ADVANTAGE—Shopper's Advantage Online
SHOPPING—Marketplace Channel
SHOPPING AND TRAVEL—Travel Channel
SHOPPING & TRAVEL—Travel Channel

Chapter 6 Keywords from A to Z

SHORTHAND—Online Shorthands
SHORTHANDS—Online Shorthands
SHOW TIMES—MovieLink
SHOWBIZ INFO—Showbiz News & Info
SHOWBIZ NEWS—Showbiz News & Info
SHOWS—AOL Live!
SHUTTLE—Challenger Remembered
SI—Smithsonian Online
SIDESHOW—Weekly World News
SIERRA—Sierra On-Line
SIFS—Computers & Software Channel [*Platform-dependent*]
SIGHTINGS—Sightings Online
SIGNUP—Online Campus
SIGS—Computers & Software Channel [*Platform-dependent*]
SIM—Simming Forum
SIMBA—Cowles/SIMBA Media Information Network
SIMI WINERY—Simi Winery
SIMMING—Simming Forum
SIMON—Simon & Schuster College Online
SIMON & SCHUSTER—Simon & Schuster College Online
SIMS—Simming Forum
SIMULATION AUTO—The Grandstand's Simulation Auto Racing
SIMULATION BASEBALL—The Grandstand's Simulation Baseball
SIMULATION BASKETBALL—The Grandstand's Simulation Basketball
SIMULATION FOOTBALL—The Grandstand's Simulation Football
SIMULATION GOLF—The Grandstand's Simulation Golf
SIMULATION HOCKEY—The Grandstand's Simulation Hockey
SIMULATION LEAGUES—The Grandstand's Fantasy & Simulation Leagues
SIMULATION WRESTLING—The Grandstand's Simulation Wrestling
SIMULATIONS—Graphic Simulations
SIMULATOR—Games Forum [*Platform-dependent*]
SINGAPORE—Singapore
SISTORE—The Sharper Image
SIXTY—60-Second Novelist
SKI—AOL Skiing

Chapter 6 Keywords from A to Z

SKI CONDITIONS—Ski Reports
SKI REPORTS—Ski Reports
SKI WEATHER—Ski Reports
SKI ZONE—The Ski Zone
SKIING—iSKI
SKY DIVING—Aviation Forum
SKYLINE—Virtual Airlines
SKYLINE AIRWAYS—Virtual Airlines
SLIME—Nickelodeon Online
SM—Smithsonian Magazine
SMALL BUSINESS—Your Business
SMART WATCHING—The ABC Classroom
SMARTMOUTHS—Smart Mouths
SMITHFIELD—Gwaltney Hams & Turkeys
SMITHSONIAN—Smithsonian Online
SMITHSONIAN MAGAZINE—Smithsonian Magazine
SML—Sony Magic Link
SN LIBRARIES—Scholastic Libraries
SN LIT GAME—Bookwoman's Literature Game
SN SPACE—Space and Astronomy
SNGUESTS—Scholastic Network: Special Guests
SNLITGAME—Bookwoman's Literature Game [K-6]
SNOWBOARDING—Snowboarding Online
SOAP DIGEST—Soap Opera Digest
SOAPLINE—ABC Daytime/Soapline
SOCIAL SCIENCE—NAS Online
SOCIAL WORK—Simon & Schuster Online: Social Work Department
SOCIETY—Saturday Review Online
SOCIOLOGY—Simon & Schuster Online: Sociology Department
SOD—Soap Opera Digest
SOFT SHOP—AOL Software Shop
SOFTARC—SoftArc
SOFTDISK—Softdisk Superstore
SOFTLOGIK—SoftLogik
SOFTWARE—Software Center [*Platform-dependent*]
SOFTWARE CENTER—Software Center [*Platform-dependent*]
SOFTWARE COMPANIES—Computing Company Connection

Chapter 6 Keywords from A to Z

SOFTWARE DIRECTORY—Software Center [*Platform-dependent*]

SOFTWARE HARDTALK—Software Hardtalk with John C. Dvorak

SOFTWARE HELP—Software Center [*Platform-dependent*]

SOFTWARE LIBRARIES—Software Center [*Platform-dependent*]

SOFTWARE LIBRARY—Software Center [*Platform-dependent*]

SOFTWARE PUBLISHERS—Computing Company Connection

SOFTWARE SHOP—AOL Software Shop

SOFTWARE SUPPORT—Personal Finance Software Support

SOFTWARE TOOLWORKS—Mindscape

SOFTWARE UNBOXED—Software Unboxed

SOHO—Home Office Computing Magazine

SOL—Snowboarding Online

SOLIII—Sol III Play-by-Email Game

SONY—Sony Magic Link

SOPHCIR—Sophisticated Circuits

SOS—Wall Street SOS Forum

SOUND—Stereo Review Online

SOUND ROOM—Sound Room*

SOUNDBITES—Soundbites Online

SOURCERER—The Hub: Sourcerer

SOUTH—Digital Cities: South

SOUTH AFRICA—South Africa

SOUTH DIGC—Digital Cities: South

SOUTH DIGIAL CITY—Digital Cities: South

SOUTHEAST—Digital Cities: South

SPA—Longevity Magazine Online

SPACE—National Space Society

SPACE A&B—Space: Above & Beyond

SPACE ABOVE AND BEYOND—Space: Above & Beyond

SPACE: ABOVE AND BEYOND—Space: Above & Beyond

SPACE ABOVE & BEYOND—Space: Above & Beyond

SPACE COAST—Florida's Space Coast

SPACE SHUTTLE—Challenger Remembered

SPACEY—The Hub: Space

SPAIN—Spain

SPAS—Longevity Magazine Online

SPC—Software Publishing Corporation

Chapter 6 Keywords from A to Z

SPEAKERS—Stereo Review Online
SPECIAL INTERESTS—Life, Styles & Interests Channel
SPECTRUM—Spectrum HoloByte
SPECULAR—Specular International
SPEEDBOATS—Boating Online
SPEEDWAY—ABC Sports' REV Speedway
SPIDER—Spider Island Software
SPIDER ISLAND—Spider Island Software
SPIN—Spin Online
SPIN ONLINE—Spin Online
SPINNING—Needlecrafts/Sewing Center
SPIRITS—Food & Drink Network
SPIRITUAL—Spiritual Mosaic
SPOOFS—TV Spoofs
SPORTING NEWS—The Sporting News
SPORTS—Sports Channel
SPORTS ARCHIVE—AOL Sports Archive
SPORTS BOARDS—The Grandstand's Sports Boards
SPORTS CHAT—The Grandstand's Chat Rooms
SPORTS CIRUIT—New England Sports Network
SPORTS EVENTS—AOL Sports Live
SPORTS HOT—What's Hot in Sports
SPORTS LIBRARIES—The Grandstand's Libraries
SPORTS LINK—Sports Channel
SPORTS LIVE—AOL Sports Live
SPORTS NEWS—Sport News
SPORTS ROOMS—The Grandstand's Chat Rooms
SPOTLIGHT—AOL Live! Spotlight
SPRING—Computing Spring Fling
SPRINT—Sprint Annual Report (Old)
SRO—Saturday Review Online
SRO SALON—Saturday Review Online: Conference Room
SRS—SRS Labs -or- Transgender Community Forum
SRS LABS—SRS Labs
SSI—Strategic Simulations
SSS—Craig Anderton's Sound Studio & Stage
SSS NEWS—Sound, Studio, Stage News
SSSI—SSSi

Chapter 6 Keywords from A to Z

ST. LOUIS CARDINALS—Major League Baseball Team. St. Louis Cardinals

ST PAUL—Digital Cities: Minneapolis - St. Paul MN

ST PAUL DIGC—Digital Cities: Minneapolis - St. Paul MN

ST PAUL DIGITAL CITY—Digital Cities: Minneapolis - St. Paul MN

ST PETERSBURG—Ditial Cities: Tampa - St. Petersburg FL

ST PETERSBURG DIGC—Ditial Cities: Tampa - St. Petersburg FL

STAC—STAC Electronics

STAFF—Staff Development Special Interest Group

STAMPS—The Exchange

STAR WARS—Star Wars Simulator Forum

STAR WARS SIM—Star Wars Simulator Forum

STARBUCKS—Caffe Starbucks

STARFISH—Starfish Software

STARFLEET—Starfleet Online

STARPLAY—Starplay Productions

STARS—Galileo Mission to Jupiter [*May disappear without notice*]

STARS AND SHOWS—ABC Online: Stars and Shows [*WAOL only*]

STARTER—Help Desk [*Platform-dependent*]

STAR TREK—Star Trek Club

STATS—Pro Sports Center by STATS, Inc.

STATS BASKETBALL—Pro Basketball Center by STATS, Inc

STATS HOOPS—Pro Basketball Center by STATS, Inc.

STATS, INC.—Pro Sports Center by STATS, Inc.

STATS INC—Pro Sports Center by STATS, Inc.

STATS INC.—Pro Sports Center by STATS, Inc.

STATS, INC—Pro Sports Center by STATS, Inc.

STD—Sexually Transmitted Diseases Forum

STEAKS—Omaha Steaks

STEREO—Stereo Review Online

STEREO EQUIPMENT—Stereo Review Online

STEREO REVIEW—Stereo Review Online

STEVE CASE—Community Updates from Steve Case*

STF—STF Technologies

STF TECHNOLOGIES—STF Technologies

STOCK—StockLink: Quotes & Portfolios Area

STOCK CHARTS—Decision Point Forum

Chapter 6 Keywords from A to Z

STOCK PORTFOLIO—Your Stock Portfolio
STOCK QUOTES—StockLink: Quotes & Portfolios Area
STOCK REPORTS—Stock Reports
STOCK TIMING—Decision Point Forum
STOCKLINK—StockLink: Quotes & Portfolios Area
STOCKS—StockLink: Quotes & Portfolios Area
STORE—Marketplace Channel
STORES—Marketplace Channel
STRANGE—Parascope
STRATA—Strata, Inc.
STRATEGIC—Strategic Simulations
STRATEGIES—Business Strategies Forum
STRATEGY—Strategy & Wargaming Forum
STRIKE-A-MATCH—Boxer*Jam Gameshows [*WAOL only*]
STUDENT—The Princeton Review Online
STUDENT ACCESS—The Princeton Review Online
STUDIO—MusicSpace Studio
STUDIOWARE—Roger Wagner Publishing
STUDY—Study Skills Service
STUDY BREAK—Compton's Study Break
STUDY SKILLS—Study Skills Service
STUFFIT—Aladdin Systems, Inc.
STUMP—The Computing Rotunda
STW—Mindscape
STYL*E—Style Channel
STYLE—Style Channel
STYLE 911—Style Channel
STYLE CHANNEL—Style Channel
SUGGEST—Suggestion boxes*
SUGGESTION—Suggestion boxes*
SUIT—Style Channel
SUMMER MOVIES—New Movie Releases
SUMMER SLAM—World Wrestling Federation
SUNAIR—Virtual Airlines
SUNAIR EXPRESS—Virtual Airlines
SUNBURST—Sunburst Communications
SUNSET—Sunset Magazine
SUNSET MAGAZINE—Sunset Magazine

Chapter 6 Keywords from A to Z

SUPERBOWL—Super Bowl XXX Online
SUPERCARD—SuperCard Scripting Center
SUPERDISK—Alysis Software
SUPERLIBRARY—MacMillan Information SuperLibrary
SUPERMAC—Radius, Inc.
SUPERMAN—DC Comics Online
SUPERSTARS—World Wrestling Federation
SUPERSTORE—Softdisk Superstore
SUPPORT—Member Services*
SURF—SurfLink
SURF SHACK—The Surf Shack
SURFBOARD—SurfLink
SURFER—SurfLink
SURFERS—SurfLink
SURFING—SurfLink
SURFLINK—SurfLink
SURNAMES—Genealogy Forum
SURVIVOR—Survivor Software
SURVIVOR SOFTWARE—Survivor Software
SUSAN—The Hub: Susan
SWEDEN—Sweden
SWEDISH—Genealogy Forum
SWEETHEART—Omaha Steaks Offer
SWIMMING—The Grandstand: Other Sports
SWISS—Genealogy Forum
SWITZERLAND—Switzerland
SYMANTEC—Symantec
SYNEX—Synex
SYSOP—Member Services*
SYSTEM 7—Mac Operating Systems Forum
SYSTEM 7.0—Mac Operating Systems Forum
SYSTEM 7.1—Mac Operating Systems Forum
SYSTEM 71—Mac Operating Systems Forum
SYSTEM RESPONSE—System Response Report Area*
T SHIRT—America Online Store
T TALK—Teachers' Forum
TA—Traveler's Advantage
TA FOOTRACE—Trans-America Footrace

CHAPTER 6 KEYWORDS FROM A TO Z

TAC—Top Advisor's Corner
TACOMA—Digital Cities: Seattle/Tacoma WA
TACOMA DIGC—Digital Cities: Seattle/Tacoma WA
TACOMA DIGITAL CITY—Digital Cities: Seattle/Tacoma WA
TACTIC—Tactic Software
TAIWAN—Taiwan
TAKE 2—Take 2 Interactive Software
TAKE 2 INC—Take 2 Interactive Software
TAL—Turner Adventure Learning
TALENT—Talent Bank
TALK—People Connection Channel
TALK SHOW—Future Labs, Inc.
TAMPA—Digital Cities: Tampa - St. Petersburg FL
TAMPA COMM—Digital City Tampa: Community
TAMPA DIGC—Digital Cities: Tampa - St. Petersburg FL
TAMPA DIGITAL CITY—Digital Cities: Tampa - St. Petersburg FL
TAMPA NEWS—Digital City Tampa: News & Weather
TAMPA PEOPLE—Digital City Tampa: People
TAMPA WEATHER—Digital City Tampa: News & Weather
TAROT—The Crystal Ball Forum
TAX—Tax Forum
TAX CHANNEL—NAEA Tax Channel
TAX FORUM—Tax Forum
TAXCUT—Block Financial Software Support
TAXES—Computing Tax Corner -or- Tax Forum
TAXI—TAXI Information and Web Link
TAXLOGIC—Taxlogic
TAY—Taylor University
TAYLOR UNIVERSITY—Taylor University
TBIBM—TBS Network Earth/IBM Project [*MAOL and GAOL only*]
TCF—Transgender Community Forum
TCW—Today's Christian Woman
TEACHER—The Educator's Network
TEACHER PAGER—Teacher Pager
TEACHER'S LOUNGE—Teachers Lounge
TEACHERS—The Educator's Network
TEACHERS' LOUNGE—Teachers' Lounge

Chapter 6 Keywords from A to Z

TEACHERS LOUNGE—Teachers' Lounge

TEAM—Team Concepts

TEAM CONCEPTS—Team Concepts

TECH HELP LIVE—Member Services*

TECH LIVE—Member Services*

TECHNOLOGY—Computers & Software Channel [*Platform-dependent*]

TECHNOLOGY WORKS—Technology Works

TECHNOTORIUM—@times/The New York Times Online

TECHWORKS—Technology Works

TEEN—Teen Selections

TEEN SCENE—Teen Selections

TEENS—Teen Selections

TEKNOSYS—Teknosys Works

TEKTRONIX—Tektronix

TELECOM—Communications/Telecom/Networking Forum [*Platform-dependent*]

TELECOM FORUM—Communications/Telecom/Networking Forum [*Platform-dependent*]

TELECOMMUNICATIONS—Communications/Telecom/Networking Forum [*Platform-dependent*]

TELEPHONE—Phone Directories

TELEPHONE NUMBERS—Phone Directories

TELEPORT—Global Village Communication

TELESCAN—Telescan Users Group Forum

TELEVISION—TV Main Screen

TELLURIDE—Telluride Film Festival

TELNET—Telnet [*WAOL 2.5 only*]

TEMPLE—Digital Cities: Waco/Temple/Bryan TX

TEMPLE DC—Digital Cities: Waco/Temple/Bryan TX

TEMPLE DCITY—Digital Cities: Waco/Temple/Bryan TX

TEMPLE DIGC—Digital Cities: Waco/Temple/Bryan TX

TEMPLE TX—Digital Cities: Waco/Temple/Bryan TX

TEMPO—Affinity Microsystems

TEMPO II—Affinity Microsystems

TEMPO II PLUS—Affinity Microsystems

TEN—The Educator's Network

TENNIS—AOL Tennis

Chapter 6 Keywords from A to Z

TERMS—Terms of Service*
TERMS OF SERVICE—Terms of Service*
TEST DAY—The Princeton Review Online
TEST PREP—Kaplan Online
TEST TUBE—ABC Online: Test Tube
TEXAS INSTRUMENTS—Texas Instruments
TEXAS RANGERS—Major League Baseball Team: Texas Rangers
TG—Transgender Community Forum
TGS—Pictorius, Inc.
THE BIZ—The Biz!
THE DEAD—Grateful Dead Forum
THE ENTREPRENEUR ZONE—Your Business
THE EXCHANGE—The Exchange
THE FLORIDA KEYS—The Florida Keys
THE GRANDSTAND—The Grandstand
THE HUB—The Hub
THE HUB INDEX—The Hub: Index
THE KEYS—The Florida Keys
THE LAB—The Lab
THE MALL—Marketplace Channel
THE MOVIES—@the.movies
THE NATURE CONSERVANCY—The Nature Conservancy
THE NEW REPUBLIC—The New Republic Magazine
THE ODYSSEY PROJECT—The Odyssey Project
THE POST OFFICE—Post Office
THE SPORTING NEWS—The Sporting News
THE TOY NET—Pangea Toy Net
THE WALL—Vietnam Veterans Memorial Wall
THE WB NETWORK—The WB Network
THE WHITE HOUSE—White House Forum
THE WORLD—The World
THE ZONE—Your Business
THEATER—Saturday Review Online
THEATRE—Saturday Review Online
THESAURUS—Merriam-Webster's Thesaurus
THIRTIES—The Exchange: Communities Center
THREE SIXTY—Three-Sixty Software
THREEDO—The 3DO Company

Chapter 6 Keywords from A to Z

THRUSTMASTER—Thrustmaster
TI—Texas Instruments
TIA—True Image Audio
TICF—Investors' Exchange
TICKET—Ticketmaster
TICKETMASTER—Ticketmaster
TIES—Woman's Day Online
TIGER—TIGERDirect, Inc.
TIGERDIRECT—TIGERDirect, Inc.
TIGERS—Major League Baseball Team: Detroit Tigers
TIME—Time Message Boards
TIME DAILY—TIME Message Boards
TIME CAPSULE—CyberJustice's Istorian's Time Capsule
TIMES—@times/The New York Times Online
TIMES ART—@times: Museums & Galleries
TIMES ARTS—@times: Art & Entertainment Guide
TIMES BOOKS—@times: Books of The Times
TIMES DINING—@times: Dining Out & Nightlife
TIMES FILM—@times: Film
TIMES LEISURE—@times: Arts & Leisure
TIMES MOVIES—@times: Film
TIMES MUSIC—@times: Music & Dance
TIMES NEWS—@times/The New York Times Online
TIMES REGION—@times: The New York Region
TIMES SPORTS—@times: Sports News
TIMES STORE—@times: Store
TIMES STORIES—@times: Page One—Top Stories
TIMES THEATER—@times: Theater
TIMESLIPS—Timeslips Corporation
TIMEX—Andy Pargh/The Gadget Guru
TIP—Family Computing Forum: Tip of the Day
TIPS—Advice & Tips
TITF—What's Hot in Computing [*Platform-dependent*]
TL—Travel & Leisure Magazine
TLC—The Learning Channel
TLC ED—The Discovery Channel: Education
TLC-ED—The Discovery Channel: Education
TMS—TV Quest -or- TMS Peripherals

204

Chapter 6 Keywords from A to Z

TNC—The Nature Conservancy
TNEWS—Teachers' Newsstand
TNPC—The National Parenting Center
TNR—The New Republic Magazine
TO MARKET—Marketplace Gift Service
TO NETSCAPE—Netscape
TODAY PITCH—The Motley Fool
TODAY'S OTHER—The Hub: Today's Other News
TODAYS NEWS—Today's News Channel
TODAYS PITCH—The Motley Fool
TODD ART—The Image Exchange: Ask Todd Art
TOLL FREE—AT&T 800 Directory (WWW site)
TOM SNYDER—Tom Snyder Productions
TONY AWARDS—Playbill Online: Tony Awards Central
TONYS—Playbill Online: Tony Awards Central
TOOL—American Woodworker: Tool Reviews
TOOLKIT—Web Page Toolkit
TOOLS—American Woodworker: Tool Reviews
TOOLWORKS—Mindscape
TOON—InToon with the News
TOONS—Cartoon Network
TOONZ—InToon with the News
TOP ADVISOR—Top Advisor's Corner
TOP ADVISORS—Top Advisor's Corner
TOP COMP SITES—Top Computing Internet Sites
TOP COMPANY SITES—Companies on the Internet
TOP COMPUTING SITES—Top Computing Internet Sites
TOP MODEL—TopModel Online
TOP NEWS—Today's News Channel
TOP TIPS—Top Tips for AOL
TORONTO—Digital Cities: Toronto ON
TORONTO BLUE JAYS—Major League Baseball Team: Toronto Blue Jays
TORONTO DIGC—Digital Cities: Toronto ON
TORONTO DIGITAL CITY—Digital Cities: Toronto ON
TOS—Terms of Service*
TOS ADVISOR—Terms of Service*
TOTN—National Public Radio Outreach

CHAPTER 6 KEYWORDS FROM A TO Z

TOUR—AOL Highlights Tour

TOUR CHAMPIONSHIP—iGolf: Tour Championship

TOUR DE FRANCE—Bicycling Magazine: Tour de France Coverage

TOUR DE FROG—Bicycling Magazine: Tour de France Coverage

TOUR GUIDE—America Online Store

TOWER—Tower Records

TOWER RECORDS—Tower Records

TOY—Pangea Toy Net

TOY NET—Pangea Toy Net

TOYBUZZ—Pangea Toy Network: ToyBuzz

TOYS—The Exchange: Collector's Corner

TPI—Trivial Pursuit Interactive

TPN—The Prayer Network

TRACK—Road & Track Magazine

TRADEPLUS—How to use StockLink & Gateway Host

TRAFFIC—Traffic Center

TRAIL GUIDES—Backpacker Magazine

TRAILHEADS—MECC

TRAILS—Backpacker Magazine

TRAINING—Career Development Training

TRANSCRIPT—AOL Live! Event Transcripts

TRANSCRIPTS—AOL Live! Event Transcripts

TRANSGENDER—Transgender Community Forum

TRANSGENDER TEEN—Gay & Lesbian Community Forum Youth Area

TRANSGENDER YOUTH—Gay & Lesbian Community Forum Youth Area

TRANSPORTATION—NAS Online

TRANSSEXUAL—Transgender Community Forum

TRANSVESTITE—Transgender Community Forum

TRAVEL—Travel Channel

TRAVEL ADVISORIES—US State Department Travel Advisories

TRAVEL FORUM—Travel Forum

TRAVEL HOLIDAY—Travel Holiday Magazine

TRAVEL & LEISURE—Travel & Leisure Magazine

TRAVEL PICKS—What's Hot in Travel

TRAVELER—Travel Forum

Chapter 6 Keywords from A to Z

TRAVELERS ADVANTAGE—Traveler's Advantage
TRAVELERS CORNER—Traveler's Corner
TREASURE HUNT—AOL Treasure Hunt
TREASURES—Tell a Story
TREASURY BILLS—U.S. Treasury Securities
TREASURY BONDS—U.S. Treasury Securities
TREASURY DIRECT—U.S. Treasury Securities
TREASURY NOTES—U.S. Treasury Securities
TREASURY SECURITIES—U.S. Treasury Securities
TREK—Star Trek Club
TREKER—800-TREKKER: 24 Hour Sci-Fi Collectibles Hotline
TREKKER—800-TREKKER: 24 Hour Sci-Fi Collectibles Hotline
TRENDS—Elle Magazine Online
TRENDSETTER—Trendsetter Software
TRIANGLE—Gay & Lesbian Community Forum
TRIB—Chicago Tribune
TRIB ADS—Chicago Online: Classifieds
TRIB CLASSIFIED—Chicago Online: Classifieds
TRIB COLUMNISTS—Chicago Online: Columnists
TRIB SPORTS—Chicago Tribune: Sports Area
TRIBE—Major League Baseball Team: Cleveland Indians
TRIBUNE—Chicago Tribune
TRIMBLE—Trimble Navigation, Ltd.
TRINCULO—The Motley Fool
TRIPLE A—AAA Online
TRIPLE CROWN—ABC Triple Crown
TRIVIA—Trivia Forum
TRIVIA FORUM—Trivia Forum
TRIVIAL PURSUIT—Trivial Pursuit Interactive
TROPICAL STORM—Tropical Storm and Hurricane Info
TRUE IMAGE AUDIO—True Image Audio
TRUE TALES—True Tales of the Internet
TS—Trendsetter Software
TSENG—Tseng
TSN—The Sporting News
TSP—Tom Snyder Productions
TSR—TSR Online
TSR ONLINE—TSR Online

Chapter 6 Keywords from A to Z

TT—ABC Online: Test Tube
TULSA—Digital Cities: Tulsa OK
TULSA DC—Digital Cities: Tulsa OK
TULSA DCITY—Digital Cities: Tulsa OK
TULSA DIGC—Digital Cities: Tulsa OK
TULSA DIGITAL CITY—Digital Cities: Tulsa OK
TULSA OK—Digital Cities: Tulsa OK
TUNE UP—Tune Up Your PC
TUNE UP YOUR PC—Tune Up Your PC
TURKEY—Turkey
TURNER VISION—Andy Pargh/The Gadget Guru
TURTLE BEACH—Turtle Beach Systems
TURTLE SYS—Turtle Beach Systems
TUTORING—Academic Assistance Center
TV—Main TV Screen
TV GOSSIP—TV Shows Gossip
TV GUIDE—TV Quest
TV LISTINGS—TV Quest
TV NETWORKS—TV Networks Area
TV PEOPLE—TV People
TV SHOWS—TV Shows
TV SOURCE—TV Quest
TV SPOOFS—TV Spoofs
TV VIEWERS—TV Viewers Forum
TWENTIES—The Exchange: Communities Center
TWENTIETH—Twentieth Century Mutual Funds
TWENTIETH CENTURY—Twentieth Century Mutual Funds
TWENTIETH-CENTURY—Twentieth Century Mutual Funds
TWI—Time Warner Interactive
TWO MARKET—Marketplace Gift Service
U.S. SAVINGS BONDS—U.S. Treasury Securities
UA—Unlimited Adventures
UCAL—University of California Extension
UCPA—United Cerebral Palsy Association, Inc.
UCX—University of California Extension
UFO—Institute for the Study of Contact with Non-Human Intelligence

Chapter 6 Keywords from A to Z

UFOS—Institute for the Study of Contact with Non-Human Intelligence
UGF—User Group Forum
UHA—Homeowner's Forum
UKRAINE—Ukraine
ULTRALIGHTS—Aviation Forum
UNDIES—Style Channel
UNIQUE—Best of America Online showcase
UNITARIUM—Religion & Ethics Forum
UNITED KINGDOM—United Kingdom
UNIVERSE—UniverseCentral.Com
UNIVERSE CENTRAL—UniverseCentral.Com
UNIVERSITIES—Electronic University Network
UNIVERSITY—Electronic University Network
UNLIMITED ADVENTURES—Unlimited Adventures
UNPROFOR—Balkan Operation Joint Endeavor
UPDATE ADD—AD&D Neverwinter Nights
UPDATES—Hoover's Company Masterlist
UPGRADE—Upgrade to the latest version of AOL*
URBAN LEAGUE—National Urban League
US GAZETTEER—U.S. Census Information Web Page [*WAOL only*]
US MAIL—Fax/Paper Mail
US NEWS—U.S. & World News Area
US SAVINGS BONDS—U.S. Treasury Securities
US TREASURY SECURITIES—U.S. Treasury Securities
USA—USA Weekend
USA WEEKEND—USA Weekend
USEFUL THINGS—The Hub: Useful Things
USELESS THINGS—The Hub: Useless Things
USENET—Internet Usenet Newsgroup Area
USER GROUP—User Group Forum
USER GROUPS—User Group Forum
USER NAME—Add, change or delete screen names
USERLAND—Userland
USFSA—United States Figure Skating Association
USPS—United States Postal Service
USROBOTICS—U.S. Robotics

Chapter 6 Keywords from A to Z

UTAH—Utah Forum
UTAH FORUM—Utah Forum
UZBEKISTAN—Uzbekistan
VA—Virginia Forum
VA.—Virginia Forum
VAA—Virtual Airlines
VACATION—Preview Vacations
VACATIONS—Preview Vacations
VALLEY—Virgin's Virtual Valley
VAMPIRE—Weekly World News
VAN—AOL Roadtrips [*WAOL only*]
VANGUARD—Vanguard Online
VANGUARD ONLINE—Vanguard Online
VAS—Virtual Airlines
VB—Visual Basic Area
VCOMMS—Vanguard Online: Communications
VDISC—Videodiscovery
VEGAN—Cooking Club: Vegetarians Online
VEGETARIAN—Cooking Club
VENTANA—Ventana Communications
VERONICA—Internet Gopher
VERTIGO—DC Comics Online
VERTISOFT—Vertisoft
VETERANS—Military and Vets Club
VETS—Military and Vets Club
VETS CLUB—Military and Vets Club
VFR—Flying Magazine
VFUNDS—Vanguard Online: Mutual Funds Campus
VG—Vanguard Online
VGA PLANETS—VGA Planets
VGAP—VGA Planets
VGS—Video Games Area
VH—Virtual Christian Humor
VH1—VH1 Online
VIDEO GAME—Video Games Area
VIDEO SIG—Video Special Interest Group
VIDEO TOASTER—New Tek
VIDEO TOOLKIT—Abbate Video

Chapter 6 Keywords from A to Z

VIDEO ZONE—PC Multimedia's Video
VIDEODISC—Videodiscovery
VIDEODISCOVERY—Videodiscovery
VIDEOS—Home Video
VIDI—VIDI
VIENNA—Computing Print & Broadcast
VIETNAM—Vietnam Veterans Memorial Wall
VIEWER—Viewer Resource Center
VIEWERS—Viewer Resource Center
VIEWPOINT—Viewpoint DataLabs
VILLAGE—Village Software
VILLAGE SOFTWARE—Village Software
VILLAIN—Military City Online: Villains of Fact & Fiction
VILLAINS—Military City Online: Villains of Fact & Fiction
VIP—Style Channel
VIREX—Datawatch
VIRGIN—Virgin Records -or- Virgin Sound & Vision
VIRGIN RECORDS—Virgin Records
VIRGINIA—Virginia Forum
VIRGINIA FORUM—Virginia Forum
VIRTUAL AIRLINES—Virtual Airlines
VIRTUAL HUMOR—Virtual Christian Humor
VIRTUAL REALITY—Virtual Reality Resource Center
VIRTUAL TORCH—Virtual Torch Relay
VIRTUAL TOYS—Pangea Toy Net
VIRTUAL VALLEY—Virgin's Virtual Valley
VIRTUS—Virtus Corp.
VIRUS—Virus Information Center Special Interest Group
VIRUS2—Virus Letter*
VISALIA—Digital Cities: Fresno/Visalia CA
VISALIA CA—Digital Cities: Fresno/Visalia CA
VISALIA DC—Digital Cities: Fresno/Visalia CA
VISALIA DIGC —Digital Cities: Fresno/Visalia CA
VISALIA DIGITAL CITY —Digital Cities: Fresno/Visalia CA
VISION VIDEO—Vision Video
VISIONARY—Visionary Software
VISIONEER—Visioneer
VISUAL BASIC—Visual Basic Area

Chapter 6 Keywords from A to Z

VITAMIN EXP—Health and Vitamin Express
VITAMIN EXPRESS—Health and Vitamin Express
VITAMINS—Longevity Magazine Online
VNEWS—Vanguard Online: Vanguard News
VOICE—Your Voice
VOLLEYBALL—AVP Pro Beach Volleyball
VOLUNTEER—access.point
VOLUNTEERS—access.point
VOTE AMERICA—Vote America
VOYAGER—The Voyager Company
VOYETRA—Voyetra Technologies
VR—Virtual Reality Resource Center
VRLI—Virtual Reality Labs, Inc.
VSTATS—Vanguard Fund Information
VSTRATEGY—Vanguard Online: Planning & Strategy
VTOYS—Pangea Toy Net
VV—Vision Video
WACO—Digital Cities: Waco/Temple/Bryan TX
WACO DC—Digital Cities: Waco/Temple/Bryan TX
WACO DCITY—Digital Cities: Waco/Temple/Bryan TX
WACO DIGC—Digital Cities: Waco/Temple/Bryan TX
WACO DIGITAL CITY—Digital Cities: Waco/Temple/Bryan TX
WACO TX—Digital Cities: Waco/Temple/Bryan TX
WAHL—Andy Pargh/The Gadget Guru
WAIS—Internet Gopher
WALKTHROUGH—Virtus Corp.
WALL—Vietnam Veterans Memorial Wall
WALL STREET WORDS—Wall Street Words
WALLPAPER—Windows Wallpaper & Paint Center
WALMART—Motley Fool: FoolMart
WAND TV—ABC Online: WAND-TV in Decatur, IL
WARNER—Warner/Reprise Records Online
WARNER BROS. STORE—Warner Bros. Studio Store
WARNER BROS STORE—Warner Bros. Studio Store
WARNER BROS. STU STO—Warner Bros. Studio Store
WARNER MUSIC—Warner/Reprise Records Online
WARNER STORE—Warner Bros. Studio Store
WASH PERSONALS—Digital City Washington: Personals

Chapter 6 Keywords from A to Z

WASHINGTON—Politics Forum
WASHINGTON WEB—City Web
WATE TV—ABC Online: WATE-TV in Knoxville, TN
WATER—Boating Online
WB—The WB Network
WB STORE—Warner Bros. Studio Store
WBAY TV—ABC Online: WBAY-TV in Green Bay, WI
WBNET—The WB Network
WBRC TV—ABC Online: WBRC-TV in Birmingham, AL
WBRZ TV—ABC Online: WBRZ-TV in Baton Rouge, LA
WC CHAT—Writer's Club: Chat Rooms
WCN—World Crisis Network
WCVB TV—ABC Online: WCVB-TV in Boston, MA
WD—Woman's Day Online
WD KITCHEN—Woman's Day Kitchen
WDC—Western Digital
WDHN TV—ABC Online: WDHN-TV in Dothan, AL
WDIO TV—ABC Online: WDIO-TV in Duluth, MN
WDTN TV—ABC Online: WDTN-TV in Dayton, OH
WEAR TV—ABC Online: WEAR-TV in Pensacola, FL
WEATHER—Weather
WEATHER MALL—WSC Weather Mall
WEATHER MAPS—Color Weather Maps
WEAVING—Needlecrafts/Sewing Center
WEB—World Wide Web
WEB ART—Web Page Clip Art Creation Center
WEB BIZ—The Web Diner
WEB COMEDY—Hecklers Online
WEB DINER—The Web Diner
WEB ENTERTAINMENT—WEBentertainment
WEB HELP—The Web Diner
WEB HUMOR—Hecklers Online
WEB MAKEOVER—Web Makeover
WEB PAGE—Web Page Toolkit
WEB PAGE TOOLKIT—Web Page Toolkit
WEB PUB—Web Publishing Special Interest Group
WEB PUBLISH—Web Publishing Special Interest Group
WEB PUBLISHING—Web Publishing Special Interest Group

Chapter 6 Keywords from A to Z

WEB RESEARCH—Reference: Web Research
WEB REVIEW—Web Review [*WAOL only*]
WEB TOOLS—Reference: Web Research
WEB UNIVERSITY—Web University
WEBCRAWLER—World Wide Web
WEBD—The Web Diner
WEBSITE—The Web Diner
WEBSOURCE—Websource
WEBSTER—Merriam-Webster Dictionary
WEDDING—Wedding Workshop
WEDNESDAYS—90210 Wednesdays
WEEKLY READER—Weekly Reader News
WEEKLY WORLD NEWS—Weekly World News
WEIGAND—Weigand Report
WEIRD—Parascope
WEIRD SISTERS—The Hub: Weird Sisters
WEISSMANN—Traveler's Corner
WELCOME TO PLANET EARTH—Astronet
WELLNESS—Longevity Magazine Online
WELSH—Genealogy Forum
WEST—Digital Cities: West
WEST DIGC—Digital Cities: West
WESTERN DIGITAL—Western Digital
WESTERN EUROPEAN—Genealogy Forum
WESTWOOD—Westwood Studios
WESTWOOD STUDIOS—Westwood Studios
WFAA TV—ABC Online: WFAA-TV in Dallas/Ft. Worth, TX
WFTV TV—ABC Online: WFTV-TV in Orlando, FL
WGGB TV—ABC Online: WGGB-TV in Springfield, MA
WGTU TV—ABC Online: WGTU/WGTQ-TV in Traverse City, MI
WHAT'S HOT IN HEALTH—What's Hot in Health
WHATEVER—What's Hot This Month Showcase
WHATS HOT—What's Hot This Month Showcase
WHEELS—Wheels
WHEELS EXCHANGE—Wheels Exchange
WHFS—WHFS 99.1 FM
WHITE HOUSE—White House Forum
WHITE PAGES—ProCD National Telephone Directory Search

Chapter 6 Keywords from A to Z

WHITE SOX—Major League Baseball Team: Chicago White Sox
WHOI TV—ABC Online: WHOI-TV in Peoria-Bloomington, IL
WHTM TV—ABC Online: WHTM-TV in Harrisburg, PA
WICCA—Pagan Religions & Occult Sciences
WICS—Women in Community Service
WIDE WORLD OF SPORTS—ABC Online: Wide World of Sports
WIERD—Parascope
WILDCAT—Mustang Software
WILDCAT BBS—Mustang Software
WILDERNESS—Backpacker Magazine
WILSON—Wilson Windoware
WIMBLEDON—Wimbledon [*May disappear without notice*]
WIN—Windows Forum
WIN 500—Windows Shareware 500
WIN 95—Windows Forum
WIN FORUM—Windows Forum
WIN MAG—Windows Magazine
WIN NEWS—Windows News Area
WIN NT—Windows NT Resource Center
WINDHAM—Windham Hill
WINDHAM HILL—Windham Hill
WINDOWS—Windows Services
WINDOWS 500—Windows Shareware 500
WINDOWS 95—Windows Forum
WINDOWS FORUM—Windows Forum
WINDOWS MAG—Windows Magazine
WINDOWS MAGAZINE—Windows Magazine
WINDOWS NT—Windows NT Resource Center
WINDOWS TIPS—Family Computing Forum: Tip of the Day
WINDOWWARE—Wilson Windowware
WINDSURFING—Sailing Forum
WINE—Food & Drink Network
WINERIES—Food & Drink Network
WINERY—Food & Drink Network
WINNER—AOL Contest Area
WINNER'S CIRCLE—ABC Track
WINSOCK—Winsock Central [*WAOL only*]
WIRED—Wired Magazine

Chapter 6 Keywords from A to Z

WIRELESS—Wireless Communication
WISE GUYS—Hecklers Online
WIXT TV—ABC Online: WIXT-TV in Syracuse, NY
WIZARD—Wizard World
WIZARD WORLD—Wizard World
WJBF TV—ABC Online: WJBF-TV in Augusta, GA
WJCL TV—ABC Online: WJCL-TV in Savannah, GA
WKBW TV—ABC Online: WKBW-TV in Buffalo, NY
WKRC TV—ABC Online: WKRC-TV in Cincinnati, OH
WKRN TV—ABC Online: WKRN-TV in Nashville, TN
WLOS TV—ABC Online: WLOS-TV in Asheville, NC
WLOX TV—ABC Online: WLOX-TV in Biloxi, MS
WLS—WLS Chicago
WMBB TV—ABC Online: WMBB-TV in Panama, FL
WMDT TV—ABC Online: WMDT-TV in Salisbury, MD
WMUR TV—ABC Online: WMUR-TV in Manchester, NH
WNEP TV—ABC Online: WNEP-TV in Scranton/Wilkes-Barre, PA
WOKR TV—ABC Online: WOKR-TV in Rochester, NY
WOLFF BOOKS—Internet Connection Store
WOLO TV—ABC Online: WOLO-TV in Columbia, SC
WOMAN—Woman's Day Online
WOMAN BOARDS—Women's Interests: Message Boards
WOMAN COLLECTIONS—Women's Interests: Arts and Letters
WOMAN NEWS—Women's Interests: News
WOMAN VOICES—Women's Interests: Organizations
WOMAN'S DAY—Woman's Day Online
WOMANS DAY—Woman's Day Online
WOMEN—Women's Interests
WOMEN CLASS—Women's Interests: Educational Opportunities
WOMEN MAIN—Women's Interests
WOMEN ONLY—Consumer Reports Complete Drug Reference Search
WOMEN ROUND—Women's Interests: Community
WOMEN SPOTLIGHT—Women's Interests
WOMEN WEB—Women's Interests: Web Sites
WOMEN'S HEALTH—Women's Health Forum
WOMEN'S HEALTH WEB—Women's Health Internet Sites

Chapter 6 Keywords from A to Z

WOMENS—Women's Interests

WOMENS HEALTH—Women's Health Forum

WOMENS SPACE—Gay & Lesbian Community Forum: Women's Space

WOMENS SPORTS—Women's Sports World

WOOD—American Woodworker

WOODSTOCK—Woodstock Online

WOODWORKER—American Woodworker

WOODWORKING—American Woodworker

WORD HISTORIES—Word Histories

WORD PERFECT—Word Perfect Support Center

WORD PROCESSING—Mac Desktop Publishing/WP Forum

WORKING—Working Software

WORKOUTS—Longevity Magazine Online

WORKSHOP—Family Computing Forum: Life's Workshop

WORLD—The World

WORLD BELIEFS—World Beliefs

WORLD CRISIS—World Crisis Network

WORLD NEWS—U.S. & World News Area

WORLD WIDE WEB—World Wide Web

WORLDVIEW—Fodor's Worldview

WORRY—CyberJustice's Worry Free Zone

WORTH—Worth Magazine Online

WORTH MAGAZINE—Worth Magazine Online

WORTH ONLINE—Worth Magazine Online

WORTH PORTFOLIO—Worth Magazine Online Portfolio

WOTV TV—ABC Online: WOTV-TV in Battle Creek, MI

WP MAG—WordPerfect Magazine

WPBF TV—ABC Online: WPBF-TV in West Palm Beach, FL

WPDE TV—ABC Online: WPDE-TV in Myrtle Beach, SC

WPTA TV—ABC Online: WPTA-TV in Fort Wayne, IN

WQAD TV—ABC Online: WQAD-TV in Moline, IL

WQOW TV—ABC Online: WQOW-TV in Eau Claire, WI

WRD—Christianity Online: Word Publishing

WRESTLING—World Wrestling Federation

WRITE—Writer's Club Chat Rooms

WRITE TO OUR STAFF—Questions*

WRITE TO STAFF—Questions*

Chapter 6 Keywords from A to Z

WRITER—Writer's Club
WRITER'S—Writer's Club
WRITER'S CLUB—Writer's Club
WRITERS—Writer's Club
WRITERS CLUB—Writer's Club
WRITERS CLUB CHAT—Writer's Club: Chat Rooms
WRITING—Writer's Club
WRONG—The McLaughlin Group
WRONG!—The McLaughlin Group
WRTV TV—ABC Online: WRTV in Indianapolis, IN
WS—Gay & Lesbian Community Forum: Women's Space
WSB TV—ABC Online: WSB-TV in Atlanta, GA
WSF—Women's Sports World
WSJV TV—ABC Online: WSJV-TV in South Bend, IN
WSW—Wall Street Words
WSYX TV—ABC Online: WSYX-TV in Columbus, OH
WTEN TV—ABC Online: WTEN-TV in Albany, NY
WTNH TV—ABC Online: WTNH-TV in Nashville, TN
WTOK TV—ABC Online: WTOK-TV in Meridan, MS
WTVC TV—ABC Online: WTVC-TV in Chattanooga, TN
WTVQ TV—ABC Online: WTVQ-TV in Lexington, KY
WVII TV—ABC Online: WVII-TV in Bangor, ME
WWF—World Wrestling Federation
WWIR—Washington Week in Review Magazine
WWN—Weekly World News
WWOS—ABC Online: Wide World of Sports
WWW—World Wide Web
WWWARDROBE—Style Channel
WXOW TV—ABC Online: WXOW-TV in LaCrescent, MN
WZZM TV—ABC Online: WZZM-TV in Grand Rapids, MI
X—Multimedia World Online
X FILES—X Files Forums
X FILES SIM—X Files Simulator Forum
XAOS—Xaos Tools
XAOS TOOLS—Xaos Tools
XCMD—XCMD Special Interest Group
XCMD SIG—XCMD Special Interest Group
XCON—Christianity Online: Contest

Chapter 6 Keywords from A to Z

XF FRIDAYS—X Files Fridays
XOL—Christianity Online
XWORDS—Crossword America
YACHTING—Sailing Forum
YACHTS—Boating Online
YANKEES—Major League Baseball Team: New York Yankees
YANKS—Major League Baseball Team: New York Yankees
YAVIASA—The Hub: You Are Very Intelligent and Somewhat Artsy
YB—Your Business
YBERSMITH—CyberSmith
YC—Your Church Magazine
YEAR—1995: The Year in Review
YEAR IN REVIEW—1995: The Year in Review
YELLOW PAGES—Business Yellow Pages
YIR—1995: The Year in Review
YM—Real Life Financial Tips
YMB—Your Mind & Body Online
YOUNG CHEFS—Young Chefs
YOUNGNESS—Longevity Magazine Online
YOUR BIZ—Your Business
YOUR BUSINESS—Your Business
YOUR BUSINESS LUNCH—Your Business Lunch
YOUR CHOICE—ABC News-On-Demand
YOUR CHURCH—Your Church Magazine
YOUR MIND AND BODY—Your Mind & Body Online
YOUR MIND & BODY—Your Mind & Body Online
YOUR MOMMA—Computing Print & Broadcast
YOUR MONEY—Your Money Area
YOUR MONEY—Real Life Financial Tips
YOUR SPORTS—NESN: New England Outdoors
YOUR TOONS—Cartoon collection
YOUTH SERVICE AMERICA—SERVEnet
YOUTHFUL—Longevity Magazine Online
YOUTHNET—National Network for Youth
YOYO—Yoyodyne Entertainment
YOYO GAMES—Yoyodyne Entertainment: Games
YOYODYNE—Yoyodyne Entertainment
YSA—SERVEnet

Chapter 6 Keywords from A to Z

YUBBA—Today's Events in AOL Live!
YUGOSLAVIA—Balkan Operation Joint Endeavor
Z—The Health Zone
<Z>—The Health Zone
ZAGAT—Zagat Restaurant/Hotel/Resort/Spa Surveys
ZAGATS—Zagat Restaurant/Hotel/Resort/Spa Surveys
ZD—ZDNet
ZDNET—ZDNet
ZEDCOR—Zedcor, Inc.
ZELOS—Zelos
ZEN—ChipNet Online: ZENtertainment
ZENTERTAINMENT—ChipNet Online: ZENtertainment
ZEOS—Zeos International Ltd.
ZIFF—ZDNet
ZIMA—Zima
ZIMA TALK—Zima Events
ZIP CODE—Zip Code Directory [*WAOL 2.5 only*]
ZIP CODE DIRECTORY—Zip Code Directory [*WAOL 2.5 only*]
ZIP CODES—Zip Code Directory [*WAOL 2.5 only*]
ZODIAC—Astronet
ZON—Zondervan Publishing House
ZONDERVAN—Zondervan Publishing House
ZONE—Your Business
ZONED—The Health Zone
ZONIE—The Health Zone
ZOOM TELEPHONICS—Zoom Telephonics
ZP—Zondervan Publishing House

Chapter 7
Keywords by Channel and Topic

If you are looking for related areas, or just want to browse, this is the place to be. The following keyword list is organized by channel (America Online department) and, hence, topic. Each keyword is sorted alphabetically under its channel heading. The easiest or most intuitive keyword is given first, followed by the area name and its alternative keywords in parentheses. The channels and topics are as follows: General, C! Computers & Software, Digital Cities, Entertainment, Games, Health & Fitness, The Hub, International, Internet Connection, Kids Only, Learning & Culture, Life Styles & Interests, Marketplace, Music Space, Newsstand, People Connection, Personal Finance, Reference Desk, Sports, Style, Today's News, Travel, Member Services (the free area), and Miscellaneous.

General Keywords

AOL GIFT—AOL Gift Certificates (GIFT CERTIFICATE)

AOLSEWHERE—AOLsewhere (AWAY, AWAY FROM HOME)

BEST OF AOL—Best of America Online Showcase (25 REASONS, UNIQUE)

BUDDY—Buddy Lists (BL, BUDDIES, BUDDY LIST, BUDDY LISTS, BUDDY MAIN)

BUDDY VIEW—Buddy View

CLOCK—Time of day and length of time online (ONLINE CLOCK)

FAX—Fax/Paper Mail (PAPER MAIL, US MAIL)

FIND—Find it on AOL!

General Keywords (continued)

GUIDE PAGER—Guide Pager (GUIDE PAGE)

HOT—What's Hot This Month Showcase (WHATEVER, WHATS HOT)

HOT TODAY—What's Hot Today!

KEYWORDS—Keyword List Area (KEYWORD, KEYWORD LIST)

MEMBERS—Member Directory (DIRECTORY, MEMBER DIRECTORY)

MARKETING PREFS—Marketing Prefs (MARKETING PREFERENCES)

MP—Multimedia Preferences (MULTIMEDIA PREFS)

MULTIMEDIA PREFS—Multimedia Preferences

NEW—New Features & Services

ORIENTATION—Orientation Express [*New Member Area*] (DISCOVER, DISCOVER America Online, DISCOVER AOL, NEWBIE, NEW MEMBER, NEW MEMBERS, ORIENTATION, ORIENTATION EXPRESS)

PERSONAL CHOICES—Personal Choices Area

PRESS—AOL Press Release Library (PRESS RELEASE)

PROFILE—Edit your member profile (CHANGE PROFILE, EDIT PROFILE, MEMBER PROFILE)

SHORTHAND—Online Shorthand (SHORTHANDS)

SOFTWARE SHOP—AOL Software Shop (AOL SOFTWARE SHOP, SOFT SHOP)

TOP TIPS—Top Tips for AOL (BEST TIPS, HOW TO, NAVIGATE, TOP TIPS)

TOUR—AOL Highlights Tour (AOL HIGHLIGHTS)

C! Computers & Software

C!—Computers & Software Channel (C&S, COMPUTER, COMPUTER FORUM, COMPUTING, COMPUTING AND SOFTWARE, COMPUTING FORUMS, FORUM, FORUMS, PC FORUMS, PC SECURITY, SIFS, SIGS, TECHNOLOGY)

@ROTUNDA—Rotunda Auditorium

ROTUNDA—Rotunda Forum Auditorium (FORUMAUD, FORUMAUDITORIUM, FORUMROT, STUMP)

Chapter 7 Keywords by Channel and Topic

COMPUTING DEPT—Computing & Software (Old Style)

FILE SEARCH—Search database of files (QUICK FIND, QUICK FINDER)

FIRST LOOK—First Look at Hot New Products (FIRST)

NPS—New Product Showcase (IIN, NETWORKS EXPO, NEW PRODUCT SHOWCASE, REDGATE)

SCHEDULE—What's Hot in Computing (CALENDAR, TITF)

SOFTWARE CENTER—Software Center (DOWNLOAD, DOWNLOADING, FILE, FILES, LIBRARIES, LIBS, SEARCH, SOFTWARE, SOFTWARE DIRECTORY, SOFTWARE LIBRARY, SOFTWARE LIBRARIES, SOFTWARE HELP)

General Interest Areas in Computers & Software

CALENDAR—What's Hot in Computing (SCHEDULE, TITF)

COBB—The Cobb Group Online (COBB GROUP)

COMPUKIDS—Compukids

COMPUTER AMERICA—Craig Crossman's Computer America (CRAIG CROSSMAN, CROSSMAN)

COMPUTER BOWL—Computer Bowl

COMPUTING NEWS—Computing News

CPB—Computing Print & Broadcast (CP&B, VIENNA, YOUR MOMMA)

FC—Family Computing Forum (FCF)

    COMPUTING LIFESTYLES—Family Computing Forum: Lifestyles & Computing

    CONTEST CENTRAL—Family Computing Forum: Contest Central

    FAMILY COMPUTING—Family Computing Resource Center

    FAMILY ALBUM—Family Computing Forum: The Family Room (FAMILY ROOM)

    FAMILY GAMES—Family Computing Forum: Family Games

    FAMILY NEWS—Family Computing Forum: News & Reviews (NEWS & REVIEWS, PRODUCT REVIEWS, REVIEWS)

    FAMILY ROOM—Family Computing Forum: Family Room (FAMILY ALBUM)

CHAPTER 7 KEYWORDS BY CHANNEL AND TOPIC

C! Computers & Software (continued)

FC TIPS—Family Computing Forum: Tip of the Day (AOL TIPS, MAC TIPS, TIP, WINDOWS TIPS)

MAX AOL—Family Computing Forum: Maximum AOL (AOL MAX, CRC, FAMILY RESOURCE, FCRC, MAXIMUM AOL)

SCRAPBOOK—Member Scrapbook

WORKSHOP—Family Computing Forum: Life's Workshop

HALL OF FAME—Downloading Hall of Fame (HOF)

KOMANDO—Kim Komando's Komputer Clinic (COMMANDO, KOMANDO CLINIC, KOMPUTER TUTOR, MR SCIENCE)

NEWSBYTES—Newsbytes (COMPUTER NEWS)

PDA—PDA/Palmtop Forum (EXPERTPAD, NEWTONBOOK, PALMTOP, PDA FORUM)

    PDA DEV—PDA Forum: Development Special Interest Group (PDA DEV SIG)

    PDA SHOP—PDA Forum: PDA Shop

PHOTODEX—Photodex

POSTCARDS—Virtual Postcard Center

SPRING—Computing Spring Fling

UGF—User Group Forum (AUG, USER GROUP, USER GROUPS)

UNIVERSE—UniverseCentral.Com (RALPH Z, RALPH ZERBONIA, UNIVERSE CENTRAL)

WEB ART—Web Page Clip Art Creation Center

WIRELESS—Wireless Communication

ZDNET—ZDNet (ZD, ZIFF)

Macintosh Forums in Computers & Software

MAC—Apple/Macintosh Forums (APPLE, MAC COMPUTING, MACINTOSH)

MAC HOT—What's Hot in Mac Computing (HOT MAC)

MAC HELP—Help Desk (ABF, AOL BEGINNERS, BEGINNER, BEGINNERS, GETTING STARTED, GETTING STARTED FORUM, HELP DESK, STARTER)

Chapter 7 Keywords by Channel and Topic

MAC SOFTWARE—Mac Software Center (MAC DOWNLOADING, MAC LIBRARIES, MAC SOFTWARE CENTER)

MAC CONFERENCE—Mac Computing Conference Center

MAC KIDS—Mac Kids World

MAC NEWS—Mac Computing News & Newsletters

MAC VIRUS—Mac Virus Information Center

APPLE UPDATE—Apple System 7.5 Update (MOS UPDATE)

MBS—Macintosh Business & Home Office Forum (4DDA ENTRY, MAC BUSINESS, APPLICATIONS, APPLICATIONS FORUM, APPS, BUSINESS FORUM, PRODUCTIVITY, PRODUCTIVITY FORUM)

MCM—Mac Communications and Networking Forum (MAC COMMUNICATION, MAC COMMUNICATIONS, MAC TELECOM, MAC TELECOMM, MTC)

DWP—Desktop & Web Publishing (MAC DESKTOP, MAC DTP, MAC WORLD PROCESSING, MDP, DTP, DESKTOP PUBLISHING, WORD PROCESSING)

MDV—Developers Forum (MAC DEVELOPMENT, PROGRAMMING, MAC PROGRAMMING, ASSEMBLY, BASIC, C, DEV, DEVELOPER, DEVELOPMENT, DEVELOPMENT FORUM)

MED—Mac Education & Technology Forum (MAC EDUCATION)

MGM—Games & Entertainment (MAC GAME, MAC GAMES, GAMES FORUM, ADVENTURE, ARCADE, SIMULATOR)

MGR—Graphic Arts & CAD Forum (MAC ART, MAC GRAPHICS, ANIMATION, ART, CAD, GRAPHICS, GRAPHIC ARTS, GRAPHICS FORUM)

MHC—HyperCard & Scripting Forum (MAC HYPERCARD, HYPERCARD)

MHW—Hardware (MAC HARDWARE, HARDWARE, HARDWARE FORUM, SILICON)

MMM—Mac Desktop Video & Multimedia Forum (MAC MULTIMEDIA, MVD, QUICKTIME)

MMS—Music & Sound Forum (MAC MUSIC, MAC SOUND, MUSIC & SOUND, MUSIC AND SOUND FORUM, MUSIC FORUM, MIDI, QMMS)

MOS—Operating Systems Forum (SYSTEM 7, MAC O/S, MAC OS, MAC OPERATING SYSTEMS, SYSTEM 7.0, SYSTEM 7.1, SYSTEM 71)

MUT—Utilities Forum (MVT, MAC UTILITIES)

C! Computers & Software (continued)

MUT AWARDS—Mac Shareware Awards (MUT AWARD)

MAC ESSENTIALS—Macintosh Essential Utilities

PC Forums in Computers & Software

HOT PC—What's Hot in PC Computing (PC FORUMS HOT, PC HOT)

PC SOFTWARE—PC Software Center

DOS 6—MS-DOS 6.0 Resource Center (DOS 60, MS DOS 6, MS DOS 60)

OS2—OS/2 Forum (IBM OS2, OS TWO)

PAP—Applications Forum (PC APS, PC APPLICATIONS, PC APPLICATIONS FORUM, APPLICATIONS, APPLICATIONS FORUM, APPS, BUSINESS FORUM, PRODUCTIVITY, PRODUCTIVITY FORUM)

COMPUKIDS—PC Applications: Kids on Computers

PDV—Development Forum (PC DEV, PC DEVELOPMENT, PC DEVELOPMENT)

PGM—Games Forum (PC GAMES, GAMES FORUM, PC GAMES FORUM, ADVENTURE, ARCADE, SIMULATOR)

PGR—Graphics Forum (PC GRAPHICS, ANIMATION, PC ANIMATION, ART, CAD, GRAPHICS, GRAPHIC ARTS, GRAPHICS FORUM, PC GRAPHICS FORUM)

PHW—Hardware Forum (PC HARDWARE, HARDWARE, HARDWARE FORUM, PC HARDWARE FORUM)

PMM—Multimedia Forum (MM)

VIDEO ZONE—PC Multimedia's Video

PMU—Music and Sound Forum (PCMU, PCMUSIC, MIDI, MUSIC & SOUND, MUSIC AND SOUND FORUM, MUSIC FORUM, PC MUSIC AND SOUND FORUM, PC MUSIC FORUM, PC SOUND, PC SOUND FORUM)

PTC—Telecom/Networking Forum (PCM, PC TELECOM, PC TELECOM FORUM, COMMUNICATIONS, NETWORKING, NETWORKING FORUM, TELECOM, TELECOM FORUM, TELECOMMUNICATIONS)

TUNE UP—Tune Up Your PC (AUTOEXEC, CONFIG, TUNE UP YOUR PC)

Chapter 7 Keywords by Channel and Topic

WIN—Windows Forum (WIN 95, WIN FORUM, WINDOWS 95, WINDOWS FORUM)

WIN NT—Windows NT Resource Center (WINDOWS NT)

Special Interest Groups in Computers & Software

3D—3D Forum (3-D, 3-D RENDERING, 3D-RENDERING, 3D RENDERING, POV, RAYTRACE, RENDERING)

MADA—MacApp Developers Association

VB—Visual Basic Area (VISUAL BASIC)

WIN 500—Windows Shareware 500 (WINDOWS 500)

WINDOWS—Windows Services

AD SIG—Advertising Special Interest Group (ADVERTISING, ADVERTISING SIG)

ADOBE—Adobe Center Menu (ADOBE PHOTOSHOP)

AECSIG—Architects, Engineers, and Construction Special Interest Group

AOP—Association of Online Professionals (ASSN ONLINE PROF)

APPLESCRIPT—AppleScript Special Interest Group

ARTISTS SPOTLIGHT—Artists' Spotlight (ARTIST'S SPOTLIGHT)

AUTODESK—Autodesk Resource Center

AWAKENED EYE—Awakened Eye Special Interest Group (AE, AWAKE EYE)

BBS—BBS Corner (BBS CORNER)

BCS—Boston Computer Society

BMUG—Berkeley Macintosh Users Group

CAD—CAD Resource Center (AUTOCAD)

COREL—Corel Special Interest Group (CORELDRAW)

CWUG—ClarisWorks User Group

DATABASE—Database Support Special Interest Group (DATABASES)

DESIGN SIG—Design Special Interest Group (DESIGNER, GRAPHIC DESIGN)

Chapter 7 Keywords by Channel and Topic

C! Computers & Software (continued)

DESKMATE—DeskMate (DES, PC DESKMATE, PC DM)

DIGITAL IMAGING—Digital Imaging Resource Center (SCANNERS)

DVORAK—Software Hardtalk with John C. Dvorak (SOFTWARE HARDTALK)

ETEXT—PDA's Palmtop Paperbacks! (EZINE)

FILEMAKER—The Filemaker Pro Resource Center

FREELANCE—Freelance Artists Special Interest Group

GROUPWARE—GroupWare Special Interest Group

IBM—IBM Forum

ILLUSTRATOR—Mac Graphics Illustrator Special Interest Group

IMAGING—Advanced Color Imaging Forum (COLOR IMAGING, PA)

ISDN—ISDN Special Interest Group

KARROS—Eric Karros Kronikles

MACHACK—MacHack (HACK, HACKER)

MACSCITECH—MacSciTech Special Interest Group

MACTIVITY—Mactivity Forum

MEDIA CENTER—Library Media Center Special Interest Group

MMS TOOL—Sound & Midi Resource Center

MS WORKS—Microsoft Works Resource Center

MULTIMEDIA—Multimedia Menu

NAQP—National Association of Quick Printers

NEWTON—Newton Resource Center (MESSAGE PAD)

NOMADIC—Nomadic Computing Discussion Special Interest Group

PALM—Palm Computing (PALM COMPUTING)

PC TOOL—PC Virtual Toolbox

PHOTOSHOP—Photoshop Special Interest Group (PHOTOSHOP SIG)

PLACES—P.L.A.C.E.S. Interest Group

POWERBOOK—PowerBook Resource Center (LAPTOP, NOTEBOOK)

Chapter 7 Keywords by Channel and Topic

POWERMAC—PowerMac Resource Center (POWER PC)

PRESCHOOL—Preschool/Early Childhood Special Interest Group (EARLY ED, EARLY EDUCATION)

PU—Programmer University (PROGRAMMER UNIVERSITY)

STAFF—Staff Development Special Interest Group (STAFF DEVELOPMENT)

SUPERCARD—SuperCard Scripting Center

VIDEO SIG—Video Special Interest Group

VIEWER—Viewer Resource Center (PLAYER, PLAYERS, VIEWERS)

VR—Virtual Reality Resource Center (VIRTUAL REALITY)

VIRUS—Virus Information Center Special Interest Group

WALLPAPER—Windows Wallpaper & Paint Center

WEB PUB—Web Publishing Special Interest Group (WEB PUBLISH, WEB PUBLISHING)

WIN NEWS—Windows News

XCMD—XCMD Special Interest Group (XCMD SIG)

Computing Company Connection

CCC—Computing Company Connection (CC, COMPANIES, HARDWARE COMPANIES, IC, INDUSTRY, INDUSTRY CONNECTION, PUBLISHERS, SOFTWARE COMPANIES, SOFTWARE PUBLISHERS)

IC HILITES—IC Hilites

3DO—The 3DO Company (COMPANY 3DO, THREEDO)

7TH—Seventh Level Software (SEVENTH)

AATRIX—Aatrix Software, Inc.

ABBATE VIDEO—Abbate Video (VIDEO TOOLKIT)

ACCESS SOFTWARE—Access Software (LINKS)

ACCOLADE—Accolade, Inc.

ACER—Acer America Corporation

ACTIVISION—Activision

ADOBE—Adobe Systems, Inc. (ALDUS)

ADVANCED—Advanced Software, Inc.

ADVSOFT—Advisor Software

C! Computers & Software (continued)

AFFINITY—Affinity Microsystems (AFFINIFILE, AUTOMATION, AUTOMATE, MACRO, MACROS, SCRIPT, SCRIPTING, SCRIPTS TEMPO, TEMPO II, TEMPO II PLUS)

AFTEREFFECTS—AfterEffects (COSA)

ALADDIN—Aladdin Systems, Inc. (STUFFIT)

ALR—Advanced Logic Research (ADVANCED LOGIC)

ALTSYS—Altsys Corporation

ALYSIS—Alysis Software (SUPERDISK)

AMBROSIA—Ambrosia Software

ANIMATED SOFTWARE—Animated Software

ANOTHER CO—Another Company

APOGEE—Apogee/3D Realms Entertainment (3D REALMS)

APPLE COMPUTER—Apple Computer

APPLEBIZ—Apple Business Consortium

ARGOSY—Argosy

ARIEL—Ariel Publishing

ARSENAL—Arsenal Commmunications

ARTEMIS—Artemis Software

ARTICULATE—Articulate Systems (ASI)

ARTIFICE—Artifice, Inc.

ASC TECH—Alpha Software Corporation (ASC TS)

AST—AST Support Forum

ASYMETRIX—Asymetrix Corporation

AT ONCE—atOnce Software

AT&T—AT&T (ATT, ATT WIRELESS)

ATLUS—Atlus Software

AVID—Avid Technology (AVID DTV)

AVOCAT—Avocat Systems (AVOCAT SYSTEMS)

BASELINE—Baseline Publishing

BASEVIEW—Baseview Products, Inc.

BEESOFT—BeeSoft (BEE)

Chapter 7 Keywords by Channel and Topic

BERKELEY—Berkeley Systems (BERK SYS, BERK SYS WIN)

BETHESDA—Bethesda Softworks, Inc. (BETHESDA SOFTWORKS, BETHSEDA)

BIT JUGGLERS—Bit Jugglers

BLIZZARD ENT—Blizzard Entertainment

BLOC DEVELOPMENT—TIGERDirect, Inc.

BLUE RIBBON—Blue RIbbon Soundworks

BOWERS—Bowers Development (APP MAKER)

BPS SOFTWARE—BPS Software (ADDONS)

BRAINSTORM—Brainstorm Products

BRODERBUND—Brøderbund

BUNGIE—Bungie Software

BYTE BY BYTE—Byte By Byte Corporation

BYTEWORKS—ByteWorks (BYTE)

CALLISTO—Callisto Corporation

CAPSTONE—Capstone Software

CARDINAL—Cardinal Technologies, Inc.

CASADY—Casady & Greene

CE SOFTWARE—CE Software

CH PRODUCTS—CH Products

CLARIS—Claris

COMMON GROUND—Common Ground Software (NO HANDS, NO HANDS SOFTWARE)

COMPAQ—Compaq

COMPUADD—CompuAdd

CONNECTIX—Connectix (RAM DOUBLER)

COOPER—JLCooper Electronics

CORBIS—Corbis Media (CORBIS MEDIA)

CPI—Computer Peripherals, Inc. (COMPUTER PERIPHERALS)

CRYSTAL—Crystal Dynamics

DATAPAK—DataPak Software (DATAPACK)

DATAWATCH—Datawatch (VIREX)

DAVIDSON—Davidson & Associates

C! Computers & Software (continued)

DAYNA—Dayna Communications

DAYSTAR—Daystar Digital

DAYTIMER—DayTimer Technologies

DEC—Digital Equipment Corporation

DELL—Dell Computer Corporation

DELTA—Delta Tao (DELTA TAO)

DELTA POINT—Delta Point

DENEBA—Deneba Software (CANVAS)

DI—Disney Interactive (DISNEY INTERACTIVE, DISNEY SOFT, DISNEY SOFTWARE)

DIAL—Dial/Data (DD)

DIAMOND—Diamond Computer Systems (DIAMOND COMPUTERS)

DIGITAL—Digital menu

DIGITAL ECLIPSE—Digital Eclipse

DIGITAL TECH—Digital Technologies

DJ—Don Johnston, Inc. (DON JOHNSTON)

DOMARK—Domark Software, Inc.

DUBLCLICK—Dubl-Click Software

DYNAWARE—Dynaware USA (DYNAWARE USA)

EDMARK—Edmark Technologies (KID DESK, PEN PAL)

ELECTRIC—Electric Image (ELECTRIC IMAGE)

EMIGRE—Emigre Fonts

EPSCONVERTER—Art Age Software

EQUIS—Equis International

EXPERT—Expert Software, Inc. (EXPERT SOFT)

EXTENSIS—Extensis Corporation

FARALLON—Farallon

FOCUS—Focus Enhancements (FOCUS ENHANCEMENTS, LAPIS)

FONTBANK—FontBank

FORMZ—auto*des*sys, Inc.

CHAPTER 7 KEYWORDS BY CHANNEL AND TOPIC

FORTE—Forte Technologies

FORTNER—Fortner Research (FORTRAN, LANGUAGE SYS)

FRACTAL—Fractal Design (FRACTAL DESIGN)

FRANCE & ASSOCIATES—France & Associates

FRANKLIN—Franklin Quest

FULLWRITE—FullWrite (AKIMBO)

FUTURE LABS—Future Labs, Inc. (TALK SHOW)

GALACTICOMM—Galacticomm

GAMETEK—Gametek

GATEWAY—Gateway 2000, Inc. (GATEWAY 2000, MOO)

GCC—GCC Technologies

GDT—GDT Softworks, Inc. (GDT SOFTWORKS)

GENERAL MAGIC—General Magic

GEO SDK—Geoworks Development

GEOWORKS—Geoworks

GIF CONVERTER—GIF Converter

GLOBAL VILLAGE—Global Village Communication (GLOBAL, TELEPORT)

GRAPHIC—Graphic Simulations (GRAPH SIM, GRAPHIC SIMULATIONS, GSC, SIMULATIONS)

GRAPHISOFT—Graphisoft

GRAPHSOFT—Graphsoft, Inc. (BLUEPRINT, MINICAD)

GRAVIS—Advanced Gravis (ADVANCED GRAVIS)

GRYPHON—Gryphon Software (GRYPHON SOFTWARE, MORPH)

GSS—Global Software Suport

HDC—hDC Corporation (HDC CORPORATION)

HP—Hewlett-Packard

    HP FAX—Hewlett-Packard: Fax Products

    HP FILES—Hewlett-Packard: Support Information Files

    HP HOME—Hewlett-Packard: Home Products Information

    HP MULTI—Hewlett-Packard: Multifunction Products

    HP PLOT—Hewlett-Packard: Plotter Products

    HP SCAN—Hewlett-Packard: Scanner Products

CHAPTER 7 KEYWORDS BY CHANNEL AND TOPIC

C! Computers & Software (continued)

    HP SCSI—Hewlett-Packard: SCSI Products

    HP SERVER—Hewlett-Packard: Server Products

    HP STORE—Hewlett-Packard: Information Storage Products

    HP VECTRA—Hewlett-Packard: Vectra Products

    HP PRN—Hewlett-Packard: Printer Products

    OMNI GO—Hewlett-Packard Omni Go 100

IBVA—IBVA Technologies (IBVA TECH)

INLINE—Inline Design (INLINE SOFTWARE)

INSIGNIA—Insignia Solutions (INSIGNIA SOLUTION)

INTEL—Intel Corporation (CONNECTION, INTEL INSIDE, PENTIUM, P6)

INTERCON—InterCon Systems Corporation

INTERPLAY—Interplay

INTREK—InTrek

INTUIT—Intuit, Inc.

IOMEGA—Iomega Corporation

ISIS—ISIS International (ISIS INTERNATIONAL)

ISLAND—Island Graphics Corporation (ISLAND GRAPHICS)

JASC—JASC, Inc. (PSP)

JL COOPER—JL Cooper Electronics

JPEGVIEW—JPEGView

KASAN—Kasanjian Research (KR, KASANJIAN)

KENSINGTON—Kensington Microwave, Ltd.

KENT MARSH—Kent*Marsh

KURZWEIL—Kurzweil Music Systems

LAWRENCE—Lawrence Productions

LEADER—Leader Technologies (LEADER TECH, TECHNOLOGIES)

LEADING EDGE—Leading Edge

LIND—Lind Portable Power

LINKSWARE—LinksWare, Inc.

Chapter 7 Keywords by Channel and Topic

LINN SOFT—Linn Software (LINN SOFTWARE)

LIVE PICTURE—Live Picture, Inc.

LOGICODE—Logicode Technology, Inc.

LUCAS—LucasArts Games (LUCAS ARTS)

MACROMEDIA—MacroMedia, Inc. (MACROMIND)

MAGIC LINK—Sony Magic Link (SML, SONY)

MAINSTAY—Mainstay

MANHATTAN GRAPHICS—Manhattan Graphics (RSG)

MARTINSEN—Martinsen's Software

MAXIS—Maxis

MAXTECH—MaxTech Corporation (GVC)

MCAFEE—McAfee Associates

MECC—MECC (TRAILHEADS)

METATOOLS—MetaTools, Inc. (BRYCE, HSC, HSC SOFTWARE, KPT, KPT BRYCE)

METROWERKS—Metrowerks

METZ—Metz

METRICOM—Metricom, Inc. (RICOCHET)

MGX—Micrografx, Inc. (MICROGRAFX)

MICRO J—Micro J Systems, Inc.

MICROFRONTIER—MicroFrontier, Ltd.

MICROMAT—MicroMat Computer Systems

MICROPROSE—MicroProse

MICROSEEDS—Microseeds Publishing, Inc.

MINDSCAPE—Mindscape (SOFTWARE TOOLWORKS, STW TOOLWORKS)

MICROSOFT—Microsoft Resource Center (MS SUPPORT)

MIRROR—Mirror Technologies

MOBILEMEDIA—MobileMedia (PCS)

MORGAN DAVIS—Morgan Davis Group

MOTOROLA—Motorola (ENVOY, MARCO)

MOTU—Mark of the Unicorn

MSA—Management Science Associates

Chapter 7 Keywords by Channel and Topic

C! Computers & Software (continued)

MSKB—Microsoft Knowledge Base (KNOWLEDGE BASE)

MSTATION—Bentley Systems, Inc.

MUSTANG—Mustang Software (MUSTANG SOFTWARE, QMODEM, WILDCAT, WILDCAT BBS)

MYOB—Best! Ware

NCT—Next Century Technologies

NEC—NEC Technologies (NEC TECH)

NEOLOGIC—NeoLogic

NETSCAPE—Netscape (TO NETSCAPE)

NEW TEK—New Tek (LIGHT WAVE, VIDEO TOASTER)

NEW WORLD—New World Computing

NIKON—Nikon Electronic Imaging

NILES—Niles and Associates (ENDNOTE)

NISUS—Nisus Software

NOVELL—Novell Desktop Systems (DIGITAL RESEARCH, DIGITAL RESEARCH INC, DRI)

NOW—Now Software

OBJECT FACTORY—Object Factory

OLDUVAI—Olduvai Software, Inc.

ON—ON Technology

ONYX—Onyx Technology

OPCODE—Opcode Systems, Inc. (OPCODE SYSTEMS)

OPTIMA—Optima Technology

OPTIMAS—OPTIMAS Corporation (BIOSCAN)

OPTIMAGE—Philips Media OptImage

ORIGIN—Origin Systems (ORIGIN SYSTEMS)

PACEMARK—PaceMark Technologies, Inc.

PACKER—Packer Software

PARSONS—Parsons Technology

PASSPORT—Passport Designs

PC DATA—PC Data Forum

Chapter 7 Keywords by Channel and Topic

PC PC—Personal Computer Peripherals

PEACHPIT—The Macintosh Bible/Peachpit Forum (MAC BIBLE, MACINTOSH BIBLE)

PEACHTREE—Peachtree Software

PICTORIUS—Pictorius, Inc. (PEREGRINE, PROGRAPH, TGS)

PIERIAN—Piereian Spring Software (PIERIAN SP)

PIXEL—Pixel Resources

PKWARE—PKWare, Inc.

PPI—Practical Peripherals, Inc. (PRACTICAL PERIPHERALS)

PRAIRIE—Prairie Group (PRARIE SOFT)

PRINT ARTIST—Print Artist Special Interest Group (IA, INSTANT ARTIST, INSTANT ARTIST 1)

PROVUE—ProVUE Development

PSION—Psion

QQP—Quantum Quality Productions

QUALITAS—Qualitas

QUARK—Quark, Inc.

RADIUS—Radius, Inc. (SUPERMAC)

RASTEROPS—Truevision

RAY—Ray Dream (RAY DREAM)

REACTOR—Reactor

RESNOVA SOFTWARE—ResNova Software (RESNOVA)

ROGER WAGNER—Roger Wagner Publishing (HYPERSTUDIO, STUDIOWARE)

ROLAND—Roland Corporation U.S.

RYOBI—Ryobi

SERIUS—Serius

SHAREWARE SOLUTIONS—Shareware Solutions

SIERRA—Sierra On-Line (DYNAMIX)

SOFTARC—SoftArc

SOFTDISK—Softdisk Superstore (SUPERSTORE)

SOFTLOGIK—SoftLogik

SOFTWARE UNBOXED—Software Unboxed (BROADCAST SOFTWARE)

C! Computers & Software (continued)

SOPHCIR—Sophisticated Circuits

SPECULAR—Specular International

SPECTRUM—Spectrum HoloByte

SPIDER—Spider Island Software (SPIDER ISLAND)

SPRINT—Sprint Annual Report (Old)

SRS LABS—SRS Labs (3D AUDIO, 3D SOUND)

SSSI—SSSi

STAC—STAC Electronics

STARFISH—Starfish Software

STARPLAY—Starplay Productions

STF—STF Technologies (STF TECHNOLOGIES)

STRATA—Strata, Inc.

STRATEGIC—Strategic Simulations (SSI)

SUNBURST—Sunburst Communications

SURVIVOR—Survivor Software (SURVIVOR SOFTWARE)

SYNEX—Synex

SYMANTEC—Symantec (5TH GENERATION, CENTRAL, CENTRAL POINT, CPS, DELRINA, FIFTH, NORTON, PETER NORTON)

TACTIC—Tactic Software (NEW ERA, NUBASE)

TAKE 2—Take 2 Interactive Software (TAKE 2 INC)

TEAM CONCEPTS—Team Concepts (TEAM)

TECHWORKS—Technology Works (TECHNOLOGY WORKS)

TEKTRONIX—Tektronix

THREE SIXTY—Three-Sixty Software

THRUST MASTER—Thrustmaster

TI—Texas Instruments (TEXAS INSTRUMENTS)

TIGER—TIGERDirect, Inc. (TIGERDIRECT)

TIMESLIPS—Timeslips Corporation

TRENDSETTER—Trendsetter Software (TS)

TRIMBLE—Trimble Navigation, Ltd. (GPS)

TSENG—Tseng

Chapter 7 Keywords by Channel and Topic

TSP—Tom Snyder Productions (TOM SNYDER)

TURTLE BEACH—Turtle Beach Systems (TURTLE SYS)

TWI—Time Warner Interactive

USERLAND—Userland

VENTANA—Ventana Communications

VDISC—Videodiscovery

VERTISOFT—Vertisoft

VIDI—VIDI

VIEWPOINT—Viewpoint DataLabs

VILLAGE—Village Software (VILLAGE SOFTWARE)

VIRTUS—Virtus Corp. (WALKTHROUGH)

VISIONARY—Visionary Software

VISIONEER—Visioneer (PAPERPORT)

VOYAGER—The Voyager Company

VOYETRA—Voyetra Technologies

VRLI—Virtual Reality Labs, Inc.

VV—Vision Video (VISION VIDEO)

WESTERN DIGITAL—Western Digital (WDC)

WESTWOOD—Westwood Studios (WESTWOOD STUDIOS)

WILSON—Wilson Windoware (WINDOWWARE)

WORD PERFECT—Word Perfect Support Center

WORKING—Working Software

XAOS—Xaos Tools (XAOS TOOLS)

ZEDCOR—Zedcor, Inc.

ZELOS—Zelos

ZOOM TELEPHONICS—Zoom Telephonics

Digital Cities

DIGITAL CITY—Digital Cities (DCITY NATIONAL, DCN, DC NATIONAL, DIGC, DIG CITY, DIG CITY NATIONAL, DIG CITY USA, DIGITAL CITIES, DIGITAL CITY NATIONAL, DIGITAL CITY US, DIGITAL USA)

Chapter 7 Keywords by Channel and Topic

Digital Cities (continued)

ALASKA—Digital Cities: Alaska (ALASKA DC, ALASKA DCITY, ALASKA DIGC, ALASKA DIGITAL CITY, DC ALASKA, DCITY ALASKA, DIGC ALASKA, DIGITAL CITY ALASKA)

ALBANY—Digital Cities: Albany, New York (ALBANY DC, ALBANY DCITY, ALBANY DIGC, ALBANY DIGITAL CITY, ALBANY NY, DC ALBANY, DCITY ALBANY, DIGC ALBANY, DIGITAL CITY ALBANY)

ALBUQUERQUE—Digital Cities: Albuquerque/Santa Fe, New Mexico (DC ALBUQUERQUE, DCITY ALBUQUERQUE, DIGC ALBUQUERQUE, ALBUQUERQUE, ALBUQUERQUE DC, ALBUQUERQUE DCITY, ALBUQUERQUE DIGC)

ATLANTA—Digital City Atlanta, Georgia (ATLANTA DIGITAL CITY, DC ATLANTA, DC HOTLANTA, DIGC ATLANTA, DIGC HOTLANTA, DIGITAL CITY ATLANTA, HOTLANTA)

AUSTIN—Digital Cities: Austin, Texas (AUSTIN DC, AUSTIN DCITY, AUSTIN DIGC, AUSTIN DIGITAL CITY, AUSTIN TX, DC AUSTIN, DCITY AUSTIN, DIGC AUSTIN, DIGITAL CITY AUSTIN)

BAY CITY—Digital Cities: Bay City, Michigan (BAY CITY DC, BAY CITY DCITY, BAY CITY DIGC, BAY CITY MI, DC BAY CITY, DCITY BAY CITY, DIGC BAY CITY)

BRYAN—Digital Cities: Waco/Temple/Bryan, Texas (BRYAN DC, BRYAN DCITY, BRYAN DIGC, BRYAN DIGITAL CITY, BRYAN TX, DC BRYAN, DCITY BRYAN, DIGC BRYAN, DIGITAL CITY BRYAN)

BUFFALO—Digital Cities: Buffalo, New York (BUFFALO DC, BUFFALO DCITY, BUFFALO DIGC, BUFFALO DIGITAL CITY, BUFFALO NY, DC BUFFALO, DCITY BUFFALO, DIGC BUFFALO, DIGITAL CITY BUFFALO)

CITY WEB—City Web (DC WEB, WASHINGTON WEB)

DALLAS—Digital Cities: Dallas - Ft. Worth, Texas (DALLAS DIGC, DALLAS DIGITAL CITY, DC DALLAS, DIGC DALLAS, DIGITAL CITY DALLAS)

DAYTON—Digital Cities: Dayton, Ohio (DAYTON DC, DAYTON DCITY, DAYTON DIGC, DAYTON DIGITAL CITY, DAYTON OH, DC DAYTON, DCITY DAYTON, DIGC DAYTON, DIGITAL CITY DAYTON)

DC EVENT—Digital City: The Event Source

DC FUN—Digital City: Entertainment

DC MARKETPLACE—Digital City: Marketplace

DC NEWS—Digital City: News/Weather

DC PEOPLE—Digital City: People

Chapter 7 Keywords by Channel and Topic

DENVER—Digital Cities: Denver, Colorado (DC DENVER, DENVER DIGC, DENVER DIGITAL CITY, DIGC DENVER, DIGITAL CITY DENVER)

DETROIT—Digital Cities: Detroit, Michigan (DC DETROIT, DETROIT DIGC, DETROIT DIGITAL CITY, DIGC DETROIT, DIGITAL CITY DETROIT)

EL PASO—Digital Cities: El Paso, Texas (DC EL PASO, DCITY EL PASO, DIGC EL PASO, DIGITAL CITY EL PASO, EL PASO DC, EL PASO DCITY, EL PASO DIGC, EL PASO DIGITAL CITY, EL PASO TX)

EUGENE—Digital Cities: Eugene, Oregon (DC EUGENE, DCITY EUGENE, DIGC EUGENE, DIGITAL CITY EUGENE, EUGENE DC, EUGENE DCITY, EUGENE DIGC, EUGENE DIGITAL CITY, EUGENE OR)

FLINT—Digital Cities: Flint, Michigan (DC FLINT, DCITY FLINT, DIGC FLINT, DIGITAL CITY FLINT, FLINT DC, FLINT DCITY, FLINT DIGC, FLINT DIGITAL CITY, FLINT MI)

FRESNO—Digital Cities: Fresno/Visalia, California (DC FRESNO, DCITY FRESNO, DIGC FRESNO, DIGITAL CITY FRESNO, FRESNO CA, FRESNO DC, FRESNO DCITY, FRESNO DIGC, FRESNO DIGITAL CITY)

FT WORTH—Digital Cities: Dallas - Ft. Worth, Texas (DC FORT WORTH, DIGC FT WORTH, DIGITAL CITY FT WORTH, FT WORTH DIGC, FT WORTH DIGITAL CITY)

HOUSTON—Digital Cities: Houston, Texas (DC HOUSTON, DIGC HOUSTON, DIGITAL CITY HOUSTON, HOUSTON DIGC, HOUSTON DIGITAL CITY)

JOIN DIGITAL CITY—Register as a Digital Citizen (DC JOIN, DIGITAL CITY JOIN, JOIN DC)

LA COMM—Digital City Los Angeles: Community

LA PEOPLE—Digital City Los Angeles: People

LA TOUR—Digital City Los Angeles: City Tour

LA WEATHER—Digital City Los Angeles: News & Weather (LA NEWS)

LOS ANGELES—Digital Cities: Los Angeles (DC LA, DC LOS ANGELES, DIGC LA, DIGC LOS ANGELES, DIGITAL CITY LA, LA DIGC, LA DIGITAL CITY, LOS ANGELES DIGC)

MIAMI—Digital Cities: Miami - Ft Lauderdale, Florida (DC FT LAUDERDALE, DIGC FT LAUDERDALE, DIGC MIAMI, DIGITAL CITY MIAMI, FT LAUDERDALE DIGC, MIAMI DIGC, MIAMI DIGITAL CITY)

MIAMI COMM—Digital City Miami: Community

Digital Cities (continued)

MIAMI PEOPLE—Digital City Miami: People

MIAMI WEATHER—Digital City Miami: News & Weather (MIAMI NEWS)

MIDWEST—Digital Cities: Midwest (DC MIDWEST, DIGC MIDWEST, DIGITAL CITY MIDWEST, MIDWEST DIGC, MIDWEST DIGITAL CITY)

MINNEAPOLIS—Digital Cities: Minneapolis - St. Paul, Minnesota (DC MINNEAPOLIS, DIGC MINNEAPOLIS, MINNEAPOLIS DIGC)

NAPLES—Digital Cities: Ft. Myers/Naples, Florida (DC NAPLES, DCITY NAPLES, DIGC NAPLES, DIGITAL CITY NAPLES, NAPLES DC, NAPLES DCITY, NAPLES DIGC, NAPLES DIGITAL CITY, NAPLES FL)

NEW BEDFORD—Digital Cities: New Bedford, Massachusetts (DC NEW BEDFORD, DCITY NEW BEDFORD, DIGC NEW BEDFORD, NEW BEDFORD DC, NEW BEDFORD DCITY, NEW BEDFORD DIGC, NEW BEDFORD MA)

NEW ORLEANS—Digital Cities: New Orleans, Louisiana (DC NEW ORLEANS, DCITY NEW ORLEANS, DIGC NEW ORLEANS, NEW ORLEANS DC, NEW ORLEANS DCITY, NEW ORLEANS DIGC, NEW ORLEANS LA)

PHIL MARKET—Digital City Philadelphia: Classifieds

PHIL TOUR—Digital City Philadelphia: City Tour

PHILADELPHIA—Digital Cities: Philadelphia, Pennsylvania (DC PHILA, DC PHILADELPHIA, DC PHILLY, DIGC PHILA, DIGC PHILADELPHIA, DIGC PHILLY, DIG CITY PHILLY, DIGITAL CITY PHILLY, PHILA DIGITAL CITY, PHILADELPHIA DIGC, PHILLY DIG CITY, PHILLY DIGITAL CITY)

RENO—Digital Cities: Reno, Nevada (DC RENO, DCITY RENO, DIGC RENO, DIGITAL CITY RENO, RENO DC, RENO DCITY, RENO DIGC, RENO DIGITAL CITY, RENO NV)

SAGINAW—Digital Cities: Saginaw, Michigan (DC SAGINAW, DCITY SAGINAW, DIGC SAGINAW, SAGINAW DC, SAGINAW DCITY, SAGINAW DIGC, SAGINAW MI)

SAN DIEGO—Digital Cities: San Diego, California (DC SAN DIEGO, DC SD, DIGC SAN DIEGO, DIGC SD, DIGITAL CITY SD, SAN DIEGO DIGC, SD, SD DIGC, SD DIGITAL CITY)

SAN FRANCISCO—Digital Cities: San Francisco, California (DC SAN FRANCISCO, DC SF, DIGC SAN FRANCISCO, DIGC SF, DIGITAL CITY SF, SAN FRANCISCO DIGC, SF DIGC, SF DIGITAL CITY)

Chapter 7 Keywords by Channel and Topic

SANTA FE—Digital Cities: Albuquerque/Santa Fe, New Mexico (DC SANTA FE, DCITY SANTA FE, DIGC SANTA FE, DIGITAL CITY SANTA FE, SANTA FE DC, SANTA FE DCITY, SANTA FE DIGC, SANTA FE DIGITAL CITY)

SD COMM—Digital City San Diego: Community

SD NEWS—Digital City San Diego: News & Weather (SD WEATHER)

SD PEOPLE—Digital City San Diego: People

SD TOUR—Digital City San Diego: City Tour

SEATTLE—Digital Cities: Seattle/Tacoma, Washington (DC SEATTLE, DIGC SEATTLE, DIGITAL CITY SEATTLE, SEATTLE DIGC, SEATTLE DIGITAL CITY)

SF COMM—Digital City San Francisco: Community

SF NEWS—Digital City San Francisco: News & Weather (SF WEATHER)

SF PEOPLE—Digital City San Francisco: People

SF TOUR—Digital City San Francisco: City Tour

SHADOW—Traffic Center (SHADOW BROADCASTING, SHADOW TRAFFIC, TRAFFIC)

SOUTH—Digital Cities: South (DC SOUTH, DIGC SOUTH, DIGITAL CITY SOUTH, SOUTH DIGC, SOUTH DIGITAL CITY, SOUTHEAST)

ST PAUL—Digital Cities: Minneapolis - St. Paul, Minnesota (DC ST PAUL, DIGC ST PAUL, DIGITAL CITY ST PAUL, ST PAUL DIGC, ST PAUL DIGITAL CITY)

ST PETERSBURG—Ditial Cities: Tampa - St. Petersburg, Florida (DC ST PETERSBURG, DIGC ST PETERSBURG, ST PETERSBURG DIGC)

TACOMA—Digital Cities: Seattle/Tacoma, Washington (DIGC TACOMA, DIGITAL CITY TACOMA, TACOMA DIGC, TACOMA DIGITAL CITY)

TAMPA—Digital Cities: Tampa - St. Petersburg, Florida (DC TAMPA, DIGC TAMPA, DIGITAL CITY TAMPA, TAMPA DIGC, TAMPA DIGITAL CITY)

TAMPA COMM—Digital City Tampa: Community

TAMPA NEWS—Digital City Tampa: News & Weather (TAMPA WEATHER)

TAMPA PEOPLE—Digital City Tampa: People

Digital Cities (continued)

TAMPA WEATHER—Digital City Tampa: News & Weather (TAMPA NEWS)

TEMPLE—Digital Cities: Waco/Temple/Bryan, Texass (DC TEMPLE, DCITY TEMPLE, DIGC TEMPLE, TEMPLE DC, TEMPLE DCITY, TEMPLE DIGC, TEMPLE TX)

TORONTO—Digital Cities: Toronto, Ontario (DC TORONTO, DIGC TORONTO, DIGITAL CITY TORONTO, TORONTO DIGC, TORONTO DIGITAL CITY)

TULSA—Digital Cities: Tulsa, Oklahoma (DC TULSA, DCITY TULSA, DIGC TULSA, DIGITAL CITY TULSA, TULSA DC, TULSA DCITY, TULSA DIGC, TULSA DIGITAL CITY, TULSA OK)

VISALIA—Digital Cities: Fresno/Visalia, California (DC VISALIA, DCITY VISALIA, DIGC VISALIA, DIGITAL CITY VISALIA, VISALIA DC, VISALIA DIGC, VISALIA DIGITAL CITY, VISALIA CA)

WACO—Digital Cities: Waco/Temple/Bryan, Texas (DC WACO, DCITY WACO, DIGC WACO, DIGITAL CITY WACO, WACO DC, WACO DCITY, WACO DIGC, WACO DIGITAL CITY, WACO TX)

WASH PERSONALS—Digital City Washington: Personals

WEST—Digital Cities: West (DC WEST, DIGC WEST, DIGITAL CITY WEST, WEST DIGC)

Entertainment

ENTERTAINMENT—Entertainment Channel (E, GOSSIP, PLAY, REC CENTER, RECREATION, RECREATION CENTER)

;)—Hecklers Online (;-), COMPUTER GAMES, HECKLE, HECKLER, HECKLER ONLINE, HECKLER'S ONLINE, HECKLERS, HECKLERS ONLINE, HO, HOL, JOKE, LIMERICK, WEB COMEDY, WEB HUMOR, WISE GUYS)

    HECKLERS CLUBS—Hecklers Online: Clubs (HECKLING CLUBS, HO CLUBS)

90210—90210 Wednesdays (90210 WEDNESDAYS, BEVERLY HILLS, BEVERLY HILLS 90210, WEDNESDAYS)

ABC—ABC Online

    ABC AUDITORIUM—ABC Online Auditorium (ABC EVENTS, ABC GUESTS, ABC TRANSCRIPTS, FRIDAY AT 4)

    ABC BETA—ABC Online: Beta Area

    ABC GMA—ABC Good Morning America (GMA, GOOD MORNING AMERICA, JOEL SIEGEL)

Chapter 7 Keywords by Channel and Topic

ABC HELP—ABC Online Help

ABC KIDZINE—ABC KIDZINE (ABC KIDS, KIDZINE)

ABC LOVE—ABC Love Online (LOVE ONLINE, LUV)

ABC NEWS VIEWS—ABC Online: News Views (NEWS VIEWS)

ABC PRIME TIME—ABC Prime Time (ABC ENTERTAINMENT)

ABC RADIO—ABC Radio (PAUL HARVEY)

ABC STARS—ABC Online: Stars and Shows (STARS AND SHOWS)

ABC STATIONS—ABC Online: Stations (ABC STATION)

ABC VIDEO—ABC Online: Video Store

AOOL—ABC Online: America Out Of Line (AMERICA OUT OF LINE)

KAAL TV—ABC Online: KAAL-TV in Rochester, MN

KABC TV—ABC Online: KABC-TV in Los Angeles, CA

KAIT TV—ABC Online: KAIT-TV in Jonesboro, AR

KAKE TV—ABC Online: KAKE-TV in Wichita, KS

KESQ TV—ABC Online: KESQ-TV in Palm Springs, CA

KEZI TV—ABC Online: KEZI-TV in Eugene, OR

KFSN TV—ABC Online: KFSN-TV in Fresno, CA

KGO—KGO: San Francisco Newstalk AM 810

KGO TV—ABC Online: KGO-TV in San Francisco, CA

KGTV TV—ABC Online: KGTV-TV in San Diego, CA

KGUN TV—ABC Online: KGUN-TV in Tucson, AZ

KHBS TV—ABC Online: KHBS/KHOG-TV in Fort Smith, AR

KIFI TV—ABC Online: KIFI-TV in Idaho Falls, ID

KIVI TV—ABC Online: KIVI-TV in Boise, ID

KMBC TV—ABC Online: KMBC-TV in Kansas City, MO

KMGH TV—ABC Online: KMGH-TV in Denver, CO

KNTV TV—ABC Online: KNTV-TV in San Jose, CA

KNXV TV—ABC Online: KNXV-TV in Phoenix, AZ

KOAT TV—ABC Online: KOAT-TV in Albuquerque, NM

Chapter 7 Keywords by Channel and Topic

Entertainment (continued)

KOCO TV—ABC Online: KOCO-TV in Oklahoma, OK
KODE TV—ABC Online: KODE-TV in Joplin, MO
KQTV TV—ABC Online: KQTV-TV in St. Joseph, MO
KTBS TV—ABC Online: KTBS-TV in Shreveport, LA
KTKA TV—ABC Online: KTKA-TV in Topeka, KS
KTRK TV—ABC Online: KTRK-TV in Houston, TX
KTVX TV—ABC Online: KTVX-TV in Salt Lake City, UT
KTXS TV—ABC Online: KTXS-TV in Abilene, TX
KVIA TV—ABC Online: KVIA-TV in El Paso, TX
KVUE TV—ABC Online: KVUE-TV in Austin, TX
WAND TV—ABC Online: WAND-TV in Decatur, IL
WATE TV—ABC Online: WATE-TV in Knoxville, TN
WBAY TV—ABC Online: WBAY-TV in Green Bay, WI
WBRC TV—ABC Online: WBRC-TV in Birmingham, AL
WBRZ TV—ABC Online: WBRZ-TV in Baton Rouge, LA
WCVB TV—ABC Online: WCVB-TV in Boston, MA
WDHN TV—ABC Online: WDHN-TV in Dothan, AL
WDIO TV—ABC Online: WDIO-TV in Duluth, MN
WDTN TV—ABC Online: WDTN-TV in Dayton, OH
WEAR TV—ABC Online: WEAR-TV in Pensacola, FL
WFAA TV—ABC Online: WFAA-TV in Dallas/Ft. Worth, TX
WFTV TV—ABC Online: WFTV-TV in Orlando, FL
WGGB TV—ABC Online: WGGB-TV in Springfield, MA
WGTU TV—ABC Online: WGTU/WGTQ-TV in Traverse City, MI
WHOI TV—ABC Online: WHOI-TV in Peoria-Bloomington, IL
WHTM TV—ABC Online: WHTM-TV in Harrisburg, PA
WIXT TV—ABC Online: WIXT-TV in Syracuse, NY
WJBF TV—ABC Online: WJBF-TV in Augusta, GA
WJCL TV—ABC Online: WJCL-TV in Savannah, GA
WKBW TV—ABC Online: WKBW-TV in Buffalo, NY
WKRC TV—ABC Online: WKRC-TV in Cincinnati, OH

Chapter 7 Keywords by Channel and Topic

WKRN TV—ABC Online: WKRN-TV in Nashville, TN
WLOS TV—ABC Online: WLOS-TV in Asheville, NC
WLOX TV—ABC Online: WLOX-TV in Biloxi MS
WMBB TV—ABC Online: WMBB-TV in Panama, FL
WMDT TV—ABC Online: WMDT-TV in Salisbury, MD
WMUR TV—ABC Online: WMUR-TV in Manchester, NH
WNEP TV—ABC Online: WNEP-TV in Scranton/W-B, PA
WOKR TV—ABC Online: WOKR-TV in Rochester, NY
WOLO TV—ABC Online: WOLO-TV in Columbia, SC
WOTV TV—ABC Online: WOTV-TV in Battle Creek, MI
WPBF TV—ABC Online: WPBF-TV in West Palm Beach, FL
WPDE TV—ABC Online: WPDE-TV in Myrtle Beach, SC
WPTA TV—ABC Online: WPTA-TV in Fort Wayne, IN
WQAD TV—ABC Online: WQAD-TV in Moline, IL
WQOW TV—ABC Online: WQOW-TV in Eau Claire, WI
WRTV TV—ABC Online: WRTV in Indianapolis, IN
WSB TV—ABC Online: WSB-TV in Atlanta, GA
WSJV TV—ABC Online: WSJV-TV in South Bend, IN
WSYX TV—ABC Online: WSYX-TV in Columbus, OH
WTEN TV—ABC Online: WTEN-TV in Albany, NY
WTNH TV—ABC Online: WTNH-TV in Nashville, TN
WTOK TV—ABC Online: WTOK-TV in Meridan, MS
WTVC TV—ABC Online: WTVC-TV in Chattanooga, TN
WTVQ TV—ABC Online: WTVQ-TV in Lexington, KY
WVII TV—ABC Online: WVII-TV in Bangor, ME
WXOW TV—ABC Online: WXOW-TV in LaCrescent, MN
WZZM TV—ABC Online: WZZM-TV in Grand Rapids, MI
AEN—American Entertainment Network
ASSASSINS—Assassins
BABYLON 5—Babylon 5 (BABYLON)
BEATLES ANTHOLOGY—The ABC Rock & Road Beatles Anthology
BONKERS—60-Second Novelist: BOnKeRs Trivia (BONK)

Chapter 7 Keywords by Channel and Topic

Entertainment (continued)

BROKEN ARROW—Broken Arrow

CANNES—Cannes Film Festival

CARTOON NETWORK—Cartoon Network (TOONS)

CARTOONS—The Cartoons Forum

CASTING—The Casting Forum (ACTING, ACTORS, ACTRESSES, CASTING FORUM)

CINDY—Cindy Adams: Queen of Gourmet Gossip (ADAMS, CINDY ADAMS)

CINEMAPOV—CinemaPOV (CPOV)

CJ CONTESTS—CyberJustice Contests

COMEDY CENTRAL—Comedy Central

COMEDY PUB—The Comedy Pub (COMEDY, HUMOR, JENNY FLAME, LOL, PUB)

COMIC STRIP—Comic Strip Centennial (POSTAL STAMPS)

COMICS—Comics Selection

COMPUTOON—CompuToon Area

CONTEST—AOL Contest Area (CONTEST AREA, CONTESTS, WINNER)

COURT TV—Court TV's Law Center (COURTROOM TELEVISION, LAW, LAW CENTER, OJ)

CRITIC—Critic's Choice (CRITICS, CRITICS CHOICE)

CYBERJUSTICE—CyberJustice

    COURTS—CyberJustice's Courts of Karmic Justice

    GAZETTE—CyberJustice's Gazette Online/Email

    DOROTHY—CyberJustice's Oasis of Xaiz

    JUDGMENT—CyberJustice's Record Your Judgment

    KENNEHORA—CyberJustice's Kennehora Junction (KENNEHORA JUNCTION)

    KIVETCH—CyberJustice's Worry, Complain & Sob

    LOCALS—CyberJustice's Meet The Locals

    POLLS—CyberJustice's Arch of Public Opinion Polls

    QUIKJUSTICE—CyberJustice's Reward & Punishment

    TIME CAPSULE—CyberJustice's Istorian's Time Capsule

Chapter 7 Keywords by Channel and Topic

WORRY—CyberJustice's Worry Free Zone

CYBERSERIALS—Cyberserials (CYBERSOAPS, SERIALS)

DC COMICS—DC Comics Online (BATMAN, DC COMICS ONLINE, MAD, MAD MAGAZINE, MILESTONE, PARADOX, SUPERMAN, VERTIGO)

DC CHAT—DC Comics Online: Chat Rooms

DEADLY—Deadly Games

DILBERT—Dilbert Comics (DILBERT COMICS, DILBOARD)

DISNEY—Disney Services

DISNEY JOBS—Disney Jobs

DREALMS—DragonRealms (DRAGONREALMS)

E!—E! Entertainment Television

EATS—Good Morning America Recipes

ECHAT—Entertainment Chat (ENTERTAINMENT CHAT, HOT CHAT)

EW—Entertainment Weekly (ENTERTAINMENT WEEKLY)

EXTRA—EXTRA Online (ACE VENTURA, ACE VENTURE STORE)

FAVORITE FLICKS—Favorite Flicks! (FAVE FLICKS, OLD FAVES)

FERNDALE—Ferndale

FOLLYWOOD—Follywood

FRASIER—Fraiser Tuesdays (FRAISER TUESDAYS)

FRIDAY AT 4—ABC Online Auditorium (ABC AUDITORIUM, ABC EVENTS, ABC GUESTS, ABC TRANSCRIPTS)

FUNNIES—The Funny Pages

GAME SITES—WWW Game Sites (GS)

GERALDO—The Geraldo Show (GERALDO SHOW)

HOLLYWOOD—Hollywood Online (HOLLYWOOD ONLINE)

HOLLYWOOD PRO—The Biz! (HOL PRO)

HOROSCOPE—Horoscopes (HOROSCOPES)

HOT AIR—Global Challenger Balloon Race

HOT ENTERTAINMENT—What's Hot in Entertainment (DAILY FIX, ENT SPOT, ESPOT, FIX, HOT ENT, HOT ENTERTAINMENT)

HYPR—Hypractv8 with Thomas Dolby

Chapter 7 Keywords by Channel and Topic

Entertainment (continued)

IG—Intelligent Gamer Online (IG ONLINE, INTELLIGENT GAMER)

IMPROVISATION—The IMPROVisation Online (IMPROV)

KIDS CHOICE—Nickelodeon: Kids' Choice Awards

LIFETIME—Lifetime Television (LIFETIME TV, LIFETIME TELEVISION)

LOIS & CLARK—Lois & Clark (L & C, L AND C, LOIS AND CLARK)

LOST TV SHOWS—Lost & Found TV Shows (CANCELLED TV SHOWS, FALL TV, FALL TV SHOWS, FOUND TV, GONER TV, LOST TV, NEW TV SEASON)

LOTTERY—Lotteries

MAY—Mad About You Fan Forum (MAD ABOUT, MAD ABOUT YOU, MAD ABOUT YOU SUNDAYS)

MCL—McLaughlin Group (GROUP, MCLAUGHLIN, MCLAUGHLIN GROUP, WRONG, WRONG!)

MELROSE—Melrose Mondays (MELROSE MONDAYS)

MOVIE FORUMS—Movie Forums Area

MOVIE REVIEW DB—Movie Review Database (CINEMAN, CINEMAN SYNDICATE, FILM REVIEW DATABASE, FILM REVIEW DB, FILM REVIEWS DATABASE, MOVIE REVIEW DATABASE, MOVIE REVIEWS DATABASE, MRD)

MOVIE REVIEWS—Movie Reviews

MOVIELINK—MovieLink (777-FILM, 777-FILM ONLINE, HOW TIMES)

MOVIES—@the.movies (@ THE MOVIES, @THE.MOVIES, CINEMA, FILMS, MOVIE, THE MOVIES)

MOVIES WEB—Movies on the Web

MOVIEVISIONS—MovieVisions (FILM STUDIOS)

MTV—MTV Online

   MTV NEWS—MTV News

   HOT SPOT—MTV Online: Hot Spot

   KRANK—MTV Online: Krank

   MUSIC NEWS—MTV Online: News

MYSTERIES—Mysteries from the Yard (BOOKSHOP, HOLMES, MFTY, MYSTERIES FROM THE YARD, SHERLOCK, SHERLOCK HOLMES)

Chapter 7 Keywords by Channel and Topic

NEW MOVIES—New Movie Releases (NEW FILM, NEW FILMS, NEW MOVIE, NEW MOVIE RELEASES, NEW RELEASES, SUMMER MOVIES)

NEWSGRIEF—NewsGrief (NG)

NEWSLETTER—Games & Entertainment Newsletter

NICK AT NITE—Nick at Nite (NAN, NICK @ NITE, TV LAND)

NOT NBC—NBC...NOT! (NBC)

OPRAH—Get Movin' With Oprah

OSCAR—Academy Awards (ACADEMY AWARDS, OSCARS)

PARASCOPE—Parascope (ALIENS, CONSPIRACY, PERISCOPE, PS, PSCP, SCOPE, STRANGE, WEIRD, WIERD)

PBM—Play-By-Mail Forum (PLAY-BY-MAIL)

    PBM CLUBS—Play-By-Mail Clubs & Messaging

PLAYBILL—Playbill Online (BROADWAY)

QB1—NTN's QB1

RADIO—Entertainment's Radio Forum (RADIO FORUM, SATELLITES)

RICKI LAKE—The Ricki Lake Show

RR—ABC Online: Rock & Road (R&R, ROCK & ROAD)

SCIFI—The Sci-Fi Channel

SEX—Entertainment [*just try it*]

SHOWBIZ INFO—Showbiz News & Info (SHOWBIZ NEWS)

SIGHTINGS—Sightings Online

SMARTMOUTHS—Smart Mouths

SOD—Soap Opera Digest (DIVA, DIVA LA DISH, SOAP DIGEST)

SOUNDBITES—Soundbites Online (SATIRE)

SPACE A&B—Space: Above & Beyond (SPACE ABOVE & BEYOND, SPACE ABOVE AND BEYOND, SPACE: ABOVE AND BEYOND)

STAR WARS—Star Wars Sim Forum (STAR WARS SIM)

STARFLEET—Starfleet Online (ACADEMY)

TELLURIDE—Telluride Film Festival

TEST TUBE—ABC Online: Test Tube (TT)

THE BIZ—The Biz!

Chapter 7 Keywords by Channel and Topic

Entertainment (continued)

TICKETMASTER—Ticketmaster (TICKET)

TONY AWARDS—Playbill Online: Tony Awards Central (TONYS)

TREASURES—Tell a Story

TV—Main TV Screen (TELEVISION)

TV GOSSIP—TV Shows Gossip

TV GUIDE—TV Quest (LISTINGS, TV LISTINGS, TV SOURCE)

TV NETWORKS—TV Networks Area

TV PEOPLE—TV People

TV SHOWS—TV Shows

TV SPOOFS—TV Spoofs (SPOOFS)

TV VIEWERS—TV Viewers Forum

VGAP—VGA Planets (VGA PLANETS)

VH1—VH1 Online

VIDEOS—Home Video (HOME VIDEO)

VIRGIN—Virgin Records -or- Virgin Sound & Vision

VIRGIN RECORDS—Virgin Records

WB—The WB Network (FROG, MICHIGAN J FROG, THE WB NETWORK, WBNET)

WEB ENTERTAINMENT—WEBentertainment

WHFS—WHFS 99.1 FM (99.1, HFS, MODERN ROCK)

WIZARD—Wizard World (ANIME, COLLECTING, IQ, MANGA, WIZARD WORLD)

WLS—WLS Chicago

WWN—Weekly World News (ASK SERENA, BATBOY, BIGFOOT, DEAR DOTTI, ED ANGER, ELVIS, NESSIE, SATAN, SIDESHOW, VAMPIRE, WWN, WEEKLY WORLD NEWS)

X FILES—X Files Forums

X FILES SIM—X Files Sim Forum

XF FRIDAYS—X Files Fridays

YOUR TOONS—Cartoon collection

CHAPTER 7 KEYWORDS BY CHANNEL AND TOPIC

Games

GAMES—Games Channel (AOL GAME FORUMS, GAME, GAMES & ENTERTAINMENT, GAMES CHANNEL)

ABM—Adventures by Mail (ADVENTURES BY MAIL, MONSTER ISLAND, QUEST)

AIR WARRIOR—Air Warrior (KESMAI)

AMERICON—America Online Gaming Conference

AT—Hecklers Online: Antagonistic Trivia (AI INC, ANTAG, ANTAGON, ANTAGONIST, ANTAGONISTS, ANTAGONIST TRIVIA, ANTAGONISTIC TRIVIA, ATG)

BOXER—Boxer*Jam Gameshows (BOXER JAM, BOXER*JAM, STRIKE-A-MATCH)

CA—Crossword America (XWORDS)

CASINO—RabbitJack's Casino (RABBITJACK'S CASINO, RABBITJACKS CASINO)

CCGF—Collectible Card Games Forum (COLLECT CARDS)

CGW—Computer Gaming World (CGW, COMPUTER GAMING, COMPUTER GAMING WORLD)

CHIPNET—ChipNet Online (CHIP)

DOWNLOAD GAMES—Download Online Games* (GAMES DOWNLOAD)

FED—Federation (FEDERATION)

FELLOWSHIP—Fellowship of Online Gamers/RPGA Network (FOG, RPGA, RPGA NETWORK)

FFGF—Free-Form Gaming Forum (RDI)

FLIGHT SIM—Flight Sim Resource Center (CRASH, FIREBALL, FLIGHT, FLIGHT CENTER, FLIGHT SIMS, FLIGHT SIMULATIONS, FSRC)

GAME BASE—Game Base

GAME DESIGN—Game Designers Forum (GAME DESIGNER, GAME DESIGNERS)

GAMEPRO—GamePro Online

GAMES PARLOR—Games Parlor (GAME ROOMS, PARLOR)

GAMEWIZ—Dr. Gamewiz Online (DR GAMEWIZ, GAMEWIZ INC)

GC ACTION—Games Channel: Action

GC CLASSIC—Games Channel: Classic Games

Games (continued)

GC CONTESTS—Games Channel: Contests

GC INFO—Games Channel: Gaming Information

GC KNOWLEDGE—Games Channel: Knowledge Games

GC NEWS—Games Channel: News

GC PERSONA—Games Channel: Persona Games

GC RPG—Games Channel: Role Playing Games

GC SIMULATION—Games Channel: Simulation Games

GC SPORTS—Games Channel: Sports Games

GC STRATEGY—Games Channel: Strategy Games

GEMSTONE—GemStone III (GEMSTONE III)

GIX—Gaming Information Exchange

HOT GAMES—What's Hot in AOL Games (GC HOT)

MODUS—Modus Operandi (MODUS OPERANDI)

MURDER—Murder Mysteries Online (CYBERSLEUTH, I FORSOOTH, MMO, MURDER MYSTERY, MURDER MYSTERIES)

NAGF—Non-Affiliated Gamers Forum

NINTENDO—Nintendo Power Source (NOA, NINTENDO POWER SOURCE)

NTN—NTN Trivia (COUNTDOWN, NTN TRIVIA)

OGF—Online Gaming Forums (GAMING, ONLINE GAMING)

PRESIDENT 96—President '96

RPG—Role-Playing Forum (ROLE PLAYING)

SCORPIA—Scorpia's Lair (SCORPIA'S LAIR, SCORPIAS LAIR)

SIM—Simming Forum (SIMMING, SIMS)

SOL III—Sol III Play-by-Email Game

STRATEGY—Strategy & Wargaming Forum (CHESS)

TRIVIA—Trivia Forum (TRIVIA FORUM)

TRIVIAL PURSUIT—Trivial Pursuit Interactive (TPI)

TSR—TSR Online (TSR ONLINE)

UA—Unlimited Adventures (UNLIMITED ADVENTURES)

VIRTUAL AIRLINES—Virtual Airlines (LYNX, LYNX AIRWAYS, SKYLINE, SKYLINE AIRWAYS, SUNAIR, SUNAIR EXPRESS, VAA, VAS)

YOYO—Yoyodyne Entertainment (YOYODYNE)

    YOYO GAMES—Yoyodyne Entertainment: Games

Health & Fitness

HEALTH—Health Channel (MEDICINE)

ACS—American Cancer Society (ACS NATL)

ALA—America Lung Association (AMERICAN LUNG, AMERICAN LUNG ASSOC)

ALTERNATIVE MEDICINE—Alternative Medicine Forum

ARFA—American Running & Fitness Association

CANCER—Cancer Forum

CEREBRAL PALSY—United Cerebral Palsy Association (UCPA)

CHILDREN'S HEALTH—Children's Health Forum

COLUMBIA/HCA—Columbia's Health Today (COLUMBIA/HCA, COLUMBIANET, COLUMBIA.NET. HEALTH TODAY, ONE SOURCE, SENIOR FRIENDS)

CRUSADE—Avon's Breast Cancer Awareness Crusade Online

DEPENDENCY—Dependency and Recovery Issues

DIABETES—American Diabetes Association (AMERICAN DIABETES)

FITNESS—Fitness Forum (EXERCISE)

HEALTH FOCUS—Health Focus

HEALTH LIVE—Health Speakers and Support Groups

HEALTH RESOURCES—Health Resources (HEALTH MAGAZINES, HEALTH REFERENCE)

HEALTH WEB—Health Web Sites

HEALTH ZONE—The Health Zone (CHOCOLATE, CYBERSLIM, IHRSA, HZ, QUALITY, Z, ZONED, ZONIE, <Z>)

HOT HEALTH—What's Hot in Health (WHAT'S HOT IN HEALTH)

HRS—Better Health & Medical Forum (BETTER HEALTH)

IMH—Issues in Mental Health

MEN'S HEALTH—Men's Health Forum

MENS' HEALTH WEB—Men's Health Internet Sites

Chapter 7 Keywords by Channel and Topic

Health & Fitness (continued)

MENTAL HEALTH—Mental Health Forum

MENTAL HEALTH WEB—Mental Health Web Sites

MULTIPLE SCLEROSIS—Multiple Sclerosis Forum

NAMI—National Alliance of Mentally Ill

NEW YEAR—Have a Healthy New Year!

NMSS—National Multiple Sclerosis Society

PEN—Personal Empowerment Network (EMPOWERMENT)

PSYCHOLOGY—Psychology Forum

SELF-HELP—Self-Help Area

WOMEN'S HEALTH—Women's Health Forum (WOMENS HEALTH)

WOMEN'S HEALTH WEB—Women's Health Internet Sites

The Hub

HUB—The Hub (THE HUB)

ARTSPEAK—The Hub: ArtSpeak

BRIDGES—The Hub: Even More Bridges of Madison County

CALENDAR GIRLS—The Hub: Calendar Girls

CELEBRITY—The Hub: Celebrity Sightings

CHANNEL ZERO—The Hub: Channel Zero

CLICK HERE—The Hub: Click Here

CYRANO—The Hub: Cyrano

FUZZY—The Hub: Fuzzy Memories

GET A LIFE—The Hub: Get A Life

GIGABYTES—The Hub: Gigabytes Island

GWPI—The Hub: Global Worldwide Pictures International, Ltd.

HEAVEN—The Hub: Heaven

HITCHHIKER—The Hub: John the Hitchhiker (HITCHIKER)

HOT BUTTON—The Hub: The Hot Button

HUB INDEX—The Hub: Index (HUB CONTENTS, THE HUB INDEX)

Chapter 7 Keywords by Channel and Topic

KENS GUIDE—The Hub: Ken's Guide to the Bible

KONSPIRACY—The Hub: Konspiracy Korner

MEANWHILE—The Hub: Meanwhile

MODERN LIVES—The Hub: Modern Lives

MONOLITH—The Hub: Monolith

OTHER NEWS—The Hub: The Other News

SOURCERER—The Hub: Sourcerer

SPACEY—The Hub: Space

SUSAN—The Hub: Susan

TODAY'S OTHER—The Hub: Today's Other News

USEFUL THINGS—The Hub: Useful Things

USELESS THINGS—The Hub: Useless Things

WEIRD SISTERS—The Hub: Weird Sisters

YAVIASA—The Hub: You Are Very Intelligent and Somewhat Artsy

International

AUSTRALIA—Australia

AUSTRIA—Austria

BELGIUM—Belgium

BULGARIA—Bulgaria

CAMEROON—Cameroon

CANADA—AOL Canada (AOL CANADA, CANADA, CANADIAN)

CANADA CHAT—AOL Canada: Chat

CZECH REPUBLIC—Czech Republic

DENMARK—Denmark

EGYPT—Egypt

FINLAND—Finland

GREECE—Greece

GUAM—Guam

HONG KONG—Hong Kong

HUNGARY—Hungary

CHAPTER 7 KEYWORDS BY CHANNEL AND TOPIC

International (continued)

ICELAND—Iceland

INTERNATIONAL—International Channel (AOL INTERNATIONAL, AOL WORLD, FRANCE, GERMANY, INTERNATIONAL US, INTL, JAPAN)

IRELAND—Ireland

ISRAEL—Israel (AOL ISREAL, AOL ISRAEL, ISREAL)

ITALY—Italy

KAZAKHSTAN—Kazakhstan

KOREA—Korea

LATVIA—Latvia

LUXEMBOURG—Luxembourg

MALAWI—Malawi

MALTA—City Guide to Malta

MEXICO—Mexico

N MARIANA ISLANDS—Northern Mariana Islands

NETHERLANDS—Netherlands

NEW ZEALAND—New Zealand

NIGERIA—Nigeria

NORWAY—Norway

PAPUA—Papua New Guinea (NEW GUINEA, PAPUA NEW GUINEA)

PHILIPPINES—Philippines

POLAND—Poland

PORTUGAL—Portugal

PUERTO RICO—Puerto Rico

RUSSIA—Russia

SINGAPORE—Singapore

SOUTH AFRICA—South Africa

SPAIN—Spain

SWEDEN—Sweden

SWITZERLAND—Switzerland

TAIWAN—Taiwan

Chapter 7 Keywords by Channel and Topic

THE WORLD—The World (COUNTRIES, WORLD)

TURKEY—Turkey

UKRAINE—Ukraine

UNITED KINGDOM—United Kingdom

UZBEKISTAN—Uzbekistan

Internet Connection

INTERNET—Internet Connection Channel (INTERNET CENTER, INTERNET CONNECTION, NET)

7 WONDERS—Seven Wonders of the Web (SEVEN WONDERS)

ANSWERMAN—Answer Man

    AM GLOSSARY—AnswerMan: Glossary

COMP SITES—Computing Internet Sites (COMPUTING SITES)

CYBERLOVE & LAUGHTER—Cyberlove & Laughter

CYBERSMITH—CyberSmith (CSMITH, CYBERCAFE, NET HEAD JED, NET HEAD RED, YBERSMITH)

DEAD END—The Dead End of the Internet

FTP—File Transfer Protocol

GNN—GNN Best of the Net

GOPHER—Internet Gopher (VERONICA, WAIS)

HOME PAGE—Personal WWW Publishing Area (PP)

HTTP—What is http?

INTERNET CHAT—Internet Chat (INET CHAT, NET CHAT)

INTERNET EMAIL—Internet E-Mail (INET EMAIL)

INTERNET EXCHANGE—Internet Exchange (INET EXCHANGE, NET EXCHANGE)

INTERNET GRAPHICS—Internet Graphic Sites

INTERNET MAGAZINES—Internet Computing Magazines (INET MAGS, INET MAGAZINES, INTERNET MAGS)

INTERNET NEWS—Internet Newsstand ('NET NEWS, NET NEWS, INTERNET NEWSSTAND)

INTERNET ORGS—Internet Organizations (INTERNET.ORGS, INET ORGS, NET ORGS)

INTERNET QUESTIONS—Internet Questions*

Chapter 7 Keywords by Channel and Topic

Internet Connection (continued)

INTERNET SOFTWARE—Internet Software (NET LIBRARY, NET SOFT, NET SOFTWARE)

MAIL GATEWAY—Mail Gateway

MAILING LISTS—Internet Mailing Lists (LISTSERV)

MY PLACE—My Place (for FTP sites)

NAVISOFT—Navisoft

NET CHAT—Internet Chat (INET CHAT, INTERNET CHAT)

NET SUGGESTIONS—Internet Suggestions

NETGIRL—NetGirl

> NETGIRL PERSONALS—NetGirl: Personals

NETORGS—Net.Orgs

NEWSGROUPS—Internet Usenet Newsgroup Area (KEEPER, NEWSGROUP, USENET)

PRO'S CORNER—Pro's Corner (CORNER EARL'S GARAGE, EARLS GARAGE, GARAGE, NET EXPERT, PROS CORNER, PRO'S, PROS)

ROADTRIP—AOL Roadtrips (AOL ROADTRIP, BUS, VAN, ROADTRIPS, RT)

SCOOP—Newsgroup Scoop

TOP COMP SITES—Top Computing Internet Sites (TOP COMPUTING SITES)

TOP COMPANY SITES—Companies on the Internet

TRUE TALES—True Tales of the Internet

WEB—World Wide Web (WEBCRAWLER, WORLD WIDE WEB, WWW)

WEB DINER—The Web Diner (DINER, DINER CREW, HTML HELP, WEB BIZ, WEBD, WEB DINER, WEB HELP, WEBSITE)

WEB MAKEOVER—Web Makeover

WEB REVIEW—Web Review

WEB UNIVERSITY—Web University

WEBSOURCE—Websource

WINSOCK—Winsock Central (TELNET)

Chapter 7 Keywords by Channel and Topic

Kids Only

KIDS—Kids Only Channel (KIDS ONLY)

BLACKBERRY—Blackberry Creek (BLACKBERRY CREEK)

BOOKS ON BREAK—Just Books!

KIDS OUT—Kids Out: London's Family Events Guide (KO)

KIDS QUEST—The Quest CD-ROM Companion to AOL's Kids Only Channel

KIDS WB—Kids' Warner Brothers Online (KIDS' WB)

KIDS WEB—Kid's Top Internet Sites

KIDSBIZ—KidsBiz

KIDSOFT—Club KidSoft (CLUB KIDSOFT)

KO HELP—Kids' Guide Pager

NICK—Nickelodeon Selections

NICKELODEON—Nickelodeon Online (ORANGE, SLIME)

POG—KidzBiz' POG Area (POGS)

WEEKLY READER—Weekly Reader News

Learning & Culture

LEARNING—Learning & Culture Channel (EDUCATION, LEARN, LEARNING & REFERENCE, LEARNING AND REFERENCE, LEARNING CENTER)

AAC—Academic Assistance Center (RESEARCH, TUTORING)

ABC CLASS—The ABC Classroom (ABC CLASSROOM, SMART WATCHING)

ADOPTION—Adoption Forum

AFT—American Federation of Teachers

AFTERWARDS—Afterwards Cafe (ARTS, OPERA, POETRY)

ALF—American Leadership Forum

ALUMNI HALL—Alumni Hall (ALUMNI)

AOL EDUCATION—America Online Education Initiative

AOL FAMILIES—AOL Families (DAD, DADS, FATHER, FATHERS, MOM, MOMS, MOTHER, MOTHERS, PARENT, PARENTING, PARENTS, PIN)

Chapter 7 Keywords by Channel and Topic

Learning & Culture (continued)

ASKERIC—AskERIC (ACCESS ERIC, ERIC)

BARRONS—Barrons Booknotes (BOOKNOTES)

BIOLOGY—Simon & Schuster Online: Biology Department

BOOKS—Book Areas

BULL MOOSE—Bull Moose Tavern

CAMPUS—Online Campus (CLASSES, IES, REGISTER, SIGNUP)

CAREERS—Career Selections (CAREER)

CHANNEL ONE—Channel One Network Online (CHANNEL 1, HACIENDA)

CHARTER—Charter Schools Forum (CHARTER SCHOOL, CHARTER SCHOOLS)

CHILD SAFETY—Child Safety Brochure

COLLEGE—College Selections

COLLEGE BOARD—College Board

COMPOSER—Composer's Coffeehouse (COMPOSER'S, COMPOSERS)

COMPTONS—Compton's NewMedia Forum

COMPTONS ENCYCLOPEDIA—Compton's Living Encyclopedia

COMPTONS SOFTWARE—Compton's Software Library

CONTACTS—Employer Contacts Database

CORCORAN—Corcoran School of Art

COURSES—Online Courses (INTERACTIVE ED, INTERACTIVE EDUCATION)

COURSEWARE—Electronic Courseware (ECS)

CRIMINAL JUSTICE—Simon & Schuster Online: Criminal Justice Department

CSPAN—C-SPAN (CSPAN ONLINE)

　　CSPAN BUS—C-SPAN in the Classroom (CSPAN CLASS, CSPAN CLASSROOM, CSPAN SCHOOLS)

CSUC—California State University (CHICO)

CYBERLAW—CyberLaw/CyberLex (COMPUTER LAW, CYBERLEX)

DOCL—Dictionary of Cultural Literacy (DCL)

DSC—The Discovery Channel (DISCOVERY)

CHAPTER 7 KEYWORDS BY CHANNEL AND TOPIC

DCI CHAT—The Discovery Channel: Chat (DISCOVERY CHAT)

DSC ED—The Discovery Channel: Education (DSC-ED, DISCOVERY ED, TLC ED, TLC-ED)

ED ADVISORY—Education Advisory Council Online (EDA)

EDUCATION CONNECTION—Compton's Education Connection

ELECTION HANDBOOK—Student's Election Handbook

ENGLISH—Simon & Schuster Online: English Department

EPARTNERS—Electronic Partnerships

ESH—Electronic Schoolhouse (SCHOOLHOUSE)

EUN—Electronic University Network (UNIVERSITIES, UNIVERSITY)

EXAM PREP—Exam Prep Center

EXCELLENCE—Access Excellence (ACCESS EXCELLENCE)

FAM HOT—What's Hot in AOL Families

GEOGRAPHY— Simon & Schuster Online: Geography Department

GIFTED—Gifted Online

GMAT—Kaplan Online or The Princeton Review (BUSINESS SCHOOL, GRADUATE SCHOOL, GRE, LAW SCHOOL, LSAT, MCAT, MEDICAL SCHOOL, SAT)

GOALS 200—Goals 2000: National Education Act

GRE—Kaplan Online or The Princeton Review (BUSINESS SCHOOL, GMAT, GRADUATE SCHOOL, LAW SCHOOL, LSAT, MCAT, MEDICAL SCHOOL, SAT)

GWU—George Washington University

HEM—Home Education Magazine

HH KIDS—Homework Help

HOMER—Homer's Page at The Odyssey Project (HOMER'S PAGE)

HOMESCHOOL—Homeschooling Forum (HOMESCHOOLING)

HOMEWORK—Homework Area (HOMEWORK HELP)

HOT TOPICS—Hot Topics

HUMAN SEXUALITY—Simon & Schuster Online: Human Sexuality Department

INTERNATIONAL CAFE—International Cafe (FOREIGN, LANGUAGES)

Chapter 7 Keywords by Channel and Topic

Learning & Culture (continued)

JOBS—Help Wanted Ads (HELP WANTED)

KAPLAN—Kaplan Online (ACT, GREENBERG, NCLEX, NURSING, TEST PREP)

L&C HOT—What's Hot in Learning & Culture (LC HOT, LEARNING & CULTURE HOT)

L&C STORE—Learning & Culture Store

LANGUAGE—International Languages

LITERACY—Adult Literacy & Education Forum (READ)

MATHEMATICS—Simon & Schuster Online: Mathematics Department

MANAGER—Manager's Network (MANAGER'S, MANAGER'S NETWORK, MANAGING)

MCINTIRE—University of Virginia Alumni/McIntire School of Commerce (MCINTIRE ALUMNI)

MONTESSORI— Montessori Schools (MONTESSORI SCHOOLS)

NAPC—Employment Agency Database

NAS—NAS Online (AGRICULTURE, ENGINEERING, MATH, SOCIAL SCIENCE, TRANSPORTATION)

NEA PUBLIC—National Education Association Public Forum

NAESP—NAESP Web Link

NATURE— The Nature Conservancy (THE NATURE CONSERVANCY, TNC)

NMAA—National Museum of American Art (AMERICAN ART)

NMAH—National Museum of American History (AMERICAN HISTORY)

NOLO—Nolo Press' Self-Help Law Center (NOLO PRESS, LAWYER)

NPC—National Parenting Center (NATIONAL PARENTING, TNPC)

ODYSSEY—The Odyssey Project (GEOGRAPHIC, NATIONAL GEOGRAPHIC, NGS, ODY, ODYSSEY PROJECT, THE ODYSSEY PROJECT)

PARENT ADVICE—Princeton Review Informed Parent

PHS—Practical Homeschooling

PHYS ED—Simon & Schuster Online: Health, Physical Education & Recreation Department

Chapter 7 Keywords by Channel and Topic

POLITICAL SCIENCE—Simon & Schuster Online: Political Science Department

PR—The Princeton Review Online (PRINCETON, PRINCETON REVIEW, STUDENT, STUDENT ACCESS, TEST DAY)

PRINCIPALS—National Principals Center Web link

READING ROOM—The Reading Room

S&S—Simon & Schuster College Online (A&B, ALLYN & BACON, COLLEGE ONLINE, KIRSHNER, PH, PRENTICE HALL, SIMON, SIMON & SCHUSTER)

SAT—Kaplan Online -or- The Princeton Review (BUSINESS SCHOOL, GMAT, GRADUATE SCHOOL, GRE, LAW SCHOOL, LSAT, MCAT, MEDICAL SCHOOL)

SCHOLARS—Scholars' Hall (SCHOLAR'S HALL, SCHOLARS' HALL, SCHOLARS HALL)

SCHOLASTIC—Scholastic Network Preview Area

SCOUTING—Scouting Forum (SCOUTS)

SI—Smithsonian Online (MUSEUM, MUSEUMS, SMITHSONIAN)

SN LIBRARIES—Scholastic Libraries

SN LIT GAME—Bookwoman's Literature Game

SN SPACE—Space and Astronomy

SN GUESTS—Scholastic Network: Special Guests

SOCIAL WORK—Simon & Schuster Online: Social Work Department

SOCIOLOGY—Simon & Schuster Online: Sociology Department

STUDY—Study Skills Service (STUDY SKILLS)

STUDY BREAK—Compton's Study Break

T TALK—Teachers' Forum

TAL—Turner Adventure Learning

TALENT—Talent Bank

TEACHER—The Educator's Network (TEACHERS, TEN)

TEACHER PAGER—Teacher Pager

TEACHERS' LOUNGE—Teachers' Lounge (TEACHER'S LOUNGE, TEACHERS LOUNGE)

TNEWS—Teachers' Newsstand

THE LAB—The Lab

CHAPTER 7 KEYWORDS BY CHANNEL AND TOPIC

Learning & Culture (continued)

TLC—The Learning Channel

TRAINING—Career Development Training

UCAL—University of California Extension (CMIL, UCX)

Life, Styles & Interests

LIFESTYLES—Life, Styles & Interests Channel (CLUBS, COMMUNITY CENTER, HOBBIES, INTEREST, LIFESTYLES & HOBBIES, LIFESTYLES & INTEREST, LIFESTYLES & INTERESTS, SPECIAL INTERESTS)

1010—A Day in the Life of Cyberspace

24 HOURS—24 Hours of Democracy Web site

AAFMAA—Army and Air Force Mutual Aid Association

AARP—American Association of Retired People

> AARP ANNUITY—AARP Annuity Program (AARP ANNUIT)
>
> AARP BANK 1—AARP Credit Card Services
>
> AARP HARTFORD—AARP Auto & Homeowners Program (AARP HART)
>
> AARP NY LIFE—AARP Life Insurance Program (AARP LIFE)
>
> AARP PRU—AARP Group Health Insurance
>
> AARP SCUDDER—AARP Investment Program (AARP FUND)

ACCESSPOINT—access.point (ACCESS.POINT, CHARITY, CITIZEN, CIVIC, COMMUNITY, DONATION, DONATIONS, NOT-FOR-PROFIT, PHILANTHROPY, VOLUNTEER, VOLUNTEERS)

ACLU—American Civil Liberties Union (CIVIL LIBERTIES)

ADVICE—Advice & Tips (TIPS)

AFROCENTRIC—Afrocentric Culture (AFRICA, AFRICAN-AMERICAN, BLACK-AMERICAN, BLACK AMERICAN, BLACKS)

AGOL—Assemblies of God Online

AIDS—AIDS and HIV Resource Center (HIV)

AIDS QUILT—Gay & Lesbian Community Forum Aids Scrapbook (GLCF QUILT, PLF QUILT)

ARIZONA—Arizona Central (ARIZONA CENTRAL, AZ CENTRAL, PHOENIX)

Chapter 7 Keywords by Channel and Topic

AZ ALT—Arizona Central: ALT. (AZ ALT.)

AZ BEST—Arizona Central: The Best

AZ CALENDARS—Arizona Central: Plan On It (AZ FUN)

AZ CAROUSING—Arizona Central: Carousing (AZ CONCERTS)

AZ COMMUNITY—Arizona Central: Your Community

AZ COMPUTERS—Arizona Central: Computers

AZ COUCHING—Arizona Central: Couching (AZ TV)

AZ DESTINATIONS—Arizona Central: Destinations (AZ TRAVEL, AZ TRIPS)

AZ DINING—Arizona Central: Dining (AZ EATS, AZ PENELOPE)

AZ ENTERTAINMENT—Arizona Central: At Ease (AZ AT EASE)

AZ FILMS—Arizona Central: Films (AZ MOVIES)

AZ GOLF—Arizona Central: Golf

AZ HOUSE—Arizona Central: House/Home (AX GARDENING, AZ HOME)

AZ KTAR—Arizona Central: KTAR Talk Radio

AZ LIFE—Arizona Central: Your Life

AZ MONEY—Arizona Central: Your Money (AZ BUSINESS)

AZ NEWSLINE—Arizona Central: Newsline (AZ NEWS)

AZ PHOTOS—Arizona Central: Photos

AZ PREPS—Arizona Central: Preps (AZ HIGH SCHOOLS)

AZ SCHOOLS—Arizona Central: Schools

AZ SCOREBOARD—Arizona Central: Scoreboard (AZ SCORES)

AZ SMALL BUSINESS—Arizona Central: Small Business (AZ BIZ)

AZ SOUNDOFF—Arizona Central: Sound Off (AZ BENSON, AZ CARTOON, AZ COLUMNS, AZ EDITORIALS, AZ LETTERS, AZ OPINIONS)

AZ SPORTS—Arizona Central: Sports (AZ ASU, AZ CARDS, AZ DIAMONDBACKS, AZ SUNS, AZ U OF A)

AZ SPORTS CALENDARS—Arizona Central: Plan On It (AZ SPORTS SCHEDULE)

Chapter 7 Keywords by Channel and Topic

Life, Styles & Interests (continued)

AZ STARDUST—Arizona Central: Stardust (AZ THEATER, AZ THEATRE)

AZ VOLUNTEERS—Arizona Central: Volunteers

ARTISTS—Artists on America Online (ARTIST)

ASK TODD ART—The Image Exchange: Ask Todd Art (ASK TODD, TODD ART)

ASTRONET—Astronet (AMERICAN ASTROLOGY, ASTROLOGY, ASTROMATES, CAROLE 2000, CHINESE ASTROLOGY, COSMIC MUFFIN, FINANCIAL ASTROLOGY, GENIE EASY, INTERACTIVE ASTROLOGY, KRAMER, WELCOME TO PLANET EARTH, ZODIAC)

ASTRONOMY—Astronomy Club

AVIATION—Aviation Forum (AIRPLANE, AIRSHOWS, AV FORUM, FLY, GENERAL AVIATION, JET, SKY DIVING, ULTRALIGHTS)

BABY BOOMERS—Baby Boomers Area (BABY BOOMER)

BC—Christian Books & Culture (BOOKS & CULTURE)

BERNIE—Bernie Siegel Online

BETHEL—Bethel College and Seminary

BICYCLE—The Bicycle Network (BFA, BIKENET)

BIRDING—Birding Selections

BOOKNOOK—The Book Nook (BOOK)

BOSTON—Digital City: Boston (BOSTON ONLINE)

BRATS—Overseas Brats

BTS—Bethel Theological Seminary

CAMERA—Photography Selections

CAPITAL—Politics (CAPITAL CONNECTION, CONGRESS, DEBATE, GOVERNMENT, ISSUES, POLITICS, PUBLIC POLICY, WASHINGTON)

CARS—Car/Cycle Selections (AUTOMOBILE, AUTOMOTIVE, CAR, MOTORCYCLE, MOTORCYCLES)

CATHOLIC—Catholic Community (POPE)

CHRISTIANITY—Christianity Online (<><, CHRIST, XOL)

    CCDA—Christian Community Development Association

    CCG—Christian College Guide (CHRISTIAN COLLEGES)

Chapter 7 Keywords by Channel and Topic

CCI—Christian Camping International (CHRISTIAN CAMPING)

CEC—Christian Education Center (CHRISTIAN EDUCATION)

CLN—Christianity Online: Church Leaders Network (CHURCH LEADERS, CHURCH LEADERS NETWORK, LEADERS NETWORK)

CLS—Christianity Online Classifieds (CHROL CLASSIFIEDS CO CLASSIFIEDS)

CM—Christian Ministries Center

CMS—Christian Media Source (CHRISTIAN MEDIA)

CN—Christianity Online Newsstand (CNEWS, CO NEWS)

CO FAMILY—Christianity Online: Marriage/Family Forum (CHRISTIAN FAMILY, CHRISTIAN FAMILIES, CO FAMILIES)

CO HOLIDAY—Christianity Online: Holidays and COntests (CO HOLIDAYS, H&H, HOLI, HOLIDAYS & HAPPENINGS)

CO INTERESTS—Christianity Online: Associations & Interests (ASSN, CO ASSOCIATIONS)

CO KIDS—Christianity Online: Kids (CHRISTIAN KID, CHRISTIAN KIDS)

CO LIVE—Christianity Online Chat & Live Events (CHRISTIAN CONNECTION, CHROL CHAT, FELLOWSHIP HALL)

CO MEN—Christianity Online: Men (CHRISTIAN MAN, CHRISTIAN MEN, CO MAN)

CO SINGLES—Christianity Online: Singles (CHRISTIAN SINGLE, CHRISTIAN SINGLES, CO SINGLE, CO SINGLES)

CO TEENS—Christianity Online: Campus Life's Student Hangout (CHRISTIAN STUDENT, CHRISTIAN STUDENTS, CO STUDENT, CO STUDENTS, CO TEEN, CO YOUTH)

COW—Christianity Online: Women (CHRISTIAN WOMAN, CHRISTIAN WOMEN, CO WOMAN, CO WOMEN)

CPC—Christian Products Center (CHRISTIAN PRODUCTS)

RC—Christian Resource Center (CHROL RESOURCES)

WRD—Christianity Online: Word Publishing

XCON—Christianity Online: Contest (CON, CO CONTEST)

CLUBS & INTERNET—Life, Styles & Interest's Top Internet Sites

CE—Consumer Electronics (ALARM, AUTO SOUND, BEEPER, CELLULAR, CELLULAR PHONE, CONSUMER ELECTRONICS, HOME AUDIO, PAGER, SECURITY)

Life, Styles & Interests (continued)

CHALLENGER—Challenger Remembered (ASTRONAUTS, KENNEDY SPACE, KENNEDY SPACE CENTER, SHUTTLE, SPACE SHUTTLE)

CHICAGO—Chicago Online (CHICAGO ONLINE, COL)

    COL BUSINESS—Chicago Online: Business Guide

    COL CALENDAR—Chicago Online: Calendar & Almanac

    COL CHAT—Chicago Online: Chat

    COL EDUCATION—Chicago Online: Education Guide (COL EDUCATE)

    COL FILES—Chicago Online: Libraries

    COL LIFESTYLES—Chicago Online: Lifestyles

    COL MALL—Chicago Online: Mall

    COL MARKETPLACE—Chicago Online: Marketplace

    COL MEDIA—Chicago Online: Media Guide

    COL NEWS—Chicago Online: News, Business & Weather

    COL PLANNER—Chicago Online: Planner

    COL SPORTS—Chicago Online: Sports

    COL TECH—Chicago Online: Technology Guide

    COL TICKET—Chicago Online: Ticketmaster

    COL VISITOR—Chicago Online: Visitor Guide

CIVIL WAR—The Civil War Forum

COOKBOOK—Celebrity Cookbook (CELEBRITY)

COOKING CLUB—Cooking Club

CORKSCREWED—Corkscrewed Online

CRAFTS—Craft Selections

CYBER 24—24 Hours in Cyberspace

CYBERVIEWS—This Week's Best Cyberviews (CYBERVIEW)

DAILY LIVING—Daily Living

DC—Digital Cities -or- DC Comics

DEAF—Deaf & Hard of Hearing Forum

DEPT 56—Department 56 Collecting (DEPARTMENT 56)

DIALOGUE—American Dialogue (AMERICAN DIALOGUE, BKG)

Chapter 7 Keywords by Channel and Topic

DIS—DisABILITIES Forum (BLIND, DISABILITIES, DISABILITY, PHYSICALLY DISABLED)

DO SOMETHING—Do Something! (DS)

EGG—Electronic Gourmet Guide (EGG BASKET)

ENVIRONMENT—Environment Forum (EARTH, EFORUM)

ENVIRONMENTAL ED—Earth Day / Environment

ETHICS—Religion & Ethics Forum (ATHEISM, BAHA'I, BUDDHISM, CHRISTIAN, CREED, DENOMINATION, ECCLESIASTICAL, HINDUISM, ISLAM, METAPHYSICS, NEW AGE, PHILOSOPHY, PERSUASION, RELIGIONS, SECT, UNITARIUM)

EXCHANGE—The Exchange (BOATS, COINS, COLLECTOR, OUTDOORS, RAILROADING, STAMPS, THE EXCHANGE)

    ANTIQUES—The Exchange: Collector's Corner (TOYS)

    COMMUNITIES—The Exchange: Communities Center (AFRICAN AMERICAN, AMERICAN INDIAN, ASIAN, MEN, NATIVE AMERICAN, ORGANIZATIONS, THIRTIES, TWENTIES)

    GUNS—The Exchange: Interests & Hobbies

    H&C—The Exchange: Home & Careers

FAMILY—Family Areas

FOLKWAYS—Folklife & Folkways

FOOD—Everything Edible! (AOL DINER, BEVERAGES, CHEF, CHEFS, COOK, COOKING, COOKS, DINE, DINING, EVERYTHING EDIBLE, FOOD & DRINK, GOURMET, KITCHEN, RESTAURANT, RESTAURANTS)

FDN—Food & Drink Network (BEER, BREW, BREWING, CIGAR, CIGARS, HOME BREW, HOME BREWING, PIPE, PIPES, WINE, WINERIES, WINERY)

FOTF—Focus on the Family (DOBSON, FOF)

    BREAKAWAY—Focus on Family: Breakaway Magazine (BOYS)

    BRIO—Focus on Family: Brio Magazine (GIRLS)

FREEMAIL—FreeMail, Inc.

FREETHOUGHT—Freethought Forum

GADGET GURU—Andy Pargh/The Gadget Guru (ANDY PARGH, ELECTRONICS, GADGET, GURU, PANASONIC, PARGH, PRIMESTAR, RCA, RUBBERMAID, TIMEX, TURNER VISION, WAHL)

GARDEN—Gardening Online Selections (GARDENING)

Chapter 7 Keywords by Channel and Topic

Life, Styles & Interests (continued)

GENDER—Transgender Community Forum (CROSSDRESSER, CROSSDRESSING, F2M, GLCF TCF, M2F, SRS, TCF, TG, TRANSGENDER, TRANSSEXUAL, TRANSVESTITE)

GENEALOGY—Genealogy Forum (AFRICAN, AUSTRIAN, BRITISH, DANISH, DUTCH, EASTERN EUROPEAN, GENEALOGY CLUB, GREEK, IMMIGRATION, IRISH, ITALIAN, NEW ENGLAND, NEWSLETTERS, NORWEGIAN, ROOTS, SCANDINAVIAN, SCOT, SCOTCH, SURNAMES, SWEDISH, SWISS, WELSH, WESTERN EUROPEAN)

GENERATIONS—Generations

GLCF—Gay & Lesbian Community Forum (BI, BISEXUAL, GAY, HOMOSEXUAL, LAMDA, LESBIAN, PINK TRIANGLE, PRIDE, PROUD, QUEER, TRIANGLE)

>   GAYME—Gay & Lesbian Community Forum: Gaymeland (BISEXUAL TRIVIA, GAY TRIVIA, GAYME, GAYMELAND, GAYMES, GENDER TRIVIA, LESBIAN TRIVIA)
>
>   GLCF BOARDS—Gay & Lesbian Community Forum Boards (GAY BOARDS, GAY MESSAGE, LESBIAN BOARDS, LESBIAN MESSAGE)
>
>   GLCF CHAT—Gay & Lesbian Community Forum Events and Conferences (GAY CHAT, GLCF EVENT, GLCF EVENTS, LESBIAN CHAT)
>
>   GLCF H2H—Gay & Lesbian Community Forum Heart to Heart (GLCF HEART, GLCF HEART TO HEART, H2H, HEART TO HEART)
>
>   GLCF LIBRARY—Gay & Lesbian Community Forum Libraries (GAY SOFTWARE, GLCF SOFTWARE, LESBIAN LIBRARY, LESBIAN SOFTWARE)
>
>   GLCF NEWS—Gay & Lesbian Community Forum News (GAY NEWS, GLCF POLITICS, LESBIAN NEWS, LESBIAN POLITICS)
>
>   GLCF ORGS—Gay & Lesbian Community Forum Organizations (GAY ORG, GAY ORGS, GLCF ORG, GLCF ORGANIZATIONS, LESBIAN ORG, LESBIAN ORGS)
>
>   GLCF TRAVEL—Gay & Lesbian Community Forum Travel (GAY TRAVEL, LESBIAN TRAVEL)
>
>   GLCF YOUTH—Gay & Lesbian Community Forum Youth Area (BI TEEN, BI YOUTH, BISEXUAL TEEN, BISEXUAL YOUTH, GAY YOUTH, GLCF TEEN, LESBIAN TEEN, LESBIAN YOUTH, TRANSGENDER TEEN, TRANSGENDER YOUTH)

Chapter 7 Keywords by Channel and Topic

WS—Gay & Lesbian Community Forum: Women's Space (GLCF WOMAN, GLCF WOMEN, WOMENS SPACE)

GOOD LIFE—Your Good Life

GOVERNING—Governing Magazine

HAM—Ham Radio Club (AMATEUR RADIO, HAM RADIO)

HATRACK—Hatrack River Town Meeting (ALVIN, ENDER, HATRACK RIVER TOWN, ORSON SCOTT CARD)

HERITAGE—Heritage Foundation (HERITAGE FOUNDATION, REVIEW)

HISPANIC—Hispanic Selections

HOBBY—Hobby Central (HOBBY CENTRAL)

HOME—House & Home Area

HOME OWNER—Homeowner's Forum (HOME OWNERS, UHA)

HOUSENET—HouseNet (BUILDING, CARPENTRY)

HUM—Virtual Christian Humor (;-D, VH, VIRTUAL HUMOR)

IMAGE—Image Exchange (IMAGE EXCHANGE)

JEWISH—Jewish.COMMunity (JCOL, JEWISH COMMUNITY)

    JEWISH ARTS—Jewish Arts

    JEWISH BOARDS—Jewish Message Boards

    JEWISH CHAT—Jewish Chat Room

    JEWISH DOWNLOADS—Jewish File Downloads

    JEWISH EDUCATION—Jewish Education

    JEWISH ELECTIONS—Jewish Israeli Elections (ISRAEL ELECTIONS)

    JEWISH FOOD—Jewish Food

    JEWISH HOLIDAYS—Jewish Holidays (JEWISH HOLIDAY, PASSOVER)

    JEWISH NEWS—Jewish News

    JEWISH SINGLES—Jewish Singles (JEWISH MATCHMAKER)

    JEWISH STORE—Jewish Store

    JEWISH YOUTH—Jewish Youth

JOKES—Jokes! Etc.

KIDCARE—KidCare

KODAK—Kodak Photography Forum

Life, Styles & Interests (continued)

KODAK WEB—Kodak Web Site

KWM WEB—Korean War Memorial Home Page

LAMBDA RISING—Lambda Rising Bookstore Online (GAY BOOKS, LAMBDA)

LATINONET—LatinoNet Registration

LEGAL—Online Legal Areas (LEGAL SIG, LIN)

LIBERTARIAN—Libertarian Party Forum—LIBERTARIAN PARTY, LIBERTARIANS

LOVE@AOL—Love@AOL (AMOR, AMOR, DATE, DATING SERVICE, DATING SERVICES, LOVE, LOVE AT AOL, LOVER, LUST, LUV, MATCHMAKER, MATCHMAKING, PASSION)

LOVE SHACK—The Love Shack

MAM—Mad About Music (FLASH)

MARS—Men Are From Mars (MEN ARE FROM MARS, JOHN GRAY)

MASS—Massachusetts Governor's Forum (MASS., MASSACHUSETTS)

MCO—Military City Online (DEFENSE, MC, MILITARY CITY, MILITARY CITY ONLINE)

    MCO BASES—Military City Online: Worldwide Military Installations Database

    MCO COMM—Military City Online: Communications

    MCO HQ—Military City Online: Headquarters

    MCO SHOP—Military City Online: Shop

    MCO TOUR—Military City Online: Tour

MEDLINE—Medline

MERCURY—Mercury Center (MERCURY CENTER, SAN JOSE)

    MC BUSINESS—Mercury Center Business & Technology Area

    MC COMMUNICATION—Mercury Center Communication

    MC ENTERTAINMENT—Mercury Center Entertainment Area

    MC LIVING—Mercury Center Bay Area Living Area

    MC NEW—San Jose Mercury News

    MC NEWS—Mercury Center In the News Area

    MC SPORTS—Mercury Center Sports Area

Chapter 7 Keywords by Channel and Topic

MC TALK—Mercury Center Communication

MES—Messiah College (MESSIAH)

MICHIGAN—Michigan Governor's Forum—MICHIGAN GOVERNOR

MILITARY—Military and Vets Club (VETERANS, VETS, VETS CLUB)

MIN—Minirth Meier New Life Clinics (MINIRTH MEIER, MMNLC, NEW LIFE)

MOMS ONLINE—Moms Online (MOM, MOMS, MOTHER)

MOSIAC—Spiritual Mosiac

MOUSEPAD—Image Exchange: Gallery of the Mousepad (MANTICORE)

NECN—New England Cable News (CABLE NEWS, NEW ENGLAND CABLE, NEW ENGLAND CABLE NEWS, NEW ENGLAND NEWS)

NEIGHBORHOODS—Neighborhoods, USA (NEIGHBORHOODS, USA)

NETNOIR—NetNoir (NET_NOIR, NET_NOIRE, NETNOIR, NETNOIRE, NOIR-NET, NOIRE_NET, NOIRENET)

NEW PRODUCTS—New Product News (NEW PRODUCT)

NNFY—National Network for Youth (NNY, YOUTHNET)

NONPROFIT—access.point: Nonprofit Professionals Network

NPN—Non-Profit Network (NON PROFIT, NON PROFIT NETWORK)

NSS—National Space Society (SPACE)

NUL—National Urban League (URBAN LEAGUE)

OAO—Outdoor Adventures Online (ADVENTURE, OUTDOOR, OUTDOOR ADVENTURE)

OC—Owens Corning

OUTDOOR FUN—The Exchange: Outdoor Fun

PAGAN—Pagan Religions & Occult Sciences (MAGICK, MAGICKAL, WICCA)

PARENT SOUP—Parent Soup (IVILLAGE, PARENT'S SOUP, PARENTS SOUP)

    PARENT SOUP CHAT—Parent Soup: Chat

    PARENT SOUP LOCAL INFO—Parent Soup: Local Information

Chapter 7 Keywords by Channel and Topic

Life, Styles & Interests (continued)

PARKS—America's National Parks (NCPA)

PET—Pet Care Forum (ANIMAL, ANIMALS, PET CARE, PETS)

PHOTO—Photography Area (PHOTOGRAPHY)

PHOTOS—Popular Photography Online (CAMERAS, POP PHOTO, POPULAR PHOTOGRAPHY)

PICTURES—Pictures of the World

PLANET EALING—Planet Ealing

PLANETOUT—PlanetOut (PNO)

PLF—The Positive Living Forum (POSITIVE LIVING)

PSC—Public Safety Center (EMERGENCY, EMERGENCY RESPONSE, ERC, PUBLIC SAFETY, SAFETY)

PSYCH ONLINE—Psych Online (ONLINE PSYCH)

QUILTING—Quilting Forum (QUILT, QUILTERS)

RBO—Ringling Online (RBO, RINGING, RINGLING BROS, RINGLING ONLINE)

RELIGIONS—Religion & Ethics Forum (ATHEISM, BAHA'I, BUDDHISM, CHRISTIAN, CREED, DENOMINATION, ECCLESIASTICAL, ETHICS, HINDUISM, ISLAM, METAPHYSICS, NEW AGE, PHILOSOPHY, PERSUASION, SECT, UNITARIUM)

RNU—Religion News Update (RELIGION NEWS)

ROMANCE GROUP—Writer's Club: Romance Writers & Readers

SCUBA—Scuba Club (GO SCUBA)

SELF HELP—Self-Help Area (SELF-HELP)

SENIOR—SeniorNet

SERVENET—SERVEnet (SERVENET, YOUTH SERVICE AMERICA, YSA)

SF—Science Fiction & Fantasy (ANALOG, ASIMOV, FANTASY, HORROR, MYSTERY, SCI FI, SCI-FI, SCIENCE FICTION)

SIMI WINERY—Simi Winery

SPIRITUAL—Spiritual Mosaic

SSS—Craig Anderton's Sound Studio & Stage (ANDERTON)

    SSS NEWS—Sound, Studio, Stage News

STD—Sexually Transmitted Diseases Forum

TAY—Taylor University (TAYLOR UNIVERSITY)

Chapter 7 Keywords by Channel and Topic

TEEN—Teen Selections (TEEN SCENE, TEENS)

THE WALL—Vietnam Veterans Memorial Wall (VIETNAM, WALL)

TPN—The Prayer Network (PRAYER NET)

TREK—Star Trek Club (STAR TREK)

UTAH—Utah Forum (UTAH FORUM)

VILLAINS—Military City Online: Villains of Fact & Fiction (SCOUNDREL, SCOUNDRELS, VILLAIN)

VIRGINIA—Virginia Forum (VIRGINIA FORUM, VA, VA., OLD DOMINION)

VOTE AMERICA—Vote America

WCN—World Crisis Network (WORLD CRISIS)

WEDDING—Wedding Workshop

WHEELS EXCHANGE—Wheels Exchange (CAR PHOTOS, MEMBERS' RIDES, MEMBERS RIDES)

WHITE HOUSE—White House Forum (CLINTON, THE WHITE HOUSE)

WOMEN—Women's Interests (WOMENS, WOMEN MAIN, WOMEN SPOTLIGHT)

    WOMAN BOARDS—Women's Interests: Message Boards

    WOMAN COLLECTIONS—Women's Interests: Arts and Letters

    WOMAN NEWS—Women's Interests: News

    WOMAN VOICES—Women's Interests: Organizations

    WOMEN CLASS—Women's Interests: Educational Opportunities

    WOMEN ROUND—Women's Interests: Community

    WOMEN WEB—Women's Interests: Web Sites

WORLD BELIEFS—World Beliefs

WRITERS—Writer's Club (WRITER, WRITER'S, WRITER'S CLUB, WRITERS CLUB, WRITING)

    WC CHAT—Writer's Club: Chat Rooms (WRITERS CLUB CHAT, WRITE)

YMB—Your Mind & Body Online (MIND & BODY, MIND AND BODY, YOUR MIND & BODY, YOUR MIND AND BODY)

YOUNG CHEFS—Young Chefs

ZON—Zondervan Publishing House (ZP, ZONDERVAN)

Chapter 7 Keywords by Channel and Topic

Marketplace

MARKETPLACE—Marketplace Channel (MALL, SHOPPING, STORE, STORES, THE MALL)

2MARKET—Marketplace Gift Service (CD, TO MARKET, TWO MARKET)

800-TREKKER—800-TREKKER: 24 Hour Sci-Fi Collectibles Hotline (1-800-TREKKER, 1-800-TREKER, 800-TREKER, TREKER, TREKKER)

AMEX—American ExpressNet (AMERICAN EXPRESS, EXPRESSNET)

AOL ENTERPRISE—AOL Enterprise (AOL BUSINESS, AOL ENTERPRISES, ENTERPRISE, ENTERPRISES)

AOL STORE—America Online Store (AMERICA ONLINE STORE, AOL PRODUCTS, MUG, T SHIRT, TOUR GUIDE)

AUTOVANTAGE—AutoVantage (AUTO, AV)

AVON—Avon

BARGAINS—Checkbook Bargains

BLOCKBUSTER—Blockbuster Music's Online Store

BOOKSTORE—Online Bookstore (READ USA)

BRAINSTORMS—Brainstorms Store

CADILLAC—Cadillac WWW Home Page

CHEESECAKES—Eli's Cheesecakes (CHEESECAKE, ELI, ELI'S, ELI'S CHEESECAKES, ELIS CHEESECHAKES)

CHEFS CATALOG—Chef's Catalog (CHEF'S CATALOG)

CLASSIFIEDS—AOL Classifieds (AOL CLASSIFIED, AOL CLASSIFIEDS, CLASSIFIED, CLASSIFIEDS ONLINE)

COLLECTIBLES—Collectibles Online (COLLECT, COLLECTIBLES ONLINE)

COMPUTER EXPRESS—Computer Express

DOWNTOWN—Downtown AOL (DOWNTOWN AOL, DT, DT AOL)

DOWNTOWN MSG—Downtown AOL Message Boards

EAGLE—Eagle Home Page

EDDIE BAUER—Eddie Bauer

ELI CONTEST—Eli's Cheesecakes Contest

FAMILY SHOWCASE—Family Product Showcase

278

Chapter 7 Keywords by Channel and Topic

FAO SCHWARZ—F.A.O. Schwarz (FAO)

FEDEX—Federal Express Online

FELISSIMO—Felissimo

FOSSIL—Fossil Watches and More (FOSSIL WATCHES)

FOUR RESOURCES—AT&T Home Business Resources (4RESOURCES)

FRAGRANCE—The Fragrance Counter (COLOGNE, PERFUME)

    CLEARANCE—The Fragrance Counter: Clearance Counter

FREESHOP—The FreeShop Online (FREESHOP ONLINE)

GIFT SERVICES—Marketplace Gift Services

GLOBAL PLAZA—Global Plaza

GM—General Motors Web Site

GODIVA—Godiva Chocolatiers

GREET STREET—Greet Street Greeting Cards (GREET ST)

GUCCI—Gucci Parfums Counter

GUESS—Guess, Inc

GWALTNEY—Gwaltney Hams & Turkeys (SMITHFIELD, HAMS)

HALLMARK—Hallmark Connections (CARDS, HALLMARK CONNECTIONS)

HAMMACHER—Hammacher Schlemmer (HAMMACHER SCHLEMMER)

HANES—One Hanes Place (BALI, CHAMPION, L'EGGS, PLAYTEX)

HEALTH EXP—Health and Vitamin Express (HEALTH EXPRESS, RX, VITAMIN EXP, VITAMIN EXPRESS)

ICS—Internet Connection Store (IC STORE, INTERNET STORE, NET STORE, NET BOOKS, WOLFF BOOKS)

INFINITI—Infiniti Online (INFINITI ONLINE)

JCPENNEY—JCPenney

KIDSOFT STORE—KidSoft Superstore

LENS—Lens Express (LENS EXPRESS)

LILLIAN VERNON—Lillian Vernon (LILLIAN)

MAMA—Mama's Cucina by Ragu (ITALIAN FOOD, MAMA'S CUCINA, PASTA, RAGU, SAUCE)

MCFAMILY—McFamily Community (MCDONALD'S)

Chapter 7 Keywords by Channel and Topic

Marketplace (continued)

MOONSTONE—Moonstone Mountaineering

NEW AUTO—AutoVantage: New Car Summary (CAR INFO, CAR SUMMARY, NEW AUTO, NEW CAR)

NISSAN—Nissan Online

OFFICEMAX—OfficeMax Online (OFFICE)

OLDS—Oldsmobile/Celebrity Circle (CELEBRITY CIRCLE, OLDSMOBILE)

OMAHA—Omaha Steaks (OMAHA STEAKS, STEAKS)

PAUL FREDERICK—Paul Frederick MenStyle

PEAPOD—Peapod Online

PERFUME—The Fragrance Counter (COLOGNE, FRAGRANCE)

PICTUREPLACE—PictureWeb & PicturePlace (PIC, PICTUREWEB)

PORK—Pork Online

PREMIER—Dinner On Us Club (EAT, EAT OUT, DINE OUT, PD, PREMIER DINING)

PRICE—Price Online (PRICE ONLINE)

PUR—PUR Drinking Water Systems

REI—REI Recreation Equipment, Inc.

ROMANCE STORE—Romance Store

SA—Shopper's Advantage Online (COMPUSTORE, SHOPPERS ADVANTAGE)

SHARPER IMAGE—The Sharper Image (SI STORE)

STARBUCKS—Caffe Starbucks (CAFFE STARBUCKS)

SWEETHEART—Omaha Steaks Offer

TOWER—Tower Records (RECORD, RECORDS, TOWER RECORDS)

TOY NET—Pangea Toy Net (BEANIE, BEANIE BOY, CRISPY, PANGEA, PANGEA TOYNET, THE TOY NET, TOY, VIRTUAL TOYS, VTOYS)

TOYBUZZ—Pangea Toy Network: ToyBuzz (PLAYMATES)

USPS—United States Postal Service

CHAPTER 7 KEYWORDS BY CHANNEL AND TOPIC

WB STORE—Warner Bros. Studio Store (WARNER BROS. STORE, WARNER BROS. STUSTO, WARNER BROS STORE, WARNER STORE)

WINDHAM HILL—Windham Hill (WINDHAM)

ZIMA—Zima

ZIMA TALK—Zima Events

MusicSpace

MUSICSPACE—MusicSpace

CHICAGO SYMPHONY—Chicago Symphony Orchestra Online

CODA—Coda Music Tech (CMT, CODA MUSIC)

DEAD—Grateful Dead Forum (:), GRATEFUL DEAD, THE DEAD)

    GD STORE—Grateful Dead Forum Store

DRUM—Drum Magazine

GUITAR—America Online Guitar Special Interest Group (GTR, GUITAR SIG)

HOB—House of Blues Online (BLUES, HOUSE OF BLUES, JAZZFEST

MMC—Music Message Center

MUCHMUSIC—MuchMusic Online (MUCHMUSIC ONLINE)

MUSIC MEDIA—Music Media

MUSIC TALK—MusicSpace Communications

MUSIC WEB—MusicSpace WEB TopStops

ROCKLINE—Rockline Online (CRAZY HORSE, HITS)

ROCKNET—RockNet Information & Web Link (ROCKLINK)

STUDIO—MusicSpace Studio

TAXI—TAXI Information and Web Link

VALLEY—Virgin's Virtual Valley (PEANUTS, VIRTUAL VALLEY)

WARNER—Warner/Reprise Records Online (REPRISE, WARNER MUSIC)

WOODSTOCK—Woodstock Online

Chapter 7 Keywords by Channel and Topic

Newsstand

NEWSSTAND—Newsstand Channel (MAGAZINES)

ASTROGRAPH—Astrograph

ATLANTIC—The Atlantic Monthly Online (ATLANTIC MONTHLY, ATLANTIC ONLINE, FICTION, IDEAS)

AZ CACTUS—Arizona Central: Cactus League Classifieds

BACKPACKER—Backpacker Magazine (BACKCOUNTRY, CAMPING, ECOTOURISM, HIKER, HIKING, OUTDOOR GEAR, TRAIL GUIDES, TRAILS, WILDERNESS)

BETTER LIVING—Ideas for Better Living (IDEAS FOR BETTER LIVING)

BIC MAG—Bicycling Magazine (BICYCLING, BICYCLING MAGAZINE, MOUNTAIN BIKE)

BIG TWIN—Big Twin Online: The All-Harley Magazine (HARLEY, HARLEY DAVIDSON)

BOAT—Boating Online (BOAT, FISH, FISHING, INBOARD, MARINE, OUTBOARD, POWER BOATS, SPEED BOATS, WATER, YACHTS)

BP MARKETPLACE—Backpacker Online's Marketplace

BV CHAT—Orlando Sentinel Online: Black Voices' Chat

BW—Business Week Online (BIZ WEEK, BW ONLINE, BUSINESS WEEK)

    BW SEARCH—Business Week: Search

CANCER JOURNAL—Cancer Journal from Scientific American (CANCER J SCIAM)

CAR AND DRIVER—Car and Driver Magazine (DRIVING)

CAREER NEWS—USA Today Industry Watch section

CC MAG—Christian Computing Magazine (CHRISTIAN COMPUTING)

CH—Christian History Magazine (CHRISTIAN HISTORY)

CHILDREN'S SOFTWARE—HomePC Magazine: Children's Software

CL—Campus Life Magazine (CAMPUS LIFE)

CNN—CNN Newsroom Online (CNN GUIDES, CNN NEWSROOM, DEMOCRACY, NGUIDES)

Chapter 7 Keywords by Channel and Topic

CNS—Catholic News Service (CATHOLIC NEWS, CATHOLIC NEWS SERVICE)

COLUMNS—Columnists & Features Online (COLUMNISTS, FEATURES)

COMPUTER LIFE—Computer Life Magazine (CLIFE, JUST DO IT, LIFE)

CONSUMER—Consumer Reports (CONSUMER REPORTS, CONSUMERS, WOMEN ONLY)

COWLES—Cowles/SIMBA Media Information Network (COWLES SIMBA, INSIDE MEDIA, MEDIA, MEDIA INFORMATION, SIMBA)

CR—Christian Reader (CHRISTIAN READER)

CT—Christianity Today (CHRISTIANITY TODAY)

CYCLE—Cycle World Online (CYCLE WORLD, CYCLING, HELMETS, MOTORCYCLING)

DIGIZINES—Digizine Sites on the Web (CYBERZINES, EZINES)

DISNEY MAGAZINE—Disney Adventures Magazine (DISNEY ADVENTURES)

DR WHO—Doctor Who Online (DOCTOR WHO)

DRUG REFERENCE—Consumer Reports Complete Drug Reference Search

ELLE—Elle Magazine Online (BEAUTY, CLOTHES, CLOTHING, DESIGN, DESIGNERS, FASHION, MODELS, TRENDS)

FAMILY LIFE—Family Life Magazine Online

FAMILY PC—FamilyPC Online (GAMESTER, GIGABRAIN, MEGA NEWS, MEGAZINE, MEGAZONE)

FLYING—Flying Magazine (AIRCRAFT, AIRCRAFTS, AIRPORTS, FLYING MAG, FLYING MAGAZINE, IFR, PILOTS, VFR)

GEN NEXT—Generation Next (GENERATION NEXT, NEXT)

HACHETTE—Hachette Filipacchi Magazines (HFM MAGNET WORK, MAGNET, MAGNETO)

HEALTH MAGAZINE—Health Magazine

HIGHLIGHTS—Highlights for Children (HFC, HIGHTLITES, HIGHTS ONLINE)

HIGHLIGHTS CATALOG—Highlights for Children Catalog (HFT CATALOG, HFC STORE, HIGHLITES CATALOG)

HISPANIC ONLINE—HISPANIC Online (HISPANIC MAGAZINE, LATINA, LATINO)

Newsstand (continued)

HMCURRENT—Health Magazine's Current Area

HMRELATIONSHIPS—Health Magazine's Relationships Area

HMREMEDIES—Health Magazine's Remedies Area

HOME OFFICE—Home Office Computing Magazine (HOC, SOHO)

HOME PC—HomePC Magazine

@INC LIVE—Inc Live Conference Room

INTOON—InToon with the News (DEPIXION, EDITORIAL CARTOONS, KEEFE, MIKE KEEFE, TOON, TOONZ)

IWIRE—I-Wire Online (COMPUTE, I-WIRE)

LJ—Leadership Journal (LEADERSHIP, LEADERSHIP JOURNAL)

LONGEVITY—Longevity Magazine Online (ANTI-AGING, ANTI AGING, ANTI-OXIDANTS, HERBS, HOMEOPATHIC REMEDIES, MASSAGE, PLASTIC SURGERY, SPA, SPAS, VITAMINS, WELLNESS, WORKOUTS, YOUNGNESS, YOUTHFUL)

MAC HOME—Mac Home Journal (MAC HOME JOURNAL, MHJ)

MAC TODAY—Mac Today Magazine

MACWORLD—MacWorld Magazine

MARRIAGE—Marriage Partnership Magazine (MARRIAGE PARTNERSHIP, MPM)

MC ADS—Mercury Center Advertising (MC CLASSIFIEDS, MC MARKET)

MC TRIVIA—Mercury Center Trivia (GERTIE)

MET HOME—Metropolitan Home (METROPOLITAN HOME)

MIRABELLA—Mirabella Magazine (MIRABELLA ONLINE)

MMW—Multimedia World Online (MMW NEWS, MMW WORLD, MULTIMEDIA WORLD)

  MMW CLINIC—Multimedia World Online's Clinic

  MMW LIBRARY—Multimedia World Online's Library

  MMW NEWS—Multimedia World Online (MMW, MMW WORLD)

  MMW OFFICE—Multimedia World Online's Office

  MMW PAVILION—Multimedia World Online's Pavilion

  MMW TEST TRACK—Multimedia World Online's Test Track

Chapter 7 Keywords by Channel and Topic

MMW WELCOME—Multimedia World Online's Welcome Area

MOBILE—Mobile Office Online (PORTABLE, PORTABLE COMPUTING)

MSCOPE—Standard & Poor's Marketscope

NAA—Newspaper Association of America (ASNE, NVN)

NCR—National Catholic Reporter (CATHOLIC REPORTER)

NEW REPUBLIC—The New Republic Magazine (THE NEW REPUBLIC, TNR)

NEWS LIBRARY—Mercury Center Newspaper Library (MC LIBRARY, NEWSPAPER LIBRARY)

NEWS & VIEWS—USA Weekend: News & Views (N&V)

NEWSHOUND—Mercury Center Newshound (MCPR, MERCPR, PERSONAL REPORTER)

NEWSPAPERS—Newspapers selection (LOCAL NEWSPAPERS, LOCALNEWS, NEWSPAPER)

NEWSWEEK—Newsweek Magazine

NUTRITION—Nutrition Forum

OMNI—OMNI Magazine Online (OMNI MAGAZINE, OMNI ONLINE)

OSKARS—Oskar's Magazine (OSKAR'S)

OSO—Orlando Sentinel Online (ORLANDO, ORLANDO SENTINEL)

   OSO AUTO—Orlando Sentinel Online: Autos

   OSO BASEBALL—Orlando Sentinel Online: Baseball

   OSO BEACH—Orlando Sentinel Online: Beach (OSO BEACHES)

   OSO BLACK—Orlando Sentinel Online: Black Voices (BLACK VOICES, BLACK-VOICES)

   OSO BUSINESS—Orlando Sentinel Online: Business

   OSO CHAT—Orlando Sentinel Online: Chat

   OSO CLASSIFIEDS—Orlando Sentinel Online: Classified Ads (OSO CLASSIFIED)

   OSO COLLEGE FOOTBALL—Orlando Sentinel Online: College Football (OSO COLLEGE FB)

   OSO DOWNLOAD—Orlando Sentinel Online: Download Libraries

Newsstand (continued)

OSO ENTERTAIN—Orlando Sentinel Online: Entertainment

OSO HOMES—Orlando Sentinel Online: Homes

OSO JOBS—Orlando Sentinel Online: Jobs (OSO WANT ADS)

OSO LIVING—Orlando Sentinel Online: Living

OSO MAGIC—Orlando Sentinel Online: Magic (OSO MAGIC MAG)

OSO MERCHANDISE—Orlando Sentinel Online: Merchandise

OSO MOVIES—Orlando Sentinel Online: Movies

OSO NET—Orlando Sentinel Online: OSOnet

OSO PHOTOS—Orlando Sentinel Online: Photos

OSO POLITICS—Orlando Sentinel Online: Government (OSO GOVERNMENT)

OSO PREDATORS—Orlando Sentinel Online: Predators

OSO RELIGION—Orlando Sentinel Online: Religion News

OSO SERVICES—Orlando Sentinel Online: Services (OSO SERVICE)

OSO SOUND OFF—Orlando Sentinel Online: Sound Off

OSO SPACE—Orlando Sentinel Online: Space

OSO SPORTS—Orlando Sentinel Online: Sports

OSO STORM—Orlando Sentinel Online: Hurricane Survival Guide

OSO THEME PARK—Orlando Sentinel Online: Theme Parks

OSO TO DO—Orlando Sentinel Online: Things To Do

OSO TOP—Orlando Sentinel Online: Top Stories

OSO TRANS—Orlando Sentinel Online: Transportation

OSO WEATHER—Orlando Sentinel Online: Weather

PC TODAY—PC Today (PC CATALOG)

PC WORLD—PC World Online (PC WORLD ONLINE)

PCW NETSCAPE—PC World: Netscape

ROAD—Road & Track (AUTOS, R&T, ROAD & TRACK, TRACK)

ROGUE—Motley Fool's Rogue (JIM'S BRAIN)

Chapter 7 Keywords by Channel and Topic

SATURDAY—Saturday Review Online (CLASSICAL MUSIC, LITERATURE, READING, SAT REV, SATURDAY REVIEW, SOCIETY, SRO, THEATER, THEATRE)

    SRO SALON—Saturday Review Online: Conference Room

SCI AM—Scientific American (SCIENCE, SCIENTIFIC, SCIENTIFIC AMERICAN)

    SA MED—Scientific American Medical Publications

    SAF—Scientific American: Frontiers (FRONTIERS)

SM—Smithsonian Magazine (SMITHSONIAN MAGAZINE)

SPIN—Spin Online (SPIN ONLINE)

STEREO—Stereo Review Magazine (AMPLIFIERS, AUDIO, CDS, HOME THEATER, SOUND, SPEAKERS, STEREO EQUIPMENT, STEREO REVIEW)

SUNSET—Sunset Magazine (SUNSET MAGAZINE)

TCW—Today's Christian Woman

TIME—Time Message Boards

TIME DAILY—TIME Message Boards

@TIMES—@times/The New York Times Online (AT TIMES, NEW YORK, NEW YORK CITY, NEW YORK TIMES, NYC, NYT, NY TIMES, TIMES, TIMES NEWS)

    TIMES ART—@times: Museums & Galleries

    TIMES ARTS—@times: Art & Entertainment Guide

    TIMES BOOKS—@times: Books of the Times

    @TIMES CROSSWORD—The New York Times Crosswords (CROSSWORD, CROSSWORDS, NYT CROSSWORD, NYT CROSSWORDS)

    TIMES DINING—@times: Dining Out & Nightlife

    TIMES FILM—@times: Film (TIMES MOVIES)

    TIMES LEISURE—@times: Arts & Leisure (LEISURE)

    TIMES MUSIC—@times: Music & Dance (DANCE)

    TIMES REGION—@times: The New York Region

    TIMES SPORTS—@times: Sport News

    TIMES STORE—@times Store (NYT STORE, @TIMES STORE)

    TIMES STORIES—@times: Page One-Top Stories

    TIMES THEATER—@times: Theater

Newsstand (continued)

TOP MODEL—TopModel Online

TOUR DE FRANCE—Bicycling Magazine: Tour de France Coverage

TRIBUNE—Chicago Tribune (CHICAGO TRIBUNE, TRIB)

    COL ENTERTAINMENT—Chicago Tribune: Local Entertainment Guide

    COL GOVERNMENT—Chicago Tribune: Election '96 (COL GOVT)

    COL TRAFFIC—Chicago Tribune: Traffic Updates

    NEWS QUIZ—Chicago Tribune: News Quiz

    TRIB ADS—Chicago Online: Classifieds (TRIB CLASSIFIED)

    TRIB COLUMNISTS—Chicago Online: Columnists

    TRIB SPORTS—Chicago Tribune: Sports Area

USA—USA Weekend (USA WEEKEND)

WD KITCHEN—Woman's Day Kitchen

WIN MAG—Windows Magazine (WINDOWS MAG, WINDOWS MAGAZINE)

WIRED—Wired Magazine

WOODWORKER—American Woodworker (AMERICAN WOODWORKER, PLANS, WOOD, WOODWORKING)

    POWERTOOLS—American Woodworker: Tool Reviews (MACHINERY, POWER EQUIPMENT, POWERTOOL, TOOL, TOOLS)

WORTH—Worth Magazine Online (WORTH MAGAZINE, WORTH ONLINE)

    WORTH PORTFOLIO—Woth Magazine Online: Portfolio

WP MAG—WordPerfect Magazine

WWIR—Washington Week In Review Magazine

YC—Your Church Magazine (YOUR CHURCH)

People Connection

PEOPLE—People Connection Channel (CHAT, PC, PEOPLE CONNECTION, TALK)

Chapter 7 Keywords by Channel and Topic

AOL LIVE—AOL Live! (AOL LIVE!, AUDITORIUM, BOWL, CENTER STAGE, CHAT SCHEDULE, COLISEUM, CS, LIVE, GLOBE, LIVE!, LIVE TONIGHT, ODEON, PC AUD. SHOWS)

@AOL LIVE—AOL Live Auditorium (@AOL LIVE, AOL DEAD)

@BOWL—The Bowl Auditorium

@COLISEUM—The Coliseum Auditorium

@CYBER RAP—Cyber Rap Auditorium

@CYBERPLEX—Cyberplex Auditorium

@GLOBE—The Globe Auditorium

@MAINSTAGE—Main Stage Auditorium

@NEWS ROOM—The News Room Auditorium (@THE NEWS ROOM)

@ODEON—The Odeon Auditorium

BAUMRUCKER—Baumrucker Conference (FIRST BYTE)

DALAI LAMA—Dalai Lama Conference (DL)

DATING—Romance Connection

EVENTS—Today's Events in AOL Live! (EVENT, YUBBA)

GALLERY—Portrait Gallery

LAPUB—LaPub

PC PLAZA—People Connection Plaza

ROMANCE—Romance Channel

SPOTLIGHT—AOL Live! Spotlight

TAROT—The Crystal Ball Forum (CRYSTAL BALL)

TRANSCRIPTS—AOL Live! Event Transcripts (TRANSCRIPT)

Personal Finance

PF—Personal Finance Channel (FINANCE, MONEY, PERSONAL FINANCE)

AAII—American Association of Individual Investors

ADVISORS—Top Advisor's Corner (ADVISOR, TAC, TOP ADVISOR, TOP ADVISORS)

AIQ SYSTEMS—AIQ Systems (AIQ)

BEATY—Company Research Message Boards (ACCORDING, ACCORDING TO BOB, BEATY, BOB BEATY, BOBB)

CHAPTER 7 KEYWORDS BY CHANNEL AND TOPIC

Personal Finance (continued)

BIZ INSIDER—Herb Greenberg's Business Insider (BUSINESS INSIDER)

BOFA—Bank of America (BA, BANK AMERICA, BANK OF AMERICA, BOFA, HOME BANKING)

BUSINESS RANKINGS—Business Rankings (RANKINGS)

BUSINESS SENSE—Business Sense

CBD—Commerce Business Daily

CCB—Chicago Online: Crain's Chicago Business (CRAIN'S, CRAIN'S SMALL BIZ, CRAINS, CSB)

CENTURY—Twentieth Century Mutual Funds (20, 20TH, 21ST, CENTURY FUNDS, TWENTIETH, TWENTIETH CENTURY, TWENTIETH-CENTURY)

CITIBANK—The Apple Citibank Visa Card

COMPANY—Company Research (COMPANY RESEARCH, HQ)

COMPANY PROFILES—Hoover's Handbook of Company Profiles (CORPORATE PROFILE, CORPORATE PROFIILES)

DISCLOSURE—Disclosure Incorporated

DP—Decision Point Forum (DECISION, DECISION POINT, DPA, STOCK CHARTS, STOCK TIMING)

EDGAR—Disclosure's EdgarPlus

FIDELITY—Fidelity Online Investments Center (FID)

    FID AT WORK—Fidelity Online's Working Area

    FID FUNDS—Fidelity Online's Funds Area (FID BROKER)

    FID GUIDE—Fidelity Online's Guide Area

    FID NEWS—Fidelity Online's Newsworthy Area

    FID PLAN—Fidelity Online's Planning Area

FINANCIALS—Disclosure's Financial Statements (BALANCE SHEET, FINANCIAL STATEMENT, INCOME STATEMENT)

FIRST CHICAGO ONLINE—First Chicago Online

FOOL—The Motley Fool (COMMONS, COOKIE, COSTARD, FESTE, FOOLISH, LAUNCE, LAVATCH, MFOOL, MOTLEY, MOTLEY FOOL, PORT FOLLY, THE MOTLEY FOOL, TODAY PITCH, TODAYS PITCH, TRINCULO)

    FOOL AIR—Motley Fool: Airlines (FOOL AERO)

    FOOL BIO—Motley Fool: Biotechnology

Chapter 7 Keywords by Channel and Topic

FOOL CHEM—Motley Fool: Chemicals

FOOL CHIPS—Motley Fool: Semiconductors (FOOL SEM, SEM)

FOOL DTV—Motley Fool: Desktop Video (FOOL VID, DTV)

FOOL FOOD—Motley Fool: Food

FOOL HARD—Motley Fool: Hardware

FOOL HEALTH—Motley Fool: Health

FOOL MART—Motley Fool: FoolMart (FOOL STORE, WAL-MART)

FOOL NET—Motley Fool: Networking

FOOL OIL—Motley Fool: Oilfield Services

FOOL PAPER—Motley Fool: Paper & Trees

FOOL RAILS—Motley Fool: Railroads

FOOL REIT—Motley Fool: Real Estate (FOOL REITTO, REIT)

FOOL SOFT—Motley Fool: Software

FOOL TECH—Motley Fool: Storage Tech

FOOL UTIL—Motley Fool: Utilities

HEADHUNTER—Motley Fool: Ask the Headhunter

FUND—Morningstar Mutual Funds (FUNDS, MORNINGSTAR)

FUNDWORKS—Fundworks Investors' Center

GOVERNMENT RESOURCES—Your Government Resources

HBS PUB—Harvard Business School Publishing

HISTORICAL QUOTES—Historical Stock & Fund Quotes

HOOVER—Hoover's Business Resources (HOOVER'S, HOOVERS)

IBD—Investor's Business Daily (INVESTOR'S BUSINESS, INVESTOR'S DAILY, INVESTORS BUSINESS, INVESTORS DAILY)

IE—Investors' Exchange (ICE, TICF)

INBUSINESS—InBusiness (IBIZ, INBIZ, INTERNET BIZ)

INC.—Inc. Magazine (INC, INC MAGAZINE, INC. MAGAZINE, INC ONLINE, INC. ONLINE)

INDUSTRIES—Your Industry

INDUSTRY PROFILES—Hoover's Industry Profiles

INSIDE—Industry Insider or The Cobb Group Online

Personal Finance (continued)

INSIDER—Industry Insider

INVESTORS NETWORK—Investors' Network (IN, INVEST, INVESTING, INVESTMENT, INVESTMENTS, INVESTOR, INVESTOR'S NETWORK, INVESTORS)

KAUFMANN—The Kaufmann Fund

LINGO—Investment Lingo (INVESTMENT LINGO)

LUNCH—Your Business Lunch (BUSINESS LUNCH, YOUR BUSINESS LUNCH)

MASTERLIST—Hoover's Company MasterList (COMPANY UPDATES, HOOVERS UPDATES, UPDATES)

MIX CITICORP—Citicorp Mortgage

MIX CMBA—California Mortgage Bankers Association

MIX DATA TRACK—Data Track Systems, Inc.

MIX GENESIS—Genesis 2000

MIXSTAR—Mixstar Mortgage Information Exchange

MLS—AOL's Real Estate Center (ARM, HOME EQUITY LOANS, HOME REFINANCING, MORTGAGE, MORTGAGE RATES, MORTGAGES, NAREE, REAL ESTATE)

MUTUAL FUND—AOL Mutual Fund Center (AOL MFC, MFC, MFC 95, MUTUAL FUND 95, MUTUAL FUNDS, MUTUAL FUND CENTER)

NBR—The Nightly Business Report: Making $ense of It All

NBR REPORT—The Nightly Business Report: NBR Online Report

OMEGA—Omega Research

OSO REAL ESTATE—OSO Classified Real Estate

PCFN—PC Financial Network (PC FINANCIAL, PC FINANCIAL NETWORK)

PF SOFTWARE—Personal Finance Software Center

PFSS—Personal Finance Software Support (SOFTWARE SUPPORT)

PLUS—Plus ATM Network

PORTFOLIO—Your Stock Portfolio (STOCK PORTFOLIO)

QUOTES PLUS—Quotes Plus

REAL ESTATE—Real Estate Selections

Chapter 7 Keywords by Channel and Topic

REAL LIFE—Real Life Financial Tips (FAMILY FINANCES, FINANCIAL PLANNING, INSURANCE, JOB, PLANNING, RETIREMENT, RL, YM, YOUR MONEY)

RSP—RSP Funding Focus (SCHOLARSHIP, SCHOLARSHIPS)

SBA—Small Business Administration

SOS—Wall Street SOS Forum

STOCK REPORTS—Stock Reports

STOCKLINK—StockLink: Quotes & Portfolios (QUOTE, QUOTES, STOCK, STOCK QUOTES, STOCKS)

STRATEGIES—Business Strategies Forum (BS FORUM, BUSINESS KNOW HOW, BUSINESS STRATEGIES)

TAX—Tax Forum (TAX FORUM)

TAX CHANNEL—NAEA Tax Channel (NAEA)

TAXCUT—Block Financial Software Support (KIP, KIPLINGER)

TAXES—Computing Tax Corner -or- Tax Forum

TAXLOGIC—Taxlogic

TELESCAN—Telescan Users Group Forum

TRADEPLUS—How to use StockLink & Gateway Host (ETRADE)

TREASURY SECURITIES—U.S. Treasury Securities (NATIONAL DEBT, PUBLIC DEBT, SAVINGS BONDS, TREASURY BILLS, TREASURY BONDS, TREASURY DIRECT, TREASURY NOTES, US SAVINGS BONDS, U.S. SAVINGS BOND, US TREASURY SECURITIES)

VANGUARD—Vanguard Online (VANGUARD ONLINE, VG)

    VCOMMS—Vanguard Online: Communications

    VFUNDS—Vanguard Online: Mutual Funds Campus

    VNEWS—Vanguard Online: Vanguard News

    VSTATS—Vanguard Fund Information

    VSTRATEGY—Vanguard Online: Planning & Strategy

VOICE—Your Voice

WEIGAND—Weigand Report

WSW—Wall Street Words (WALL STREET WORDS)

YOUR BUSINESS—Your Business (BUSINESS CENTER, E-ZONE, ENTREPRENEUR ZONE, EZ, EZONE, MS BIZ, MSBC, SBC, SMALL BUSINESS, THE ENTREPRENEUR ZONE, THE ZONE, YB, YOUR BIZ, ZONE)

YOUR MONEY—Your Money

Chapter 7 Keywords by Channel and Topic

Reference Desk

REFERENCE—Reference Desk Channel (REFERENCE DESK)

800—AT&T 800 Directory Web Site (800 DIRECTORY, TOLL FREE)

BARTLETT—Bartlett's Quotations (BARTLETT'S, BARTLETTS, QUOTATION, QUOTATIONS)

COLLEGIATE—Merriam-Webster's Collegiate Dictionary (COLLEGIATE DICTIONARY, MW DICTIONARY)

COLUMBIA—Columbia Encyclopedia (CCE)

COMPUTER TERMS—Dictionary of Computer Terms

DAILY—Reference Daily Dose

DESK REFERENCE—NY Public Library Desk Reference (NY PUBLIC LIBRARY)

DICTIONARY—Dictionary Selections

GROLIER'S—Grolier's Encyclopeda (GROLIER, GROLIERS, MME, GMME)

HOT REFERENCE—Hot Reference (HOT REF, REF HOT)

KIDS DICTIONARY—Merriam-Webster's Kids Dictionary

MEDICAL DICTIONARY—Merriam-Webster's Medical Dictionary

MERRIAM—Merriam-Webster Dictionary (MERRIAM-WEBSTER, WEBSTER)

PHONE DIRECTORY—Phone Directories (PHONE BOOK, TELEPHONE, TELEPHONE NUMBERS)

PLACES RATED—Places Rated Almanac (PLACES RATED ALMANAC)

QUES DICTIONARY—Computer and Internet Dictionary

QUOTATION—Bartlett's Quotations (BARTLETT, BARTLETT'S, BARTLETTS, QUOTATIONS)

REFERENCE HELP—Reference Desk: Help

SUPERLIBRARY—MacMillan Information SuperLibrary (MACMILLAN)

THESAURUS—Merriam-Webster's Thesaurus

US GAZETTEER—U.S. Census Information Web Page

WEB RESEARCH—Reference: Web Research (WEB TOOLS)

WHITE PAGES—ProCD National Telephone Directory Search (PROCD)

WORD HISTORIES—Word Histories

YELLOW PAGES—Business Yellow Pages (ABI, ABI YELLOW PAGES, MAILING LIST)

ZIP CODES—Zip Code Directory (ZIP CODE, ZIP CODE DIRECTORY)

Sports

ABC BASEBALL—ABC Sports Major League Baseball (MLB)

ABC FIGURE SKATING—ABC Sports Figure Skating (FIGURE SKATING)

ABC FOOTBALL—ABC Sports College Football (ABC COLLEGE FOOTBALL)

ABC SPORTS—ABC Sports

ABC SPORTS STORE—ABC SPORT STORE

ABC TRACK—ABC Track (EQUIBASE, WINNER'S CIRCLE)

ABC TRIPLE CROWN—ABC Triple Crown (TRIPLE CROWN)

ABC WOMEN—ABC Sports Women's Sports (ABC WOMEN'S)

ALL STAR—MLB All-Star Ballot

AMERICA3—America-3: The Women's Team (ACUBED)

AMERICAS CUP—America's Cup 1995 (AMERICA'S CUP)

ANGELS—Major League Baseball Team: California Angels (CALIFORNIA ANGELS)

AOL SPORTS LIVE—AOL Sports Live (LIVE SPORTS, SPORTS EVENTS, SPORTS LIVE)

ASTROS—Major League Baseball Team: Houston Astros (HOUSTON ASTROS)

ATHLETICS—Major League Baseball Team: Oakland Athletics (A'S, OAKLAND A'S, OAKLAND ATHLETICS)

AUTO RACING—AOL Auto Racing (NASCAR)

BASKETBALL—NBA Basketball

BK—Burger King College Football (BURGER KING)

BLUE JAYS—Major League Baseball Team: Toronto Blue Jays (JAYS, TORONTO BLUE JAYS)

Sports (continued)

BOATING—Boating Selections (SAILING)

BOSOX—Major League Baseball Team: Boston Red Sox (BOSTON RED SOX)

BOWLS—NCAA Football Bowl Info (BOWL GAMES)

BRAVES—Major League Baseball Team: Atlanta Braves (ATLANTA BRAVES, BRAVOS)

BREWERS—Major League Baseball Team: Milwaukee Brewers (MILWAUKEE REWERS)

BUCS—Major League Baseball Team: Pittsburgh Pirates (PIRATES, PITTSBURGH PIRATES)

CAPS—Washington Capitals (CAPITALS)

CARDINALS—Major League Baseball Team: St. Louis Cardinals (ST. LOUIS CARDINALS)

CHOOSE A SPORT—Choose a Sport on AOL

CUBS—Major League Baseball Team: Chicago Cubs (CHICAGO CUBS, CUBBIES)

DODGERS—Major League Baseball Team: Los Angeles Dodgers (DOGERS, LOS ANGELES DODGERS)

DRESSAGE—Horse Forum's Dressage MiniForum

EDELSTEIN—Fred Edelstein's Pro Football Insider

EXPOS—Major League Baseball Team: Montreal Expos (MONTREAL EXPOS)

EXTREME FANS—Extreme Fans: College Hoops (EXTREME FANS, FANS)

    HOOPS BOARDS—Extreme Fans: Message Boards

FANTASY LEAGUE—The Grandstand's Fantasy & Simulation Leagues (CYBERSPORTS, FANTASY LEAGUES, SIMULATION LEAGUES)

FOOL BOWL—Fool Bowl (BOWL GAME, FIESTA BOWL, ORANGE BOWL, ROSE BOWL)

FOOL DOME—Motley Fool: The Fool Dome (FOOLBALL, FOOL SPORTS, BASEBALL WORKSHOP, BWOL)

FOOTBALL—AOL Football (COLLEGE FOOTBALL)

FRENCH OPEN—French Open

GM'S CORNER—The GM's Corner (GMS CORNER)

Chapter 7 Keywords by Channel and Topic

GOLF—AOL Golf Area

GOLF DATA—GolfCentral

GRANDSTAND—The Grandstand (The GRANDSTAND)

GS ARTS—The Grandstand's Martial Arts (The Dojo) (KARATE, MARTIAL ARTS)

GS AUTO—The Grandstand's Motor Sports (In The Pits)

ICRS—The Grandstand's Simulation Auto Racing (SIMULATION AUTO)

GS BASEBALL—The Grandstand's Baseball (Dugout)

GBL—The Grandstand's Simulation Baseball (SIMULATION BASEBALL)

FANTASY BASEBALL—The Grandstand's Fantasy Baseball

GS BASKETBALL—The Grandstand's Basketball (Off the Glass)

FANTASY BASKETBALL—The Grandstand's Fantasy Basketball

SIMULATION BASKETBALL—The Grandstand's Simulation Basketball

GS DL—The Grandstand's Simulation Basketball

GS BOXING—The Grandstand's Boxing (Squared Circle)

GS COLLECTING—The Grandstand's Collecting (Sports Cards)

GS FOOTBALL—The Grandstand's Football (50 Yard Line)

FANTASY FOOTBALL—The Grandstand's Fantasy Football

SIMULATION FOOTBALL—The Grandstand's Simulation Football (ASFL, CNFA, GCFL, GPFL, GMFL, GSFL, GUFL, NWFL, OFL, RSFL)

GSFL—The Grandstand's Simulation Football

GS GOLF—The Grandstand's Golf (On The Green)

GGL—The Grandstand's Simulation Golf (ALPT, GGL, MAC ALPT

GS HOCKEY—The Grandstand's Hockey (Blue Line)

FANTASY HOCKEY—The Grandstand's Fantasy Hockey

GSHL—The Grandstand's Simulation Hockey (SIMULATION HOCKEY)

Sports (continued)

GS HORSE—The Grandstand's Horse Sports (Post Time) (HORCE RACING, HORSE SPORTS)

GS OTHER—The Grandstand's Other Sports (Whole 9 Yards) (BOWLING, ROLLERSKATING, SWIMMING)

GS SIDELINE—The Grandstand's Sideline

GS SOCCER—The Grandstand's Soccer (The Kop)

GS SOFTWARE—The Grandstand's Sports Software Headquarters

GS SPORTSMART—The Grandstand's Sports Products (Sportsmart)

GS TRIVIA—The Grandstand's Sports Trivia (GS SPORTS TRIVIA, GRANDSTAND TRIVIA)

GS WINTER—The Grandstand's Winter Sports (The Chalet)

GS WRESTLING—The Grandstand's Wrestling (Squared Circle)

> GWA—The Grandstand's Simulation Wrestling (SIMULATION WRESTLING)

FANTASYLEAGUE(S)—The Grandstand's Fantasy & Simulation Leagues (SIMULATIONLEAGUES)

SPORTS BOARDS—The Grandstand's Sports Boards

SPORTS CHAT—The Grandstand's Chat Rooms (SPORTS ROOMS)

SPORTS LIBRARIES—The Grandstand's Libraries

HARDBALL—Baseball Daily by Extreme Fans (BASEBALL DAILY)

HOCKEY—NHL Hockey

HOCKEY TRIVIA—ABC Hockey Trivia (NTN HOCKEY TRIVIA)

HORSE—The Horse Forum (HORSES)

HORSE SPORTS—The Grandstand: Horse Sports & Racing Forum (GS HORSE, HORSE RACING)

HOT SPORTS—What's Hot in Sports (SPORTS HOT)

HTS—Home Team Sports

IDITAROD—Iditarod Trail Sled Dog Race

IGOLF—iGolf

> IGOLF HISTORY—iGolf History

Chapter 7 Keywords by Channel and Topic

INDIANS—Major League Baseball Team: Cleveland Indians (CLEVELAND INDIANS, TRIBE)

INDY—Indianapolis 500 (INDY 500)

ISKI—iSKI (MOUNTAIN, MT, SKIING)

JORDAN—Michael Jordan Area (AIR JORDAN, MF, MICHAEL JORDAN)

KARATE—The Grandstand's Martial Arts (The Dojo) (GS ARTS, MARTIAL ARTS)

KID SPORTS—New England Cable Network: Sports for Kids

LACROSSE—The Lacrosse Forum (LAX)

MARINERS—Major League Baseball Team: Seattle Mariners (M'S, SEATTLE MARINERS)

MARLINS—Major League Baseball Team: Florida Marlins (FLOIDA MARLINS)

MATT WILLIAMS—Matt Williams' Hot Corner (MATT)

METS—Major League Baseball Team: New York Mets (NEW YORK METS)

MINNESOTA TWINS—Major League Baseball Team: Minnesota Twins

MLS LIVE—The Grandstand's Major League Soccer

MOTORSPORT—Motorsport '95 Online (MOTORSPORTS)

NABER—John Naber (JOHN NABER)

NBA DRAFT—1995 NBA Draft

NCAA—NCAA Hoops (HOOPS)

NESN BASEBALL—NESN: New England Baseball (AROUND THE HORN, NEW ENGLAND BASEBALL, RED SOX, RED SOX BASEBALL)

NESN BASKTEBALL—NESN: New England Baskteball (ABOVE THE RIM, BOSTON CELTICS, CELTICS, CELTICS BASKETBALL)

NESN FOOTBALL—NESN: New England Football (NEW ENGLAND FOOTBALL, NEW ENGLAND PATRIOTS, RED ZONE)

NESN HOCKEY—NESN: New England Hockey (BOSTON BRUINS, BRUINS HOCKEY, CUTTING EDGE, NEW ENGLAND HOCKEY)

NHL—NHL Online (ABC HOCKEY, ABC NHL)

NTN BASKETBALL TRIVIA—NTN Basketball Trivia (BASKETBALL TRIVIA, HOOPS TRIVIA, NTN HOOPS TRIVIA)

OLYMPIC SHOP—The Olympic Shop (OLYMPIC STORE)

Chapter 7 Keywords by Channel and Topic

Sports (continued)

OLYMPICS—Olympic Festival Online (OLYMPIC, OLYMPIC FESTIVAL)

ON HOOPS—On Hoops Basketball (Web Page)

PADRES—Major League Baseball Team: San Diego Padres (SAN DIEGO PADRES)

PAT O—The Pat O'Brien Report (PAT O'BRIEN, PAT OBRIEN)

PHILLIES—Major League Baseball Team: Philadelphia Phillies

PLAYWELL—U.S. Golf Society Online

PRO BOWL—1996 Pro Bowl

QOTD—Grandstand's Sport Trivia Question of the Day

RANGERS—Major League Baseball Team: Texas Rangers (TEXAS RANGERS)

REDS—Major League Baseball Team: Cincinnati Reds (CINCINNATI REDS)

REV—ABC Sports' REV Speedway (ABC AUTO RACING, REV SPEEDWAY, SPEEDWAY)

ROCKIES—Major League Baseball Team: Colorado Rockies (COLORADO ROCKIES)

ROGER CLEMENS—Roger Clemens' Playoff Baseball Journal

ROYALS—Major League Baseball Team: Kansas City Royals (KANSAS CITY ROYALS)

RUNNING—AOL Sports: Running

SIMULATION FOOTBALL—The Grandstand's Simulation Football (ASFL, CNFA, GCFL, GPFL, GMFL, GSFL, GUFL, NWFL, OFL, RSFL)

SIMULATION GOLF—The Grandstand's Simulation Golf (ALPT, GGL, MAC ALPT)

SKI—AOL Skiing

SKI REPORTS—Ski Reports (SKI CONDITIONS, SKI WEATHER)

SNOWBOARDING—Snowboarding Online (ASYLUM, SOL)

SPORTING NEWS—The Sporting News (THE SPORTING NEWS, TSN)

SPORTS—Sports Channel (BOXING, SPORTS LINK)

SPORTS ARCHIVE—AOL Sports Archive

Chapter 7 Keywords by Channel and Topic

STATS—Pro Sports Center by STATS, Inc. (STATS, INC., STATS, INC, STATS INC)

STATS HOOPS—Pro Basketball Center by STATS, Inc (STATS BASKETBALL)

SURF SHACK—The Surf Shack

SURFLINK—SurfLink (SURF, SURFBOARD, SURFER, SURFERS, SURFING)

TA FOOTRACE—Trans-America Footrace

TENNIS—AOL Tennis

TIGERS—Major League Baseball Team: Detroit Tigers (DETROIT TIGERS)

TOUR CHAMPIONSHIP—iGolf: Tour Championship

TRIPLE CROWN—ABC Triple Crown (ABC CROWN, ABC TRIPLE, ABC TRIPLE CROWN)

USFSA—United States Figure Skating Association

VOLLEYBALL—AVP Pro Beach Volleyball (KING OF THE BEACH, KOB)

WHEELS—Wheels (RACING)

WHITE SOX—Major League Baseball Team: Chicago White Sox (CHICAGO WHITE SOX, CHISOX)

WIMBLEDON—Wimbledon

WSF—Women's Sports World (WOMENS SPORTS)

WWF—World Wrestling Federation (RAW, SUMMER SLAM, SUPERSTARS, WRESTLING)

WWOS—ABC Online: Wide World of Sports (WIDE WORLD OF SPORTS)

YACHTING—Sailing Forum (BOARDSAILING, WINDSURFING)

YANKS—Major League Baseball Team: New York Yankees (NEW YORK YANKEES, YANKEES)

Style

STYLE—Style Channel (A-LIST, BEAUTY 911, BODY ELECTRIC, CELEBRITIES, DESIGNER STUDIO, FACE, GIRL STUFF, GUY STUFF, MAKEOVER, MAKEUP, MODELS! MODELS!, PARTY GIRL, SCENTS, STYL*E, STYLE, STYLE CHANNEL, STYLE 911, SUIT, UNDIES, VIP, WWWARDROBE)

CHAPTER 7 KEYWORDS BY CHANNEL AND TOPIC

Today's News

NEWS—Today's News Channel (HEADLINES, NEWS AND FINANCE, NEWS & FINANCE, NEWS ROOM, NEWS TEXT, NEWS/SPORTS/MONEY, NEWSLINK, OUR WORLD, TODAY'S NEWS, TOP NEWS)

1995—1995: The Year in Review (YEAR, YIR, YEAR IN REVIEW, REVIEW)

AIDS DAILY—AIDS Daily Summary

BLIZZARD—Blizzard Fun!

BOSNIA—Balkan Operation Joint Endeavor (BALKAN, UNPROFOR, YUGOSLAVIA)

BUSINESS—Business News Area (BUSINESS NEWS)

CAMPAIGN 96—The Campaign Trail (DECISION 94)

COLOR WEATHERMAPS—Main Weather Area

CQ—Congressional Quarterly (CONGRESSIONAL)

CROATIA—Croatia

EDITOR'S CHOICE—Pictures of the Week (EDITORS CHOICE, IOTW)

ENTERTAINMENT NEWS—Entertainment News

FIRST LADY—Hillary Rodham Clinton (HILLARY)

GALILEO—Galileo Mission to Jupiter (JUPITER, NASA, STARS)

HOT NEWS—Hot News

HURRICANE—Tropical Storm and Hurricane Info (TROPICAL STORM)

MAD WORLD—Today's News: It's a Mad, Mad World...Dispatches from the Wires

MARKET—Market News (MARKET NEWS)

NEWS SEARCH—Search News Articles (NEWS WATCH, SEARCH NEWS)

SPORTS NEWS—Sport News

WEATHER—Weather

WEATHER MAPS—Color Weather Maps (COLOR WEATHER MAPS)

WORLD NEWS—U.S. & World News (US NEWS)

CHAPTER 7 KEYWORDS BY CHANNEL AND TOPIC

Travel

TRAVEL—Travel Channel (SHOPPING & TRAVEL, SHOPPING AND TRAVEL)

AAA—AAA Online (3A, TRIPLE A, A3)

ARTHUR FROMMER—Arthur Frommer's Secret Bargains (AF'S SECRET BARGAINS, SECRET BARGAINS)

B&B—Bed & Breakfast U.S.A. (BED, BED & BREAKFAST, BREAKFAST)

CRUISE CRITIC—Cruise Critic (CRUISE, CRUISE CRITICS, CRUISES, SHIP CRITIC, SHIP CRITICS)

FLORIDA—Destination Florida

   DF FOOD—Destination Florida: Restaurants and Nightlife

   DF OUT—Destination Florida: Outdoors

   DF PARKS—Destination Florida: Attractions

   DF ROOMS—Destination Florida: Places to Stay

   DF SHOP—Destination Florida: Shopping

   DF SPACE—Destination Florida: Kennedy Space Center

   DF SPORTS—Destination Florida: Sports

   DF TICKET—Destination Florida: Ticketmaster

EAASY SABRE—EAASY SABRE Travel Service (AMERICAN AIRLINES, EASY, EASY SABRE, SABRE)

EMERALD COAST—Emerald Coast

FAMILY TRAVEL—Family Travel Selections

FROMMER—Frommer's City Guides (FROMMER'S, FROMMER'S CITY GUIDES, FROMMERS, FROMMERS CITY GUIDES)

FTN—Family Travel Network (FAMILY TRAVEL NETWORK, KID TRAVEL)

GOLFIS—Golfis Forum (GOLF AMERICA, GOLF COURSES, GOLF INFORMATION, GOLF RESORTS)

HOT TRAVEL—What's Hot in Travel (TRAVEL PICKS)

INSIDE FLYER—Inside Flyer (FREQUENT FLYER)

LANIER—Lanier Family Travel Guides (LANIER FAMILY TRAVEL)

ONE WORLD—One World Travel (ONE WORLD TRAVEL, RESERVATION, RESERVATIONS)

PLAY KEYWORD—Preview Vacations' Travel Update

Travel (continued)

RPM—RPM Worldwide Entertainment & Travel (RPM TRAVEL)

SKI ZONE—The Ski Zone

SPACE COAST—Florida's Space Coast

TA—Traveler's Advantage (TRAVELERS ADVANTAGE)

THE KEYS—The Florida Keys (FLORIDA KEYS, THE FLORIDA KEYS)

TL—Travel & Leisure Magazine (TRAVEL & LEISURE)

TRAVEL ADVISORIES—U.S. State Department Travel Advisories

TRAVEL FORUM—Travel Forum (TRAVELER)

TRAVEL HOLIDAY—Travel Holiday Magazine

TRAVELERS CORNER—Traveler's Corner (WEISSMAN)

VACATIONS—Preview Vacations (PREVIEW VACATION, VACATIONS)

WORLDVIEW—Fodor's Worldview

ZAGAT—Zagat Restaurant/Hotel/Resort/Spa Surveys (ZAGATS)

Member Services

HELP—Member Services* (ASK AMERICA ONLINE, ASK AOL, ASK CS, CS LIVE, CUSTOMER SERVICE, FEEDBACK, FREE, HOTLINE, INFORMATION, SERVICE, SUPPORT, SYSOP, TECH HELP LIVE, TECH LIVE)

AMEX ART—ExpressNet Art Download* (EXPRESSNET ART)

AOLGLOBALNET—AOLGLOBALnet International Access* (GLOBALNET)

AOLNET—AOLNET*

BILLING—Accounts and Billing*

BROWSER FIX—AOL 2.6 for Macintosh*

CANCEL—Cancel Account*

CREDIT—Credit Request Form for connect problems* (CREDIT REQUEST, DOWNLOAD CREDIT, PC-LINK HOTLINE)

DESKTOP CINEMA—Desktop Cinema*

DOWNLOAD 101—Download Help* (DOWNLOAD HELP)

FRIEND—Sign On a Friend*

FRIEND IN FRANCE—France Beta Test* (FRENCH TEST)

GLOSSARY—America Online Glossary*

GPF—GPF Help*

HIGH SPEED—High Speed Access* (9600, 9600 ACCESS 9600 CENTER, MODEM, MODEM HELP)

MEMBER SUVERY—Member Survey*

MM SHOWCASE—Multimedia Showcase*

NEW AOL—Newest Version of AOL Software*

PARENTAL CONTROL*—Parental Controls

PASSWORD—Change your password* (CHANGE PASSWORD)

QUESTION—One Stop Infoshop* (QUESTIONS)

SOUND ROOM—Sound Room*

STEVE CASE—Community Updates from Steve Case* (LETTER, LETTER2)

SUGGEST—Suggestion boxes* (SUGGESTION)

SYSTEM RESPONSE—System Response Area*

TOS—Terms of Service* (TERMS, TERMS OF SERVICE, TOS ADVISOR)

UPGRADE—Upgrade to latest AOL software* (AOL PREVIEW)

VIRUS2—Virus Letter*

WRITE TO STAFF—Questions* (ASK STAFF, WRITE TO OUR STAFF)

Special

95 APPLY—AOL for Windows 95 Beta Test Application

AOL CRUISE—AOL Member Cruise (AOL MEMBER CRUISE)

AOL DIAG—AOL Diagnostic Tool

APRIL FOOLS—AOL's April Fool Area (APRIL, APRIL FOOL)

BETA APPLY—Beta Test Application Area

BURP—AOL Plays With Sounds (BELCH)

CABLE—AOL's Cable Center (BROADBAND, CABLE MODEM)

CEP—Council on Economic Priorities

CYBERSALON—Cybersalon

Special (continued)

DON'T CLICK HERE—Don't Click Here

EASTER—AOL's Easter Area

EWORLD—Apple Aloha for eWorld Alumni (ALOHA, AOLHA)

FULL DISCLOSURE—AOL's Full Disclosure for Investors (AOL FULL DISCLOSURE, AOL INVESTOR RELATIONS, AOLIR, FD, FULLD, INVESTOR RELATIONS, IR)

GREENHOUSE—AOL Greenhouse

HERITAGE—Black History Month (BLACK HISTORY)

INFORMATION PROVIDER—Information Provider Resource Center (INFORMATION PROVIDERS, IP)

ISCNI—Institute for the Study of Contact with Non-Human Intelligence (UFO, UFOS)

LATE NIGHT SURVEY—The Late Night Survey (CAN'T SLEEP, CANT SLEEP)

LOOKING GLASS—Looking Glass

LOVE MOM—I Love My Mom Because...

MEMORIAL DAY—Memorial Day 1996

MLK—Martin Luther King (MARTIN, MARTIN LUTHER, MARTIN LUTHER KING, KING)

MOTHER'S DAY—Mother's Day Area (MOTHERS DAY)

NEA—Accessing the NEA Public Forum* (NEA ONLINE)

NEWS 8—News Channel 8 (NC8, NEWS CHANNEL, NEWS CHANNEL 8)

PAGE—Page Sender (SEND PAGE)

PHOTO FOCUS—Graphics and Photo Focus Area

PRESIDENT—President's Day (CLASSROOM, PRESIDENTIAL)

PRIN—Principians Online (PRINO)

PRODIGY—Prodigy Refugees Forum (COMPUSERVE, PRODIGY REFUGEES)

SEND PAGE—Page Sender (PAGE)

TMS—TV Quest -or- TMS Peripherals

TREASURE HUNT—AOL Treasure Hunt (HUNT)

VIRTUAL TORCH—Virtual Torch Relay

WICS—Women in Community Service

APPENDIX A
KEYBOARD SHORTCUTS

America Online's most frequently used commands have key combinations you can use in lieu of the standard pull-down menus. These keyboard shortcuts make navigation much easier and faster, and I highly recommend you use them. To use a keyboard shortcut on Windows, press either the **Alt** key (located next to the **Spacebar**) or the **Ctrl** key (usually located next to the **Alt** key) and then (without releasing the **Alt** or **Ctrl** key) press the appropriate letter key. On the Macintosh, do the same thing using the **Command** key, which you'll find next to the **Spacebar** with either the Apple logo or the cloverleaf symbol on it. Other keys used in the keyboard shortcuts include the function keys (located in the very top row on the keyboard), the **Enter** key (also called the **Return** key on the Macintosh), and the **Option** key (usually located next to the **Command** key on the Macintosh). Please note that the keyboard shortcuts are different depending on whether you access America Online from Windows or a Macintosh.

Function	Windows AOL 3.0	Macintosh AOL 3.0
File menu	**Alt+f**	N/A
New file	**Ctrl+n**	**Command+n**
Open...	**Ctrl+o**	**Command+o**
Close	**Ctrl+F4**	**Command+w**
Save	**Ctrl+s**	**Command+s**
Print...	**Ctrl+p**	**Command+p**
Download manager	**Ctrl+t**	N/A
Exit (quit)	**Alt+F4**	**Command+q**

Appendix A Keyboard Shortcuts

Edit menu	**Alt+e**	N/A
Undo	**Ctrl+z**	**Command+z**
Redo	**Ctrl+y**	N/A
Cut	**Ctrl+x**	**Command+x**
Copy	**Ctrl+c**	**Command+c**
Paste	**Ctrl+v**	**Command+v**
Select all	**Ctrl+a**	**Command+a**
Check spelling	N/A	**Command+=**
Stop speaking	N/A	**Command+.**
Insert hyperlink	N/A	**Command+h**
Go To menu	**Alt+g**	N/A
Exit free area	**Ctrl+e**	**Command+e**
Channels	**Ctrl+d**	N/A
Keyword...	**Ctrl+k**	**Command+k**
Find...	**Ctrl+f**	**Command+f**
Mail menu	**Alt+m**	N/A
Compose mail	**Ctrl+m**	**Command+m**
Read new mail	**Ctrl+r**	**Command+r**
Members menu	**Alt+b**	N/A
New Instant Message	**Ctrl+i**	**Command+i**
Send an Instant Message	**Ctrl+Enter**	**Enter**
Get a member's profile	**Ctrl+g**	**Command+g**
Locate a member online	**Ctrl+l**	**Command+l**
Window menu	**Alt+w**	N/A
Cascade windows	**Shift+F5**	N/A
Tile windows	**Shift+F4**	N/A
Close all windows	N/A	**Command+Option+w**
Help	**Alt+h**	**Command+/**
Abort incoming text	**Esc**	**Command+.**

> **NOTE:** **Ctrl** (or **Command**) + **0** through **9** are do-it-yourself keyboard shortcuts that you can customize by selecting **Edit Go To Menu** from the Go To menu.

Appendix B
VirtuaLingo
Glossary of America Online Terms

VirtuaLingo is a glossary of the lingo you will hear in the many gathering places around America Online. The version that appears here is abridged specifically with you, the keyword connoisseur, in mind. The complete version—with all the technical terms, jargon, and slang you could want, in addition to useful (and trivial) information—is available online at keyword: KEYWORDS. The complete version also includes network phone numbers, filename extensions, community leader uniforms, and assorted tips and techniques. Credit goes to George Louie, who co-authored this glossary.

America Online, Inc. (AOL)

The Virginia-based online service. Formerly known as Quantum Computer Services and founded in 1985, AOL has grown rapidly in both size and scope. AOL has more than 6 million members and hundreds of alliances with major companies. America Online's stock exchange symbol is AMER. To contact AOL headquarters call 1-703-448-8700, or use 1-800-827-6364 to speak to a representative.

AOLoholic

A member of America Online who begins to display any of the following behaviors: spending most of their free time online; thinking about AOL even when offline (evidenced by the addition of shorthands to non-AOL writings); attempting to bring all their friends and family online; and/or thinking AOL is the best invention since the wheel. A 12-step plan is in devel-

Appendix B VirtuaLingo Glossary

opment. Many, but not all AOLoholics, go on to become community leaders. *See also* **member** and **community leader**.

article

A text document intended to be read online but that may be printed or saved for later examination offline. Usually articles are less than 25k, as anything larger would probably scroll off the top of your window.

auditorium

A specially equipped online "room" that allows a large group of America Online members to meet in a structured setting. Visit keyword: AOL LIVE for the latest auditorium schedules.

beta test

A period in a new product or service's development designed to discover problems (or "bugs") prior to release to the general public. America Online often selects members to beta test its new software. If you are interested in beta testing America Online software, you can apply at keyword: BETA APPLY.

bug

A problem or glitch in a product, be it software or hardware. A bug may be referred to jokingly as a "feature." You can report a problem with America Online software or services by going to keyword: QUESTIONS and clicking on **Report a Problem**.

channel

This is the broadest category of information into which America Online divides its material. Also known as *department*. See Chapter 1 for a list of channels

chat

To engage in real-time communications with other members. America Online members that are online at the same time may chat with each other in a number of ways: Instant Messages (IMs), chat/conference rooms, and auditoriums. "Chatting" provides immediate feedback from others; detailed discussions are better suited to message boards, and lengthy personal issues are best dealt with in e-mail if a member isn't currently online.

chat/conference rooms

Online areas where members may meet to communicate and interact with others. There are two kinds of chat areas: public and private. Public chat areas can be found in the People Connection area (keyword: PEOPLE) or in the many forums around America Online.

community leader

America Online members who help in the various forums and areas online. They usually work from their homes not America Online headquarters, hence they may be also known as *remotes*. Often these are Guides, Hosts, Forum leaders/assistants/consultants, and so on.

cyberspace

An infinite world created by our computer networks. Cyberspace is no less real than the real world; people are born, grow, learn, fall in love, and die in cyberspace. These effects may or may not be carried over into the physical world. America Online is an example of cyberspace created through interaction between the energies of the members, staff, and computers.

e-mail

Short for electronic mail. One of the most popular features of online services, e-mail allows you to send private communications electronically from one person to another. With America Online's e-mail system, mail can be sent directly to scores of people, carbon copied, blind carbon copied, forwarded, and it can even include attached files. E-mail can also

APPENDIX B VIRTUALINGO GLOSSARY

be sent (and forwarded) to any other service that has an Internet address.

favorite place

A feature that allows you to "mark" America Online and World Wide Web sites you'd like to return to later. These favorite places are stored in your Personal Filing Cabinet. Any WWW site can be made a favorite place, as can any America Online window with a little heart in the upper-right-hand corner of the title bar.

Instant Message (IM)

America Online's equivalent of passing notes to another person during a meeting, as opposed to speaking up in the room (chat) or writing out a letter or memo (e-mail). Instant Messages (IMs) may be exchanged between two members signed on at the same time and are useful for conducting conversations when a chat room isn't appropriate, available, or practical.

Internet

The mother of all networks is not an online service itself, but rather it serves to interconnect computer systems and networks all over the world. The Internet, originally operated by the National Science Foundation (NSF), is now managed by private companies (one of which is AOL). America Online features the Internet Connection department, which includes access to e-mail service to and from Internet addresses, USENET newsgroups, Gopher and WAIS databases, FTP, and the World Wide Web (WWW).

keyboard shortcuts

The America Online software provides keyboard command equivalents for menu selections. For example, rather than selecting **Send Instant Message** from the pull-down menu, you could type **Ctrl+i** on Windows or

Command+i on the Mac. For a complete list of these keyboard shortcuts, see Appendix A.

member

An AOL subscriber. The term *member* is embraced because AOLers are members of the online community. There are currently more than 6 million members on AOL.

message board

An area where members can post messages to exchange information, ask a question, or reply to another message. All America Online members are welcome and encouraged to post messages in message boards (or "boards"). Because messages are a popular means of communication online, message boards are organized with "folders," wherein a number of messages on a specific subject (threads) are contained in sequential order.

password

Your secret 4- to 8-character code word that you use to secure your account. Because password security is important, we've included a number of password-creation tips and reminders here. Please read these and pass them along to your friends (and enemies).

- Your password should be as long as possible (use all eight characters, if you can).
- Your password should not include any word found in your profile, any of your names (or your spouse's/kid's names), or anything commonly found in a dictionary.
- Your password should be a combination of letters and numbers.
- Try using the first letter of each word in an eight-word sentence.
- Use a word that is easy to remember and insert numbers into it such as *SU8M3ER*.

Appendix B VirtuaLingo Glossary

> (Important: Do *not* use any passwords you have ever seen used as examples.)

- Change your password often (use keyword: PASSWORD).

Personal Filing Cabinet

A special feature of the AOL software that organizes your mail, files, newsgroups postings, and favorite places. Note that everything in your Personal Filing Cabinet is stored on your hard disk.

screen name

The names, pseudonyms more often than not, that identify America Online members online. Screen names may contain no fewer than three and no more than ten characters, and they must be unique. Any one account may have up to five screen names, to accommodate family members or alter-egos, and each can have its own unique password. Either way, you cannot delete the original screen name you set up the account with, and the person that establishes the original screen name and account is responsible for all charges incurred by all five screen names. To add or delete your screen name, go to keyword: NAMES.

shorthands

The collective term for the many emoticons and abbreviations used during chat. These devices were developed by members over time to give information on the writer's emotional state when only ASCII text is available. A brief list of these is available at keyword: SHORTHANDS.

surf

To cruise in search of information not readily evident in the hope of discovering something new. Usually paired with another word to describe the type of information being sought. Keyword surfing is an excellent example.

APPENDIX B VIRTUALINGO GLOSSARY

TOS

Short for America Online's *Terms of Service*, the terms of agreement everyone agrees to when registering for and becoming a member of America Online. These terms apply to all accounts on the service(s). You can read these terms at keyword: TOS (available in the free area).

World Wide Web (WWW)

One of the more popular aspects of the Internet, this is actually an overarching term for the many hypertext documents that are linked together via a special protocol called Hypertext Transfer Protocol (or HTTP). WWW information is available on America Online, using URL addresses to get to various WWW sites, or pages, much like you use keywords.

INDEX

A

alt key, 9, 307-308
America Online, 4, 309
    accessing, 34
    billing, 34
    investing in, 52
    learning about, 36-37
    new software, 46
    press releases, 43
    questions about, 43
    problems, 35-36
    tips, 44-45
    Terms of Service (TOS), 45
    tour, 45-46

B

Boettcher, Sue, 53-54, 61, 74-75, 77-78
Brice, Stacy, 48, 59, 61, 70, 78-79
buddy lists, 34-35

C

C! Computers and Software Channel, 5, 65, 222-239
    Apple Computer, 63
    Consumer Electronics, 64
    Family Computing, 68
    Preschool/Early Childhood SIG, 57
    ZD Net, 59

channel, 4-6, 310

Chase, Kate, 61, 67, 79

classifieds, 64-65

command key, 9, 14, 307-308

community leaders, 311

conferences, 311
    AOL Live, 62-63

contests, 66

control key, 9, 14, 307-308

Corning, James, 61, 65-66

D

dictionary, 36

Digital Cities Channel, 5, 67, 239-244

Directory of Services, 11-12, 43-44

Downey, Valerie L. (KEYValerie), 22-23, 26-27, 33, 41, 44-45, 48, 51, 54-55, 57, 59, 61-62, 66-67, 69-71, 73-74, 75-76,

downloading, 37

E

enter key, 9, 307-308

Entertainment Channel, 5, 244-252
    Astronet, 50

Hatrack River Town Meeting, 71
Love@AOL, 55
Parascope, 55-56
Straight Dope, 57
Weekly World News, 58

F

favorite places, 15, 312

G

Games Channel, 5, 253-255
- Air Warrior, 48-49
- Computer Gaming World, 51
- Gemstone, 69-70
- Trivial Pursuit Interactive, 58

Gay, Mary, 33, 34
Go To menu, 14-15, 308
Guide Pager, 38

H

Hayes, Tim, 61, 68
Health & Fitness Channel, 5, 255-256
- America Running & Fitness Association (ARFA), 49-50
- KidCare, 54
- Your Good Life, 52

help
- general, 38
- Help Desk, 39
- homework, 62, 72
- members helping members (MHM), 41

INDEX

    paging a Guide, 38
    questions, 43
    Tech Help Live, 44
high speed access, 39
holidays, 39-40
Holzem, Warren, 61 69, 73
Homza Elizabeth, 33, 40-41, 43-44, 61-63
The Hub Channel, 5, 256-257

I

International Channel, 5, 257-259
    AOL World, 49
Internet Connection Channel 5, 72-73, 312
    Web Diner, 78

K

Kazdin, Genevieve, 61-62, 67, 76
KEY List, 19, 31
keyboard shortcuts, 7, 9, 307-308, 312-313
keyword trivia, 28
keywords
    about, 6-8
    bizarre, 30
    feedback, 19
    finding, 16
    general, 221-222
    hot, 12, 40, 61-79
    important, 33-46
    invalid, 16-17
    lists, 14-15, 21-31
    locating, 9-13

new, 11, 41, 47-59
online list, 10
special, 305-306
surfing, 13-14, 314
URL (WWW) addresses as, 8, 25
using, 7-8
your own, 25
Kippenbrock, Ken, 33, 36
Kids Only Channel, 5, 261
    Grandmas' Attic, 50-51
    Highlights Magazine, 52-53
    Homework Help for Kids, 72
    Kids' Warner Bros., 73
Kramarsky, Laura, 33, 37, 61, 63, 68, 71
Kummer, Carol, 61, 74

L

Learning & Culture Channel, 5, 261-266
    Academic Assistance Center, 62
    Adoption Forum, 62
    Homeschool Forum, 72
    Odyssey Project, 74-75
    Online Campus, 63-64
    Space Exploration Online, 77
    University of California Extension, 78
Life, Styles & Interests Channel, 5, 266-277
    disABILITIES Forum, 68
    Gay and Lesbian Community Forum, 70
    Jewish Community, 53-54
    Hispanic Online, 54-55
    Parent Soup, 56
    Star Trek Club: 77

INDEX

> Transgender Community Forum, 70
> Womens' Interests, 78-79
> Writers Club, 79

Louie, George (NumbersMan), 24, 61, 64-65, 309

M

Marketplace Channel, 5, 278-281
> The Free Shop, 69

Marx, Dave, 33, 34, 37-39, 43-46, 48, 51, 58, 61, 72
Mason, William, 33, 42-43
Member Services, 6, 304-305
member,
> searching, 40-41
> members helping members (MHM), 41

MusicSpace Channel, 6, 281
> Flash, 51
> Grateful Dead Forum, 67

N

Nathan, Miriam, 33, 39, 61, 72-73
Newsstand Channel, 6, 282-288
> Cable News Network (CNN), 65
> InToon (editorial cartoons), 53
> Longevity Magazine Online, 73-74
> New York Times, 74
> OMNI Magazine Online, 75
> Orlando Sentinel Online, 75-76
> Saturday Review Online, 76

O

option key, 307-308

P

parental controls, 42
passwords
    about, 313-314
    changing, 42
People Connection Channel, 6, 288-289
    AOL Live, 62-63
Personal Finance Channel, 6, 289-293
    Motley Fool, 69
    Real Life, 76
    Your Biz, 59

R

Randall, Amanda, 33, 38
ratings bar, 18, 33, 47, 61
Reference Desk Channel, 6, 294-295
Rosengarten, Hal, 61, 63-64

S

searching
    files, 37
    members, 40-41
    services, 11-12, 43-44
Sebel, Lauren, 48-49, 52-53
Shaderowfsky, Eva, 33, 35
Smith, Gwen, 33, 35-36, 48, 53
Sports Channel, 6, 295-301
    The Grandstand, 71
Stader, Terry, 61, 64
Strange, Bob (KEY Bobby), 33, 34-35, 48-49, 61, 66, 77
Style Channel, 6, 301

T

Terms of Service (TOS), 45, 315
    paging a Guide, 38
Today's News Channel, 6, 302
time, 34
Tipul, Kate, 48, 55-56, 61, 65, 78
Trautman, Kimberly, 61, 72
Travel Channel, 6, 303-304
    AAA, 48
    Cruise Critic, 66-67
    Places Rated, 56-57

U

Urban, Stephen, 48, 55

W

What's Hot on America Online, 12, 40
World Wide Web (WWW)
    about, 315
    addresses, 8, 25

Z

Zimmer, Bradley, 33, 42, 48, 52, 56-57